YES,

GOD OF THE GENTILES, TOO

The Missionary Message Of The Old Testament

David Filbeck

YES,

GOD OF THE GENTILES, TOO

The Missionary Message
Of The Old Testament

© 1994 by the Billy Graham Center, Wheaton College
Printed in the United States of America

ISBN 1-879089-14-9

To

Meghan, Rachel,
Chelsea, Michal,
Janel, Aaron

In Memory Of
Kane

Contents

Preface

The content of this book has been "burning in my soul" for more than twenty years, ever since I substituted for my good friend Dr. Cyril Simkins (who ironically was on sabbatical writing a dissertation on the subject), teaching his class on Theology of Mission. While I was not trained in the finer points of theology, I was a missionary. And because I had needed, on numerous occasions, to justify my decision to minister outside my own North American Christian context, I knew how I wanted to teach the class.

Over the intervening years I have met several former students of that class who became missionaries in other nations as well. Many have expressed gratitude for what they learned in the class. What was especially gratifying was that they had also used the contents of the class in teaching in churches and training institutes. Such feedback made the fire burn even hotter!

This book represents an integration of more than thirty years of mission service, experience, and study. But without the assistance of many others, it could not have been written. Therefore, recognition is due those who helped make this volume possible.

First, I am grateful to my mission coworkers in Thailand: David and Sharon Filbeck, Carmen Filbeck (yes, my son, daughter-in-law, and daughter) and Rick and Kathy Walden. Without their stepping in and carrying my part of the work in evangelism, church planting, and operating a Bible institute, I could not have taken the time to do the research and writing necessary for this book.

I am thankful to the Billy Graham Center at Wheaton College for reopening at the last minute the position of Missionary Scholar in Residence so that at last I could fulfill my desire of writing this book. I am thankful to Dr. James Kraakevik, Director of the Billy Graham Center, and Mrs. Jane Nelson, Coordinator for the Scholarship program, for showing faith in this project and encouraging me along the way. I am also thankful to Virginia Morris, Administrative Secretary, for making my entrance and stay at the Billy Graham Center an enjoyable experience, and to Dotsey Welliver, Editorial Coordinator, for patiently preparing the manuscript for final publication.

I am especially grateful to Dr. James Stamoolis, Dean of the Graduate School of Wheaton College. He graciously answered my letter, addressed only to the Dean (I did not know him or his name at the time), inquiring about a temporary teaching position so I could write a book. Without his thoughtfulness I would never have known of the Missionary Scholar in Residence program at the Billy Graham Center.

I am also thankful to the following faculty of Wheaton College for their criticism and suggestions: Drs. Douglas McConnell, M. E. Lorentzen, Julius J. Scott, Charles W. Weber, John McRay, Herbert M. Wolf, and Arthur F. Holmes. I am also thankful to Dr. David Howard, Vice President of the David C. Cook Foundation and to Dr. David Clark of the United Bible Societies for their comments. Their suggestions helped to make this monograph a much better book than what it would have been otherwise. However, they should not be blamed for any weaknesses and inaccuracies that remain. These are my responsibility alone.

A special word of thanks is due my wife Deloris who was willing to forgo a normal furlough year from mission field living so I could research and write this book. Through our many years of service together she has been a true and encouraging companion in the Great Commission.

This book is dedicated to my grandchildren. There is something disconcerting about seeing the closing of one's career coinciding with the beginning of a new century. It is my prayer that my grandchildren will become obedient (as their grandparents and parents have done before them) to the vision that God has revealed through his Holy Scriptures of being his witnesses to the uttermost parts of the earth.

Section 1

Foundations

CHAPTER ONE

What's Behind the Great Commission?

The graduate student from Thailand leaned over to ask me a question. In a few minutes the bell would ring, and the professor would begin teaching the class in Historical Linguistics. "Why are you a missionary in Thailand?" the student asked. "We already have a religion. Buddhism."

Fair question.

Of course, I was not the only missionary in Thailand. Or in the world. In fact, at the time probably some 45,000 missionaries served around the world. And this was not the first time I had been confronted with the question. The Thai people are understandably proud of their long history — since A.D. 1200 — as a free and independent nation. The early founders established Buddhism as the national religion and invited monks from Sri Lanka, where a purer Buddhism was practiced at the time, to come teach the Buddhist way more perfectly to the Thai people.

As a consequence thousands of Buddhist temples are now scattered throughout the kingdom, and at any one time more than 30,000 men wear the bronze robe of the Buddhist monk. Their purpose is to learn the moral precepts of the Buddha and to be examples of these precepts in daily life before their fellow citizens.

Indeed, why was I a missionary in Thailand? More currently, some thirty years later, why am I still a missionary to Thailand? And in general, why would anyone become a missionary?

Over the past 200 years, as each decade rolled by, more and more people became missionaries. In the 100 years from 1800 to 1900, for example, Protestant missionaries grew from numbering just a few to some 13,000 people serving in nations outside their own homelands (The New Schaff-Herzog Encyclopedia of Religious Knowledge).

Then, in spite of two world wars and a great depression, this number grew to 22,000 missionaries by 1945, and, in just twenty-five more years, the number leaped to 48,000 people (Ralph Winter 1970).

More than 150,000 Protestant missionaries are now scattered throughout the world (Frank Kaleb Jensen 1989). Not all are from the traditional Christian countries of North America and Europe, however. Of this huge number 39,000 missionaries come from Two-Thirds world nations of Asia and Africa (Stephen E. Burris 1992).

A Deeper Reason

What is the underlying reason for all the mission activity in the Christian church of the past 200 years? To be sure we have the command of Jesus Christ in the Great Commission when he ordered "Go, and preach the Gospel." The Great Commission, however, is not enough to explain the great surge in missionaries and mission work. When we look more closely at the Great Commission, we get a feeling that there is much more than what meets the eye. This is more than just a command containing a verb in the imperative mood.

The Great Commission of our Lord Jesus Christ is an important command, for it was repeated five times in the New Testament. Read carefully the following texts from the New Testament.

Matthew 28:18–20
Then Jesus came to them and said, "All authority in heaven and on earth has been given to me. Therefore go and make disciples of all nations, baptizing them in the name of the Father and of the Son and of the Holy Spirit, and teaching them to obey everything I have commanded you. And surely I will be with you always, to the very end of the age."

Mark 16:15–16
He said to them, "Go into all the world and preach the good news to all creation. Whoever believes and is baptized will be saved, but whoever does not believe will be condemned."

Luke 24:46–47
He told them, "This is what is written: The Christ will suffer and rise from the dead on the third day, and repentance and forgiveness of sins will be preached in his name to all nations, beginning at Jerusalem."

John 20:21–23

Again Jesus said, "Peace be with you! As the Father has sent me, I am sending you." And with that he breathed on them and said, "Receive the Holy Spirit. If you forgive anyone his sins, they are forgiven; if you do not forgive them, they are not forgiven."

Acts 1:7–8

He said to them: "It is not for you to know the times or dates the Father has set by his own authority. But you will receive power when the Holy Spirit comes on you; and you will be my witnesses in Jerusalem, and in all Judea and Samaria, and to the ends of the earth."

These are powerful words, to be sure. But, as God reminded Isaiah in his day and time, they are words that speak of something more ancient.

Isaiah 46:9–10

Remember the former things, those of long ago; I am God, and there is no other; I am God, and there is none like me. I make known the end from the beginning, from ancient times, what is still to come...

Indeed, the words of the Great Commission speak of going back to the very beginning of creation;
- of a time when sin infected the human race and men and women needed to repent;
- of a time when human life broke up into different nations and languages;
- of a time when men boldly spoke up for God to a recalcitrant people;
- of a time when men wrote the words of God for people of every age to know and understand.

Truly it is this deeper reference to things ancient that gives the Great Commission its continuing power to inspire men, women, even families with children to leave all and literally trek to the ends of the earth to preach the Good News of Jesus Christ. That something more ancient, of course, is the Old Testament, that portion of the Christian Scriptures which tells of these ancient things. But, it must be emphasized, not just bits and parts of the Old Testament: for example, the story of Rahab, a Jericho prostitute who joined the cause of Israel in the Promised Land; or the story of Jonah, a disgruntled Hebrew, who preached repentance in the foreign city of Nineveh; or a few verses from the Old Testament prophet Isaiah which said that Israel is a light to the Gentiles. The entire Old Testament is involved, from the beginning to its end.

A Missionary Message

How did I answer the graduate student who asked me why I was a missionary in her country of Thailand? I did not appeal to the Great Commission as the basis for being a missionary, for I had learned that such an appeal is unconvincing to Buddhists and, often enough, even to Christians as well.

So in the couple of minutes left before class began, I turned her attention to the Old Testament. It was God's plan as revealed through the prophets of the Old Testament, I told her, for the Gospel to be taken to the ends of the earth. I was following the missionary message of the Old Testament in going to Thailand as a missionary.

In the whole of the Old Testament, we observe a missionary message. This message, as it was being delivered through Moses, Samuel, David, and the prophets, ultimately produced a missionary interpretation in the minds and hearts of Old Testament readers.

This interpretation first became apparent among the Jews of the intertestament period, the 400 years between the closing of the Old Testament and the opening of the New Testament.

During this time Jews traveled the known world. As they came in contact with non-Jewish populations they opened up and shared with them the teachings of their Scriptures. Non-Jews began to forsake their old religions and convert to belief in the Lord, the God of Israel. In the end hundreds and thousands of people became proselytes, God-fearers, and followers of the Jewish Scriptures.

This missionary interpretation of the Old Testament was later carried over into the church of the New Testament. When the church was first established, the Old Testament was its only Bible. Apostles and evangelists, as they preached the Gospel to non-Jews, immediately found their reasons for this type of activity from the Old Testament.

The missionary message of the Old Testament still "drives" the Great Commission today. The Old Testament stands behind the Great Commission, motivating men and women from the deepest well-springs of life itself to spend their lives preaching the Gospel in other nations.

The Missionary Call

So we see that the Old Testament is the "driver" of the Great Commission. Together they perform two important functions in the missionary work of Christ's church.

To illustrate what I mean, let us look at the life of the Apostle Paul. One might think that Paul relied on the Great Commission as the basis for his mission work among the Gentiles.

As we read the New Testament we find that this expectation is only partly true. In Acts 9:15 we find another account of the Great Commission. God called Saul of Tarsus (whose other name was Paul) to be "a chosen instrument of mine to carry my name before the Gentiles and kings and the sons of Israel." Later Paul referred to his call when he wrote to the Christians in Rome.

Romans 1:1,5
Paul, a servant of Christ Jesus, called to be an apostle and set apart for the Gospel of God…Through him and for his name's sake, we received grace and apostleship to call people from all the Gentiles to the obedience that comes from faith.

Two points may be emphasized here. The first is that Paul relied on the Great Commission to justify his own personal call to be an apostle to people of other nationalities. The second is that, even in the face of a direct call from God to be an apostle, it still left unanswered a more basic question: why should nationalities other than Jews be evangelized in the first place?

To answer this question Paul turned back to the Old Testament and its promise to include the Gentiles in God's plan of salvation.

Rom. 15:8–9,12; (quoted from Isaiah 11:10)
For I tell you that Christ has become a servant of the Jews on behalf of God's truth, to confirm the promises made to the patriarchs so

that the Gentiles may glorify God for his mercy, as it is written...
"The Root of Jesse will spring up, one who will arise to rule over
the nations; the Gentiles will hope in him."

In other words, it is right and proper to evangelize in other nations
because this was God's intention from the beginning, an intention
revealed throughout the Old Testament.

It is interesting to note that a missionary of today often has the
same experience. First, he or she looks to the Great Commission ("Go,
therefore...") as the basis for his or her own personal calling to be a
missionary: what was said to the first disciples still applies today. The
Great Commission is still the reason why individuals dare to step out
from the mainstream of their lives and culture to be missionaries. They
are personally obeying the direct command of Jesus Christ.

But invoking the Great Commission often turns out to be unconvincing to church members as to why people other than their own
need to be evangelized. "After all," so the argument goes, "we have
more than enough sinners here at home to keep us busy." Or, "We
should first convert the sinners in our own country before sending
missionaries to other nations."

In the face of this argument, why should countries other than our
own be evangelized? Or, why should a church have a mission
program designed to convert people of other nationalities? Or, more
simply, "Why missions?"

The Great Commission does not give answers to these questions.
Nor was the Great Commission given to do so. To answer these
questions to the satisfaction of the church member, we must turn back
the pages of our Bibles to the Old Testament.

Missions: The Missing Dimension

This book, in preview then, is a theological study of missions
based on the Old Testament. But it is more than this. This book is a
particular way of looking at all the Scriptures. Specifically it is using
mission as a "principle for valid and meaningful interpretation of
Scripture [for] understanding the Scripture in the light of world
mission" (David J. Hesselgrave 1993).

However, in recent times this principle has been neglected in the
church and in the theological education of ministers and teachers. As
a result a serious "gap" has developed, both in the pulpit and in the
pew, in the interpretation of the Old Testament and how this large
portion of the Scriptures may and indeed should be applied today.

Many theological studies, of course, have been and will no doubt continue to be written on the message that the Old Testament has for us, each one containing valuable insights. Yet, in discussing the Old Testament the missionary dimension has more often than not been missing in the interpretation of topics and themes traditionally treated in theology.

My purpose in this regard therefore is to "fill in the gap," to present the missionary dimension to interpretation which, I believe as a missionary, any theological study must address in order to adequately explain the message of the Old Testament for our age. There are, I also believe, many benefits in recapturing the missionary dimension to Old Testament interpretation for preaching, teaching, and especially for explaining in this age of pluralism why we still have missions and missionaries.[1] There is still authority untapped in the Old Testament for the Christian evangelist.

Therefore in the many topics and texts that will be discussed in this book, I shall emphasize their missionary dimension, or in some instances, their potential for unfolding the missionary message of the Old Testament. This missionary emphasis makes contributions to the interpretation of the Old Testament text that often go unnoticed.

This is not to deny the validity of different emphases made in other theological studies on the Old Testament. But the purpose of my emphasis is to supply a long neglected dimension for a more complete interpretation. Happily it is the New Testament that exhibits this missionary dimension to the interpretation of the Old Testament.

The Old Testament was the only text or Bible that the church of the book of Acts had. The apostles and evangelists found in the Old Testament reasons for including the Gentiles in Israel's inheritance of eternal life.

The Unity Of The Scriptures

Many have noted that the Bible exhibits a structure allowing us to see a plan which is developing and leading to a goal or purpose to be fulfilled. J. Severino Croatto (1987:57), for example, states:

the Bible as a single text...establishes new relationships among its different parts, and among its distinct literary collections—legal, historical, prophetical, sapiential, evangelical, epistolary, apocalyptic, and so on. Like any structured work it has a beginning and an end—and an ordered progression between them. It runs from Genesis to Revelation along a particular route.

This observable structure of the Bible takes us back to the Old Testament for the beginning stages of the plan. Consequently our focus in this book will be on the structure of the biblical text and its meaning (Richard Jacobson 1986). To do this I will draw upon my background in the structuralism of linguistics and social anthropology (David Filbeck 1978, 1985). This is not the first time that structuralism has been used as an interpretative method for the Scriptures (Vern S. Poythress 1978), but to my knowledge it is the first time that it has been applied to the theology of mission.

Two aspects of structuralism are particularly insightful to our investigation of the biblical text. First, a structure is composed of components or parts, each performing a function. Second, when all components are brought together into a system, the whole actually adds up to more than what the individual parts suggest. That is, there is a meaning to the whole that is not apparent in its parts separately.[2]

To me, of course, the overall meaning of the biblical text—that "ordered progression" — is missions, the "flaming center" in the universal Gospel of hope (Carl E. Braaten 1977), the missing dimension in theological interpretation. Indeed, it is this missionary dimension, so often neglected in modern theological interpretation, that unifies both Old and New Testaments and coordinates their various themes into a single motif.[3] It is the logical connection between the Testaments that many modern theologians unfortunately seem to despair of ever finding (Claus Westermann 1963).

In short, the dimension of missions in the interpretation of the Scriptures gives structure to the whole Bible.[4] Any theological study of the Scriptures, therefore, must be formulated with the view of maintaining this structure. The missionary dimension to the interpretation of the Old Testament as displayed in the New Testament, I believe, accomplishes this in a way that no other theological theme can hope to match.

The plan for writing this book is to follow the progress of the biblical record from the beginning to its end, and not as a systematic arrangement of topics and issues. My primary purpose at this point is not to describe progressive revelation through the Old Testament. To be sure, God intervened and spoke to the people of the Old Testament many times and in various ways (Heb. 1:1). Rather, my approach is meant to describe the progression of understanding the will and plan—the mystery—of God (Eph. 3:4–6).

In a real sense, God said it all in calling Abraham so that all clans and nations might be blessed because of him (Gen. 12:1–3). After that, it was mainly a matter of working out the details and guiding Abraham's descendants (including Gentiles who are descendants through faith—Rom. 4:16) to maturity in fully understanding and obeying the implications of their call and election.

Winning The Lost

A word of clarification is needed at this point. Since the modern missionary movement has diversified into many different types of works, the purpose of this book is not meant to be a biblical basis or justification for every type currently conducted.

The purpose is to demonstrate the basis for cross-cultural evangelism of the lost in tribes, nations, or language groups other than our own. Even after two hundred years of the modern missionary movement, it is still not clear to many why we should actively seek to convert non-Christians who live in other nations and hold to non-Christian religions, perhaps even more fervently than we hold to Christianity. Prayerfully this book will make this necessity clearer.

Therefore, when we speak of missions in this book we are referring only to crossing boundaries of language and custom into cultures other than our own with the express purpose and goal of winning the lost to belief in Jesus Christ as Lord and Savior and establishing God's Kingdom, Christ's Church, to be a light or witness for God in those cultures.

Any other work that a missionary might do to advance this cause; such as building a hospital, teaching grade school, experimenting with planting a new variety of rice or vegetable, etc., while beneficial, is not included. These good works come and go according to the needs of time and place, and because of their very nature do not need biblical justification in an age of humanism.

But justifying the main task of missions in going and inviting the unbeliever and the lost to Jesus Christ (Mt. 11:28–30) will forever face the missionary because it appears so foolish, even unnecessary, in this world of religious pluralism and enlightened sensibilities. Providing a justification or apologetic for evangelizing non-Christians by showing that such was and is God's plan from the beginning of time is the purpose of this study.

Ultimately, of course, this book is a reflection of my own commitment to God's call to cross-cultural evangelism, of a desire to know God's will for his church today as revealed through the Scriptures, and finally, as with the Apostle Paul, this book is a reflection based on a continual and joyous wonderment of "this mystery, which for ages past was kept hidden in God, who created all things...that now, through the church, the manifold wisdom of God should be made known to the rulers and authorities in the heavenly realms, according to his eternal purpose which he accomplished in Christ Jesus our Lord" (Eph. 3:9–11).

Questions For Discussion

1. From reading this introductory chapter, do you think the Great Commission should theologically be considered as the beginning or concluding point to the Scriptural mandate for missions? Why?

2. Even though Paul was called directly to preach to the Gentiles, why did he appeal to the Old Testament to justify this activity?

3. In the mission work of the church today, to what should we appeal, the Great Commission or the Old Testament, in order to justify evangelizing ethnic groups other than our own? Why?

4. Have you ever considered that missions might be the key to interpreting and teaching the Old Testament today? If not, why not?

Endnotes

1. In this regard David J. Hesselgrave (1993) also states that using missions as a principle for interpreting the Scriptures is important in understanding biblical texts that do not deal explicitly with missions per se. For Bible interpreters, therefore, the missionary message of the Scriptures becomes an operative part of the mega-context of many, if not most, Bible books and passages. For the Old Testament specifically, Hesselgrave says that the missionary interpretation sheds new light on numerous Old Testament texts.

2. When applied to the Old Testament, for example, we may say that the various themes of the Old Testament are analogous to the components of a structure. Each theme may be the basis for a theology thus allowing for several theologies to be formulated from the Old Testament. However, when all themes or theologies are "added up," something else emerges. We may term that "something else" the theological meaning of the Old Testament around which all Old Testament themes revolve and find their interrelationships to one degree or another in forming the theological unity of the Old Testament.

3. For more discussion on the unity of the Scriptures, see Elmer A. Martens (1977) and Walter C. Kaiser, Jr. (1978). Stanley J. Grenz (1993:137) states that there is an "integrative motif of the Scriptures—a central organizational feature or orienting concept—that provides the thematic perspective in light of which all other theological concepts are understood and given their relative meaning or value." To me, it is mission that provides both the unity and integrative motif for the Scriptures.

4. J. Severino Croatto (1987:57) goes on to explain that this structure itself is part of the message of the biblical text. That is, since missions give structure to the biblical text, it is obvious that it is mission that the structure itself communicates.

CHAPTER TWO

The Missionary Message of the Old Testament

"They did not understand."

This assessment from two Thai evangelists came as we descended the mountain trail from the village where we had spent the previous night. We had been the first evangelistic team to ever proclaim the Gospel in this non-Christian village located near the Laotian border in northern Thailand. We had spent several hours in the evening playing Gospel records, witnessing, explaining Bible pictures, and answering questions. No one, though, had expressed any interest in believing our message about Jesus Christ.

The term "understand" is nearly synonymous with conversion in the thinking of Christians in northern Thailand. For if a person understands that the Gospel message is one of deliverance from the power of demons and release from the results of one's karma, then the person, it is reasoned, will surely become Christian. After all, there can be no better news than this!

Indeed, lack of understanding the Scriptures is a major obstacle in evangelism in Thailand. Many non-Christians in Thailand have reported that they have read the Bible and have even enjoyed the stories of events and miracles contained in it. They also say that they do not really understand the Bible. What they mean is that while the individual stories are clear enough (they are similar enough to present-day experiences to be recognized), it is not clear what overall meaning they should "add up to" for contemporary life in Thai society.[1]

Not understanding what the Scriptures add up to is not a problem confined to non-Christians in Thailand, however. This problem also affects Christians, especially when it comes to the Old Testament and what it should mean to Christ's church today.

At Antioch of Pisidia

What is the missionary message of the Old Testament?

This is no idle question, even though it has been a much neglected one in recent theological studies of the Old Testament. The question is important because in the 400 years immediately preceding the coming of Christ, and in the absence of a Great Commission in the Old Testament, the Jewish people witnessed to surrounding non-Jewish populations that they too must worship the God of Abraham, Isaac, and Jacob.

In other words, what "message" did the Jewish proselytizers find in the Old Testament that propelled them to witness to those outside their own religious communities? What method did the rabbis and scholars employ that allowed them to interpret the Old Testament in such a "missionary" manner, and which Paul and others in the early church took over and used so successfully in evangelizing the Roman Empire of their time?

When Paul and Barnabas, for example, on their first missionary tour arrived in Antioch of Pisidia (south central Turkey — Acts 13:13–48), they entered the local Jewish synagogue and were immediately invited to speak. Paul began his message by reviewing Jewish history in the Old Testament from Abraham through Israel's slavery in Egypt and on to the time of King David. He ended his message by proclaiming that Jesus is the fulfillment of the Scriptures as spoken through David. Afterwards many Jews and devout proselytes followed Paul and Barnabas to discuss this message more fully. Paul and Barnabas encouraged them to continue in their new-found interest in Jesus Christ.

The following Sabbath a great number of non-Jews, in addition to Jews and proselytes, gathered at the synagogue to hear Paul speak again. Upon seeing the crowd of non-Jews, the Jews became jealous and spoke against Paul and his message. Paul retorted that he and Barnabas would now turn from their Jewish brethren and preach to the Gentiles. To justify this move Paul quoted in Acts from Isaiah 49:6,

Acts 13:46–47

...We had to speak the word of God to you first. Since you reject it and do not consider yourselves worthy of eternal life, we now turn to the Gentiles. For this is what the Lord has commanded us: "I have made you a light for the Gentiles, that you may bring salvation to the ends of the earth."

Of interest here is the fact that the Apostle Paul referred to this quote as a command from the Lord. In fact, in the Greek language which he was speaking at the time, Paul used the verb entellomai which has the meaning of an explicit, definite order or command to do something specific (Johannes P. Louw and Eugene A. Nida 1988:426). However, a linguistic analysis of the following quote from Isaiah reveals no imperative verb. An imperative or command-giving verb is also lacking in the Hebrew, the original language of Isaiah 49:6.

Why did Paul at Antioch of Pisidia say that this verse from Isaiah was a specific command when linguistically the verse contains no such command?

Exegesis And Hermeneutics

The answer lies in realizing that in interpreting and understanding what the Bible means, there are really two steps involved. The first is call exegesis and the second hermeneutics.[2]

Walter David Stacy (1977:6) explains the difference between the two steps with these words.

[T]he distinction between original sense [of a text] and modern sense is a real one. This distinction is so important that it is proper to speak of two separate techniques in the field of biblical studies, one concerned with original meaning and commonly called exegesis, the other concerned with present meaning and sometimes called hermeneutics...The exegete can explain why Paul appealed to Philemon in the terms he did. The interpreter tries to translate that appeal into an attitude and a mode of conduct that are applicable today.

More specifically exegesis is the study of the biblical text linguistically in terms of its words and grammar and what the author meant by both (grammatical structure has meaning as well as words). This is the historically intended meaning that the author wanted his readers to understand. An exegesis of a text, then, is describing for readers today 1) the historical context in which the text was written, 2) the meaning, and 3) how the context and meaning interacted to show the intention of the author; i.e., what the author originally wanted to achieve in his readers' understanding.

Hermeneutics, on the other hand, takes the conclusions (linguistics and otherwise) of exegetical studies and shows at what points each conclusion links up with life today to achieve an understanding that both explains and leads to a faithful obedience to the Word under today's circumstances.

Diogenes Allen (1985:272), for instance, defines hermeneutics as "the study of the principles of how we bring [ancient text and present day interpreter] together so that understanding is possible."

Some evangelical theologians, however, object to defining hermeneutics in terms of understanding (Julius Scott in personal conversation).[3] Such a definition is reminiscent of liberal theology and the so-called "new hermeneutics" where the Scriptures are to be interpreted existentially.

But for this book my association of hermeneutics with understanding is not based on liberal theology. Rather, as the opening story of this chapter indicates, it is based on mission field experience in Thailand.[4]

Another source, perhaps more closely related to theology, is the concept of functional equivalence in translating the Scriptures.[5] In this concept the emphasis is not only on the meaning of the text but also on how readers are likely to understand the translated Scriptures (Jan de Waar and Eugene A. Nida 1986:5). For functional equivalence Johannes P. Louw and Eugene A. Nida (1988:380) define understanding as "a process by which information is used in order to arrive at a correct comprehension or evaluation."

In other words, just as the goal in translation is for readers today to understand the text as the original readers did, so the goal here theologically is for readers to understand the Old Testament as Christians of the New Testament church did.

From the above remarks, then, hermeneutics may properly be considered an extension "of the rules of exegesis...to cover all that is involved in the process of perceiving [understanding] what the biblical revelation means and how it bears on our lives;"[6] it is an updating that shows the relevance of the biblical text for today (J. Severino Croatto 1987). The system of linkages to life today that emerges from this type of updating may be called an interpretation or, more technically, a hermeneutic.

The term hermeneutic (in the singular), as used above, has a double-sided definition. On one side it is a system of interpretation that relates the various parts of the Scriptures to show overall meaning and direction of meaning in the text.

From the other side, a hermeneutic refers to a particular way of understanding the Scriptures, more precisely the overall meaning of the biblical text. That is to say, a hermeneutic is an interpretation that provides a "mapping" of the biblical record so the reader, teacher, or interpreter can organize biblical material in order to arrive at an overall understanding of the Scriptures.[7]

At this level the term hermeneutic becomes equivalent to theology, more precisely theological interpretation. In fact, a theology in this perspective is a hermeneutic for interpreting and understanding the Scriptures. However, while the two terms are equivalent they are not synonymous. A hermeneutic at this level refers not only to the meaning and message of the Scriptures in their entirety (as in theology), but also to the methods and rules one may use to arrive at that understanding of the overall meaning of the Scriptures.[8]

From the above discussion, therefore, hermeneutics (in the plural) now involves more than the analysis of short texts (such as a verse, paragraph, or chapter of Scripture). Hermeneutics includes the analysis of the overall intent and purpose of a complete text, plus demonstrating at what points the overall intent links up with life today to similarly achieve an understanding that faithfully explicates and executes the overall intent or meaning of the document.[9]

For example, the missionary message of the Old Testament may be termed the missionary hermeneutic, or more simply the hermeneutic, of the Old Testament.[10] That is, this hermeneutic, in addition to stating that the overall intent and meaning of the Old Testament is missionary in nature, also maps out how every aspect of the Old Testament should be analyzed to show how it relates and, more crucially, contributes to the task of evangelizing non-Christian populations in the world today.

Consequently there is a hermeneutical key for understanding and interpreting the Old Testament. That key is the missionary message of the Old Testament as revealed in the New Testament.

This hermeneutical key consists basically of three parts. There are a) the direct statements mentioning that nations other than Israel shall participate in God's blessing (Gen. 12:3), and b) indirect but foundational concepts found in the Old Testament that provide a deeper or more general theological level from which to justify the inclusion of the nations in his blessing.

An example of this latter is the praise of God in universal terms as Lord of heaven and earth in the Psalms (see Chapter Seven). The first two points reveal a direction to take in interpreting the Scriptures

which in turn leads to the third part, c) subjecting texts not traditionally thought as having a missionary interpretation to see how they fit
in and contribute to the missionary dimension of the Old Testament.[11]

Now let us turn back to Paul and his preaching from Isaiah to see
these two steps in Old Testament interpretation, exegesis and
hermeneutics, in action in New Testament evangelism.

Isaiah: A Missionary Interpretation

The book of Isaiah was already a 700-year-old document by New
Testament times. In other words, it needed to be interpreted and
updated to be relevant to a world of Jewish dispersion—living in
racially mixed communities with Gentiles, foreign domination, modern warfare, etc. The missionary interpretation of Isaiah was that
update; it was the hermeneutic that related an ancient document to
the circumstances of that time.

The following diagram helps us visualize what I mean. It is a
diagram of Isaiah 49:6, the verse that Paul announced as a command
(even though there was no verb in the imperative mode in the quote)
for preaching the Gospel to the Gentiles. The diagram is divided into
three parts: a text, an exegesis (here restricted to a functional analysis
of the text's two clauses) and its hermeneutic (meaning).

Text	Exegesis	Hermeneutic
I have made you a light for the Gentiles }	Topic	Meaning: A Command To Evangelize The Gentiles
That you may bring salvation to the ends of the earth }	Purpose	

The above diagram illustrates that exegetically the language of
Isaiah 49:6 consists of two parts: a topic or statement ("I have made
you...") plus the purpose of the stated topic ("...[to] bring salvation..."). Now to Paul and many of his contemporaries, the purpose

of God as revealed in this text was command enough to demand obedience in bringing salvation to the Gentiles. It is as though they were saying that God's wish was their command![12]

Paul's conclusion—that God's desire to include the nations of the earth in his salvation is to be interpreted as a command—may be termed the missionary interpretation of the Old Testament. This interpretation is the hermeneutic that yields the missionary message of the Old Testament. Briefly stated the message is this. *We see, as we read the Old Testament, that God's purpose for his people in being light for the nations of this world is also his command to us to bring salvation to the ends of the earth.*

Revealing this purpose and demonstrating its imperative from the Old Testament for us today is the thesis that will guide our look through the Old Testament to discover God's will and desire for his people.

Reviving the Missionary Interpretation of the Old Testament

I once listened to a series of five sermons on Isaiah delivered by Bible and theological professors. They addressed many topics from this Old Testament book that were deemed theologically important. However, no professor discussed the one topic that by New Testament times had become the hermeneutic for interpreting Isaiah. The missing topic was the missionary message of Isaiah which the Apostle Paul, for example, used in Antioch of Pisidia to justify his and Barnabas' proclamation of the Gospel to non-Jews.

For this reason, I believe, it is important to keep hermeneutics as something different from exegesis. Otherwise, as in the above illustration, we have only exegesis with no basis for saying how the Old Testament is to be related to a world where the majority of the population is non-Christian. Instead the Old Testament becomes what its name implies, old, a neglected part of the Bible.

But in distinguishing exegesis from hermeneutics, the two must not be divorced from each other. This unfortunately has been the case in liberal scholarship. To liberal theologians the more important task is not what the writers of the Scriptures originally meant to say (the function of exegesis) but what the Scriptures mean to us in our time and context (the function of hermeneutics).

Hermeneutics divorced from exegesis is left without grounding in what the Scriptures say (Clark H. Pinnock 1984). In the rush to be relevant to our post-modern age, liberal theologians often neglect exegesis, at which point hermeneutics (relevancy) ends up saying little or nothing on how the Scriptures (both Old and New Testaments) are to be understood—and more crucially obeyed—in a world where most of the population is non-Christian.

When either occurs (exegesis without hermeneutics or hermeneutics devoid of exegesis), the missionary message of the Old Testament is overlooked and the missionary outreach of the church takes second place.

The time has come to revive and give top priority, as the Apostle Paul did in Antioch of Pisidia, to the missionary interpretation of the Old Testament, especially as we enter the twenty-first century realizing that two-thirds of the world's population is still non-Christian. There are lessons to be learned for evangelizing the rest of the world by reviewing the Old Testament.

Unfortunately this hermeneutic or view of the Old Testament has been submerged and all but lost in the midst of other theological and hermeneutical questions of the past 500 years. Before we proceed, therefore, we should survey this history because of its impact on the interpretation and application within Christ's church of both the Great Commission and the Old Testament mission imperative that lies behind the Great Commission.

Questions For Discussion

1. Why did Paul say that Isaiah 49:6 was a command?

2. From your understanding of the two terms, is it legitimate to draw a distinction, as is done in this chapter, between exegesis and hermeneutics? Why?

3. Before reading this chapter, what message or meaning did you understand the Old Testament to have for you in this day and time?

4. From your knowledge of the book of Isaiah, what should be the major theme and application of this Old Testament prophetic book for us today? Does this differ from the interpretation of Isaiah as proposed here? If so, how does it differ?

5. How do you interpret the purposes of God as revealed in the Scriptures? Should God's purposes be viewed as commands or as statements (propositions) that contain no mandate for individuals to obey? Why?

6. Why does mission outreach from the church suffer when, a) exegesis of the Scriptures is devoid of hermeneutics, and b) hermeneutics is divorced from exegesis?

Endnotes

1. Of course, sometimes a person understands but will not convert. When this happens, Christians in northern Thailand will attribute such refusal to hardness of heart, opposition from family and neighbors, social pressure from peers, etc.

2. Many have drawn attention, in one degree or another, to the distinction between exegesis and hermeneutics (Frederick W. Danker 1987, Carl E. Braaten 1966, Anthony C. Thiselton 1980).

3. For example, Grant R. Osborne (1991:5) "oppose[s]…the practice today of using 'exegesis' for the study of the text's meaning and 'hermeneutics' for its significance in the present."

4. Insights from my background in missions and cross-cultural communication of the Gospel, in other words, provide the major motivations for distinguishing exegesis from hermeneutics.

Ever since the publication of *Mission And Message* by Eugene A. Nida (1960), for example, understanding or response on the part of the reader/listener has assumed a crucial role in effectively communicating the Gospel cross-culturally. For if the reader-listener does not understand, then how can we say that the Gospel has adequately been communicated? Indeed, the issue is as important domestically as it is cross-culturally, for as James F. Engel (1993) remarks, telling the story of Jesus in such a way that it is understood is the responsibility of the Christian communicator. The audience, Engel exclaims, is sovereign when it comes to telling the story of Jesus Christ.

In missionary evangelism there is little difference between communicating the Gospel cross-culturally and the theological interpretation of the Scriptures for recipients (listeners, readers) who are non-Christians of another culture and language. For if the purpose and message of the Bible are not understood, how can we say that the Bible has been properly interpreted? In other words, understanding must be taken into account if the Scriptures are to be adequately interpreted theologically. Or, to paraphrase Engel above, to interpret the Bible in a way that is correctly understood is the responsibility of the theologian.

5. In addition to evangelism and church planting in my missionary ministry in Thailand, I have also translated the complete New Testament into Mal, a Mon-Khmer language spoken by over 6000 people in Nan Province in northern Thailand.

6. Quoted from Article IX of the Chicago Statement On Biblical Hermeneutics (Donald K. McKim 1986:23). Even on a much broader scale than what is presented in this book, I believe that evangelical theologians should reconsider understanding and its role in hermeneutics. There are at least two reasons for this.

First, understanding is properly a hermeneutical task (see following endnote); there is no understanding of the Scriptures or any other aspect of life without hermeneutics or interpretation. Second, non-Christians often have "understandings" of Christians, the church, and the Scriptures that are both inadequate and incorrect and which prevent them from considering belief in Jesus Christ. Therefore, since two-thirds of the world is non-Christian, the overriding theological task of today is not correct exegesis or having the right hermeneutical rules for exegesis; these have long been worked out by competent scholars.

Rather, it is for theologians to assist in formulating how the Gospel message may be correctly understood, on the part of non-Christian listeners, as it is communicated in contemporary life by Christian witnesses. For a detailed study of these broader theological issues as they must relate to missiology, see John R. Davis (1993).

7. That a hermeneutic is a mapping for organizing and understanding the biblical record also finds precedent in the social sciences and their utilization in missiology for the task of interpreting and understanding culture which, in Charles Tabor's (1978) words, is a "hermeneutic task." For a more detailed discussion of social and cultural knowledge as a hermeneutic and explanatory method in the social sciences, see W. Stark (1958) (reviewed in Susan J. Hekman 1986) and Grant R. Osborne (1991:139f).

8. From this perspective a hermeneutic functions as a cognitive strategy for selecting pertinent data from the Scriptures and relating such data into a system of knowledge. For a more detailed discussion of both cognitive mapping and cognitive strategy and their role in knowledge and understanding, see David Filbeck (1985).

9. Hans-Georg Gadamer (1975), in his explanatory treatise on hermeneutics, describes this link-up of an ancient text with today's circumstances as a fusion. To Gadamer, the interpretation of a text expands from the horizon of the world of its original setting to "fuse" with the horizon of the world of the reader or interpreter who, by the very nature of the case, is living in another time and place. In a comment on the significance of Gadamer's work, D. P. Fuller (1982) summarizes that "The hermeneutical problem is not one of the correct

mastery of language, but of the proper understanding of that which takes place through the medium of language."

10. David J. Hesselgrave (1993) also uses the term hermeneutic in this sense. He states that a "missionary hermeneutic" grows out of the teaching of many Bible texts so that the texts in turn may become foundational for understanding the whole of Scripture. It functions as a pre-understanding for the interpretation of the whole Bible.

11. Such a procedure is similar to the Hermeneutic Spiral advocated in Grant R. Osborne (1991).

12. Of course this is not a new idea in Old Testament interpretation. Leonard Hodgson, writing in the *Church Quarterly Review* in 1942 (quoted in Walter C. Kaiser, Jr. 1983:16) stated that in pre-Christian Judaism the will of God was the source of obligation. It was this understanding of obligation, in other words, that the New Testament church took over in interpreting and obeying the Old Testament as well.

CHAPTER THREE

Hermeneutics and the Missionary Imperative

The age of discovery, initiated by Columbus in 1492, redirected and rejuvenated Christian missions in ways unforeseen during the previous 1000 years.[1] Explorers discovered new continents, new lands, and thousands of new ethnic groups without knowledge of the Christian religion and more importantly, unrelated to any other major religion such as Islam or the ethico-religious systems of the Far East.

These new discoveries impacted the way people would come to interpret the Scriptures with regard to missions as well. In the Roman Catholic church at the time, the conquest theory of mission was already in operation (Johannes Verkuyl 1978). In fact Columbus, in addition to his quest for new trade routes to the Far East, had set sail with the objective that new lands and peoples should also be Christianized (Kevin A. Miller 1992). For the church, then, it was only a matter of immediately accepting the challenge of planting the church in new lands and among non-Christian peoples. Between 1493 and 1820, for example, Spain sent over 15,000 missionaries to the Americas and in Mexico alone baptized 5,000,000 native Americans (Thomas S. Giles 1992).

Meanwhile back in Europe, a revolt against the Roman Catholic church was taking place. The Protestant Reformation led by Martin Luther and others stirred the continent. Unlike missions in the Roman Catholic church, Protestants were initially unaffected by the age of discovery, and only by way of a long, tortuous route would the discovery of new lands and peoples finally have a similar impact for missions in the Protestant Reformation. In fact, it would be more than 200 years before the Protestant Reformation finally "caught up" with the age of discovery and succeeded in evangelizing non-Christians in other lands.

Missions And The Protestant Reformation

In the early days a conspicuous lack of mission activity characterized Protestantism. Several reasons accounted for this. Not least among them was the way the Scriptures had come to be interpreted.

First, biblical studies were not primarily to discover what the Scriptures say about missions but to strengthen the Protestant theological position on issues such as the priesthood of all believers, the Lord's Supper, salvation by faith, the all-sufficiency of the Scriptures, etc. As a result the missionary intent of the Scriptures was all but lost in the midst of other theological concerns of the Reformation.

Second, from a hermeneutical perspective, many believed that the Great Commission was given only for the Apostles of New Testament times. Some even interpreted the Scriptures to mean that missions to non-Christian peoples were an insult to the sovereignty of God who would save the heathen without human intervention. Missions therefore would be presumptuous if not sinful for the church to initiate.

A third reason was that many Reformers believed that the second coming of Christ was imminent. In other words, there would not be enough time in the history of the world to start obeying the Great Commission by sending forth missionaries to recently discovered lands.

A fourth reason for the lack of a missionary impact on Scripture interpretation was that orthodox Protestants (those who believed the Great Commission was given only to the Apostles) opposed and sometimes persecuted other Protestants who believed that the Scriptures still mandate the church to send missionaries to evangelize non-Christians.

Nevertheless, in spite of this initial bad showing, a mission consciousness eventually developed in the Protestant Reformation. In the 17th Century, for example, Dutch missionaries followed the Dutch East India Company to foreign lands and engaged in evangelizing non-Christian peoples in addition to serving as ministers to Dutch expatriates. Also the first missionary societies, the Society for the Propagation of the Gospel in New England and the Society for Promoting Christian Knowledge, were established.

The main reason that a mission consciousness emerged, however, was due to the influence of the pietistic movement in Protestantism. The pietists believed that a close, personal relationship with God was more important than holding to correctly formulated doctrine.

This emphasis on piety in the personal life led people to understand that while the Great Commission was indeed given first to the Apostles, an interpretation of the Great Commission required that the Christians of every age should obey its commands of going and making disciples of all nations.

The earliest example of pietism combined with missionary outreach was the Moravians. In 1727 the Moravians sent out their first missionaries and by 1760 a total of 226 missionaries was serving in non-European lands.

New Beginnings

The early explorers who followed Columbus to the new world discovered not only new lands but also new peoples. At first, these peoples with their strange customs, languages, and sometimes lack of clothing according to European standards of the time, were objects of curiosity. Before long scholars of the time began to suggest theories of how and where these people fit in the general scheme of social and human evolution. Some called them savages, others called them primitive or heathen. A few saw in them a noble humanity unspoiled by modern ways of life.

But as more reports and data filtered in from faraway places, it became apparent that these people, while exotic from a European perspective, were still human beings. This consensus meant two things to the Protestant pietist. These recently discovered people were 1) sinners along with the rest of humanity and 2) therefore worthy of salvation and winning to the Kingdom of Jesus Christ.

Two English clergymen who realized these implications and who went on missions to the Americas and preached to the Indians were George Whitefield (1714-1770) and John Wesley (1703-1791). These two also came in contact with Moravian missionaries. Consequently when the great English revival occurred as the result of the preaching of these men, a concern within England for the need to send missionaries to non-Christians soon followed.

The preaching of these two men was more than just motivational, however. In their preaching they also provided a hermeneutic for interpreting the world (now including both Europe and the discoveries of new lands and peoples) in such a way that allowed people to see that preaching to non-Christians could indeed be productive. That is, the doctrine of God's sovereignty did not of necessity exclude understanding on the part of these new world peoples. They, too, were able to decide on their own whether to become Christian or not.

For example, Whitefield believed in predestination. Yet he preached that even within God's sovereignty to predestine to heaven or hell, a person still had the duty to listen and repent, to wait for that sign of predestination. Upon this basis Whitefield called the masses to repentance helping to spur the English world to revival during his lifetime.

John Wesley, on the other hand, was an Arminian believing in the person's free will to decide or reject. Since humans had freedom to act upon what was heard, Wesley likewise called the masses of the English countryside to repentance. Whitefield and Wesley disagreed and for a time parted ways over the issues of predestination and free will. Yet each, on his respective basis, went on calling the English world to repentance and revival.

Wesley found support for his thinking on human free will from a treatise on human knowledge written earlier by the English empirical philosopher John Locke (1632-1704) (Bernard Semmel 1973, Richard E. Brantley 1984). In this treatise Locke rejected the theory of innate ideas which had been a widely accepted theory since Plato (third century B.C.). In its place Locke suggested the theory that a person is born without innate ideas and that all knowledge is gained from experience.

One line of evidence that Locke used to support his theory was the idea of God. Since this idea was considered basic in human knowledge it followed that everyone should have some idea about God. However, we do not find this to be the case. Therefore, any person who has an idea about God has obtained such from learning and experience.

In other words, if humans are indeed born without innate ideas and learn of God by experience, then the heathen in other lands were also born in the same manner and could similarly learn of God and come to faith in His Son Jesus Christ. Indeed, Locke's theory showed the imperative for mission work in a way that Platonic innate ideas could not.

The writings of Locke on language were also influential. Borrowing from the humanists of the Renaissance, Locke taught that language is governed by the rules of grammar and conventional usage. Conversely language is to be interpreted and understood by the same rules. This implied that there is no sacred language as many thought Greek and Latin were. That is, Greek and Latin were no different than English, German, or any other known language of the time. It also meant that the interpretation of Scripture as recorded in Greek and

Latin should follow the rules of ordinary language and not according to special theological or ecclesiastical dictates.

Wesley incorporated these insights into his strategy for preaching the Gospel among the masses of the English countryside. In fact, it probably can be said that Wesley was Locke's interpreter in the pietistic movement of the Protestant Reformation. Through Wesley's preaching, Locke's ideas penetrated the religious masses, the segment of English society where William Carey (1761-1834), a shoe cobbler, was a member.

The Turning Point

The real turning point in Protestant missions came with William Carey who later spent his life as a missionary in India. In 1792 Carey first published a pamphlet titled *An Enquiry into the Obligation of Christians to Use Means for the Conversion of the Heathen*. It is generally recognized that this pamphlet changed the Protestant Reformation from being only an inward-looking reformation of an existing condition in the Christian religion to that of an outward-looking movement to convert and incorporate non-Christian populations into the Kingdom of Christ.

Of interest to us here are the biblical reasons which Carey gave to support the argument that Christians still had the obligation to evangelize non-Christians. He divided his pamphlet into five sections designed to counter objections to missions which were prevalent in his time.

In the first section, Carey argued against the belief that the Great Commission was given only to the Apostles. In other words, the Great Commission was still obligatory for the church in every age, including the church of the eighteenth century.

Section two gave a brief overview of mission history beginning with Acts to show that the expansion of the church into non-Christian lands was and should still be normative for the church.

Section three was a survey of the world and its population. It ended with the assertion that the heathen or non-Christian peoples were as capable of learning as (European) Christians; that is, they were as capable of faith and therefore should be evangelized.

Section four was a practical survey of how missions could be successfully accomplished. For example, ships were regularly traveling to all parts of the world, thus making transportation possible for the missionary. Because explorers and traders had gone and lived, and more importantly survived in primitive conditions, missionaries could do the same. Even the possibility of missionaries being killed should be no obstacle as the church has had martyrs throughout history. And since traders were learning other languages in order to do business, missionaries could also learn languages in order to preach the Gospel.

The fifth section set forth the duties of the church and Christians in mobilizing to send missionaries. The first duty was to pray. Then an organization should be formed, a society, composed of members from different denominations. The society should be supported by individual contributions and from the budgets of churches. At this point missionaries could be sent out.

In short, Carey dared to say through his Enquiry that the slogan of the Protestant Reformation, sola scriptura, had been subverted by having been turned into a "gag rule" on the Great Commission, for while the slogan gave a correct exegesis of the Great Commission, it prevented an interpretation for the church of the eighteenth century and beyond. Exegesis of the Great Commission was not enough, for exegesis alone produced only an ultra-literalness (or orthodoxy, as it was termed in Carey's day) of this final command of Christ. An interpretation of the Great Commission was needed to show its meaning for Christians.

The Great Century

On this basis, to use Kenneth Scott Latourette's term, the Great Century of missions was launched. Indeed, Protestant missions over the next 100 years succeeded beyond the dreams of William Carey and the few who first joined him to form a missionary society in 1792. In short, the ideas on human knowledge and language which Whitefield and Wesley put into practice during the eighteenth century found compatibility with the heart of the Protestant pietist of the nineteenth century, for these ideas gave reason and respectability to what (s)he felt about the possibility—indeed the imperative—of doing mission work among the non-Christian ethnic groups of the world.

More specifically, these views were an affirmation of the missionary's own intuition and feelings about what truth is, and above all, what God's will is today as revealed through an understanding of the Great Commission. They allowed the missionary to cogently explain what was burning in the soul, thus leading others to go also, and inspiring churches to support them.

In other words, a common sense approach was used when interpreting the Scriptures. For the first time the common person possessed a hermeneutic for arriving at the meaning of the Great Commission and making a personal decision about missions and feeling right by that decision. There was no need to depend on the expert from church or the theological university. This approach to missions reached its most productive phase in Hudson Taylor (1832-1905) when he first went as a missionary to China, and later on established the China Inland Mission based on these same common sense values.[2]

To the Protestant missionary of the nineteenth century, these views had other, more far-reaching implications. If Greek and Latin were not sacred in and of themselves, for example, then the Scriptures could be communicated by means of any other language of the world. More importantly, translating and printing the Scriptures in another language would not be blasphemous. To the contrary, Scripture translation would be a theological necessity if the full scope of the Great Commission was to be obeyed, for after making disciples of other nations, there was the additional task of teaching them to observe all things that Jesus Christ has commanded (Matthew 28:19–20), a task that could not be successful without the Scriptures first being translated into the language of the new disciples.

Consequently, during the 100 years of the nineteenth century alone, the Scriptures were translated into a total of 446 new languages. This averages out to more than 44 languages every ten years receiving translation. More revealing, though, are the statistics that during the decade of 1800 to 1810 the Scriptures were translated into 26 new languages while from 1890 to 1900 there were 100 translations (William Smalley 1991).

From all the advances in missions of the nineteenth century, it is surprising to note that no definite theology of mission was formulated (Carl E. Braaten 1977). Evidently people were too busy doing missions to do much reflecting on the Scriptural basis for their work. This failure, I believe, soon proved disastrous for the mission outreach of the Protestant Reformation. For in retrospect we now see that no theological direction was given to prepare this missionary movement for the upcoming twentieth century. The nineteenth century was an age of progress and optimism. It was hard to see that life would be any different in the future.

Missions And Hermeneutics In the Twentieth Century

Not all was positive throughout the nineteenth century. There was also a negative side. Other, darker movements soon impacted the missions of the Protestant Reformation. During the eighteenth century the Enlightenment came into being, a varied social and political movement whose followers esteemed human reasoning as the final criterion for knowing truth. As the nineteenth century dawned, a generation of philosophers emerged who expanded the ramifications of John Locke's ideas on human reason and knowledge in ways that exceeded their original application. For Locke, reason and rationalism were tools to help Christians justify belief in the basic core of Christianity. Now their role was to stand in judgment over the reasonableness of the Christianity that Locke had defended.

Due to the age of discovery, knowledge about non-Christian religions in other parts of the world increased. Stories of myths and legends filtered in from diverse lands and peoples. These stories, while different in content, were of the same genre or type as found in ancient biblical literature. Other religions also contained creation and flood stories, myths of giants, heroes and saviors, legends of great victories, etc.

This similarity raised several questions. What was the difference, if any, between the Bible and the sacred stories, myths, and legends from other religions? Was there any rationale for accepting the Bible as unique among the religious literature of the world? By what authority did modern individuals accept the Bible as unique?

This last question was especially pertinent because the Enlightenment had already rejected any notion that ecclesiastical or traditional authority as found in Roman Catholicism was reasonable for accepting the Christian Scriptures as uniquely from God.

Without any such authority the conclusion seemed obvious. Neither in its content or literary construction was the Bible unique or even particularly special. That is, the Bible had no intrinsic merit by which to commend itself as God's only word to a world rapidly expanding in knowledge about other religions.

Such a conclusion led to the destruction of confidence in the text of the Bible. Of course, exegesis of the Scriptures could still be done, but now it was a meaningless exercise. The only way that the Bible could be studied with any promise of being meaningful for the modern age was from a historical and critical viewpoint. By this method those parts of the Scriptures critically considered more mythical in nature could be eliminated. The remainder would then be the true core of the Bible which could be rationally accepted.

Before long, implications of this historical method had permeated Protestant thought and for many people, it became unthinkable to view the Bible in any other way. Furthermore this factor impacted missions. If the Bible was just one of many religious documents in the world, then no valid rationale existed for evangelism among people of other religions. Consequently many persons begin to question the need and even the legitimacy of evangelism among non-Christian people who had their own religion and sacred literature.

However, others thought that all was not lost, for within Protestantism a compromise was at hand. Evolution coupled with nineteenth century progressivism (classic liberalism) was invoked to justify missionary activity. The progress of the Christian religion through its missions was now closely tied to the progress of society in general. It made little difference if this compromise could not be supported by Scripture exegesis. This hermeneutic could still explain in meaningful language the rationale and purpose of Christian missions in an enlightened age. In other words, God's purpose in this modern age, and which therefore should be the command of the modern church as well, was to bring the good fruits of western progress to the ends of the earth.

Before long, social progress took precedence and the emphasis shifted away from evangelism to social concerns in a large segment of Protestant missions. The rationale for missions so eloquently expressed by William Carey in his interpretative essay on the Great Commission was set aside. Now it became more rational to justify missions on the basis of social progress.

Alarms over these developments were raised by fundamentalists both in missions and mission-sending churches. Fundamentalists, in seeking to preserve the fundamentals of Christian faith, quickly saw that these developments would eventually destroy missions and evangelism. But the objections proved too little and too late. The twentieth century had already dawned and the next forty years (1914-1945) of war, communism, depression, and war again, overturned the world of social progress and fundamentalist objection.

In those turbulent years Protestantism divided into two camps, liberal and fundamentalist. On the liberal side the biblical text and exegesis of the text were downgraded and hermeneutics, now often referred to as the "new hermeneutics," elevated. This further eroded confidence in the biblical text.

Exegesis, as a valid task in biblical studies, was ultimately undermined, setting the more preferred task of hermeneutics adrift without any certainty. This impacted the Great Commission in a negative way and missions in the liberal camp suffered gradual decline throughout the decades following World War II.

On the fundamentalist side several developments took place. First, fundamentalists went on the defensive to preserve what was being lost, namely the integrity of the biblical text. Without a Bible people could trust, no exegetical basis for missions existed. No grounding for the classical hermeneutic of the Great Commission would be possible.

Second, fundamentalism was redefined as conservative and evangelical Christianity; i.e., regardless of what changes take place in society and in the world, evangelizing and winning the lost to Christ were to be conserved as essential to the Gospel message.

In the decades following World War II, evangelical missions expanded beyond belief: scores of new mission agencies (formerly called missionary societies) were established and the number of new missionaries soared into the tens of thousands (Ralph Winter 1970). Even as old colonial empires disintegrated and newly independent countries emerged to fill the void, an unending supply of new missionaries arose to evangelize and establish Christ's church among non-Christian populations.

We can rejoice in the explosive growth of evangelical missions in the second half of the twentieth century. However, in making a deeper analysis of this growth, we see that its motivation is derived from the Great Commission and not based on the Old Testament mandate for mission. Since hermeneutics is largely restricted to exegesis, a missionary interpretation of the Old Testament is precluded. This is exegesis without hermeneutics, resulting in the full missionary potential of the Old Testament being overlooked and more crucially neglected in the task of evangelism that faces the church in the twenty-first century.

For example, most evangelical books on the biblical basis for missions begin with the New Testament, the Great Commission, or the person and mission of Jesus Christ as the main starting point. The Old Testament is given no role except by occasional reference to the missionary implications of the book of Jonah or the instruction in the Mosaic Law to take care of the goyim, aliens or Gentiles, who lived in Israel.

Fortunately this greater emphasis on the Great Commission has not hindered an ever increasing number of new missionaries from going to do mission work in other nations. But this should come as no surprise, for this is the function of the Great Commission. On the other hand, however, there is at least one bad side effect.

With few exceptions missions have become a department—that is, compartmentalized—in the church and are no longer her purpose in the world. Moreover evangelical theology has reinforced this compartmentalization by focusing on other topics and issues. Once more the missionary dimension of biblical interpretation goes unnoticed in the midst of other theological concerns. This reinforcement filters down to theological education and the training of Christian workers, finally settling as a mindset in the local congregation.

The compartmentalization of missions in the life of the church is an untenable position, both in theological interpretation and in practice. How then can this practice be corrected? It is said that bad theology makes for bad practice.

The converse then should be true. Good theology makes for good practice. Good theology in this case I believe is returning to the missionary message of the Old Testament. For when we see that the overall purpose of the Old Testament is to take God's message of salvation to the ends of the earth, so shall we then see that the command of the whole church will be to evangelize the non-Christian groups who live around the world.

The function of theology and theologians is to show that the ultimate purpose of the Old Testament is evangelism. In more specific terms their duty is to explicate the mission hermeneutic of the Old Testament that the church will need for the twenty-first century. This will require, in Lois McKinney's words (1993),

a reintegration of theological disciplines that will demand a radical departure from the departmentalized and compartmentalized curricula which characterize so much of theological education today. The disciplinary streams related to the study of hermeneutics will converge as understandings of historical backgrounds, literary genre, and broader biblical contexts flow into the grammatical analyses of specific Bible texts...[C]ourses...will be interdisciplinary, interactive, and dialogical. Specialization will give way to integration...In the process, missionaries will be better prepared to live and serve in a post-Enlightenment world.

The church and her missions will no doubt face increasing difficulty both in recruiting new missionaries and funding their work. The full motivational and mobilizing power for missions contained in the Old Testament will be needed in churches and theological institutions to accomplish the task of evangelizing the world in the next century.

A missionary imperative runs throughout the Old Testament. A hermeneutic or interpretation of the Old Testament that does not show this is inadequate at best, or simply false at worse.

Questions For Discussion

1. Why was a mission consciousness slow to develop in the first two centuries of the Protestant Reformation?

2. How did the pietists differ from the orthodox Protestants in their respective hermeneutic of the Great Commission?

3. How did the predestination theology of George Whitefield, the Arminian theology of John Wesley, and common sense philosophy all work together to create a more open climate for missions in the England of the late eighteenth century?

4. Beginning with John Locke, how did the Enlightenment at first help, then later hinder and ultimately undermine mission outreach?

5. What type of curriculum would you recommend for training missionaries for the post-Enlightenment future?

Endnotes

1. For a more detailed analysis of the historical period up to circa 1914 in this chapter, see Kenneth Scott Latourette (1970).

2. As an aside to the above discussion, it perhaps should come as no surprise that England, being the birthplace of common sense philosophy, provided so many missionaries for the nineteenth century.

Section II

The Mysteries of God

Chapter Four

In the Beginning

"Who was born first, teacher, Noah or Adam?"

The question came from a new Thai Christian. He was a villager whose reading ability since attending primary school some twenty years earlier had deteriorated considerably. When he started reading the Bible for the first time after his conversion, the words of Genesis came with difficulty. He had to spend so much mental effort figuring out the text word by word that he would lose the flow of the narrative. All he could remember were the two names of Noah and Adam. And since Noah was the last name he had read, it enjoyed more immediate recall in his memory. However, this caused confusion. Was the man whom he could more quickly recall born first, or was the other person, Adam, born first?

My immediate response was to consider this a problem in Christian education. So I went to work devising a line chart of Old Testament history. By drawing horizontal and vertical lines of different heights I was able to show both major and minor divisions of the Old Testament. Predictably the divisions followed what I had learned in Vacation Bible School as a child and, in more sophisticated detail, in Bible college.

The Bible From A Missionary Perspective

After having devised the line chart of biblical history, I decided to add an enhancement. I drew a simple arch across the top from Abraham to the cross to show the unity of purpose in the Bible from the promise given to Abraham to the promise fulfilled in Jesus Christ.

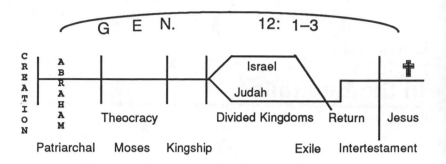

The divisions of the chart are clear. From the creation to Moses there was the Patriarchal period of biblical history in which the most prominent person was Abraham. From Moses to the cross was the period of the Law. During this time Israel's history was divided into a period of theocracy, kings, and the divided kingdoms of Israel and Judah. Israel was taken into captivity first, never to re-emerge as a nation. Judah was taken into exile to Babylon and returned seventy years later. At this point the Old Testament canon closes and there is a period of 400 years before the New Testament opens up with the Gospel of Jesus Christ.

The arch placed above the diagram, however, was revealing beyond its original educational intent. It immediately became clear that the arch revealed a missionary structure to the Scriptures. Instead of the traditional division of Old Testament and New Testament with each part further subdivided into Law, History, Poetry, and Prophets for the Old Testament, and Gospels, History, Letters, and Prophecy (Revelation) for the New Testament, the Bible now had three sections:

Section 1   Section 2   Section 3

Genesis 1–11   Genesis 12–Acts 1   Acts 2–Revelation

The first section, Genesis 1–11, establishes a description of the universals that run throughout the Scriptures.[1] These opening chapters of the Bible contain certain universals that, in Johannes Blauw's words (1962), form the "point of departure" for a theology of mission. That is, these chapters contain more than just an "ontology," a bunch of facts or descriptions, of God, creation, the fall into sin, the breakup of the human race into different language groups, etc. They also form the basis for the history that later follows in the nation of Israel. That is to say, as the human race became alienated from God as recorded throughout Gen. 1–11, so reconciliation is seen beginning from Abraham in Genesis 12.

The second section extends from Genesis 12 to the first chapter of Acts in the New Testament. This is where we find God at work through Israel to reveal his desire for all other nations of the earth; namely, that through his people, all others should come to know the salvation he has offered.

The third section goes from the second chapter of Acts to the end of Revelation. From this section we can see how the First Century Church interpreted and used the Old Testament to justify the move away from self-centeredness into the wider world in order to fulfill God's desire for the nations (Acts 13:1–3). We will not directly investigate this section of the Bible as a separate part of this book. Rather, we shall refer to the Scriptures of this section throughout, as has already been done on occasion, to show the missionary interpretation of the Old Testament in action and exposition in the New Testament church.

Universals

A missionary imperative runs throughout the Bible. It begins at Genesis 1:1 with the words "In the beginning…" and from there it forms a mandate to bring God's salvation to all nations, even to those located at the ends of the earth.

This imperative finds its basis in the way the Bible is structured. Johannes Verkuyl (1978), for example, writes:

Our best help comes from biblical studies which are carried out with great attention to the basic structure of the biblical message in all of its nuances as it relates to the mission mandate and which help us relate the message to the present situation by providing hermeneutical pointers in addition to the exegetical material.

As we stand back and view the Bible as a whole, we see that it is no secret why the canon of the Bible was structured in the way it is. The present arrangement of the books in the canon of the Scriptures "is meant to be looked at" and not "through," Terence J. Keegan (1985:135) states. "That is where the real meaning of the text is to be found." This canonical structure, as we shall see below, points to the mandate that lies behind the Great Commission to preach the Gospel throughout the earth.

This imperative has its beginnings in the universals found in the opening chapters of the Bible, and which run throughout the whole biblical record. Johannes Blauw (1962) speaks of the "universalism in the Old Testament" which forms a general perspective for a theology of mission. He writes: "When we call the message of the Old Testament 'universal,' we mean that it has the whole world in view and that it has a validity for the whole world."

The terms "universals" and "universalism" in this respect do not refer to the doctrine of universal salvation which stresses that all members of the human race, even if they have not believed in Jesus Christ, shall be saved either immediately or eventually from punishment in hell. Indeed, if universal salvation awaits all humans past, present, and future, then we have no need to continue in missions. Under the banner of universal salvation, mission is superfluous and a theology of mission is a waste of energy that could be put to better use elsewhere.

The term "universals" as used in our context here, corresponds more to what is found in philosophy. Universals there are features, real or conceptual, that form the essentials of our world and life. They are ascertainable from the particulars we observe. Viewed in this way there is a sense in which the Old Testament contains theological universals even in the midst of the religious particulars of Israel and her history. These universals, of course, are describable from our vantage point of having the New Testament (cf. 1 Pet. 1:10–12).

This universality is the basis for the missionary message of the Old Testament. These universals set the stage for revealing God's purpose to his people. They form the backdrop to the Great Commission. Indeed, they are what "drive" the Great Commission today.

God

Gen. 1:1 begins with the words "In the beginning God...," a statement startling for its simplicity because no evidence is given for his existence. Nor are any defining characteristics given which would

tell us what God is like. Rather, this chapter and the next give a picture
of God as creator. Genesis 1 is a general account of creation. Chapter
2 is a focused account which zeros in on the creation of man as male
and female.

Chapter 1 pictures God in his power and divine nature. Chapter
2 pictures the concern of God as he cares first for Adam and the
animals under his charge, and next as he creates Eve to be Adam's
helper and companion.

These two aspects of God, that he is and he is creator, point to his
universality. The message of God's universality is the "what" of
mission; it is what a missionary is sent to proclaim in another culture.
All humans are God's "offspring" the Apostle Paul reminded his
listeners in Athens (Acts 17:28).

Now what is the meaning or interpretation of these two aspects?
How should we understand them in our world today? Both topics
have occupied the attention of evangelical theologians.

For example, it has fallen to the task of theologians, in an age of
skepticism, to formulate the evidences that make God's existence
reasonable. It is not enough just to say "God is..." His existence must
be reasonable according to current rules of thought. Also, theologians
have the task of demonstrating that creation is a viable alternative in
an age of competing theories on the origins of the universe. Using the
help of Christian scientists, the creation as seen in Genesis 1–2 is
presented as a theory that accounts for more of the observations or
data of the physical world than other theories.

A third application is to show that the universality of God as
revealed in Gen. 1–2 points to monotheism and related issues. For
example, how monotheistic was Israel's belief in the beginning years?
Did YWYH (Jehovah) mean the "one" god of Israel, while at the same
time not denying existence to the gods of surrounding peoples? Was
Israel's monotheism really monolatry (a type of idolatry)? Did the
Israelites believe there were other gods in addition to theirs?

But these discussions miss the point with regard to seeing the
starting points for a theological basis of missions in Gen. 1–2, because
the themes of God's existence, creation, and monotheism are equally
important to the theology of mission.[2] Indeed, it was their missionary
implications that came to be the dominant hermeneutic for interpreting these themes in the centuries of Jewish dispersion (see Chapter
Nine) and the early New Testament church. God exists, the writer of
Heb. 11:6 exclaimed. This is an assertion of God's existence and of
absolute monotheism reminiscent of Gen. 1:1. But the meaning of the

assertion is evangelistic in nature: "anyone who comes to him must believe that he exists and that he rewards those who earnestly seek him."

The theme of God as universal creator formed the basis for Paul as he preached to the citizens of Athens.

Acts 17:24,27,30
The God who made the world and everything in it is the Lord of heaven and earth...God did this so that men would seek him and perhaps reach out for him and find him, though he is not far from each one of us...now he commands all people everywhere to repent.

It is interesting to note that this theological basis of Paul makes use of a distinction that many theologians have also used in claiming that the Old Testament has no missionary message. Johannes Blauw (1962:34) has described this as the "distinction between [a] centripetal and centrifugal missionary consciousness." Centripetal is defined as motion that proceeds in a direction inward to a center. Centrifugal is motion that proceeds in a direction away from a center. To these theologians there is only centripetal consciousness of missions in the Old Testament; i.e., the Gentiles must come to God. They have no centrifugal consciousness of going to the Gentiles.

However, in preaching to the Athenians we see that Paul had both factors in mind. Since it is God who is at the center of all things, it is expected for all to seek and hopefully find him. But since he is the Creator of all things, a command also proceeds outward from God for all to repent.

In other words, both the "centripetal and centrifugal conscious-ness" are to be kept in mind in the missionary interpretation of the Old Testament. Both are theologically true, for each leads to a different but necessary perspective on the need for human beings to know God, and on how this knowledge may be obtained.

Both perspectives moreover are kept in tension in the Old Testa-ment. We have, for example, the story of Rahab (Josh. 2) joining Israel and becoming a part of Old Testament history. But we also see Jonah going to proclaim repentance in the Gentile city of Ninevah. Conse-quently each may be used as occasion demands in the missionary expansion of the church into non-Christian territory.[3]

The basic point is this. In the Scriptures we find a missionary or evangelistic dimension in interpreting the themes of God's existence, creation, and monotheism. In this hermeneutic, it makes no difference whether nonbelievers are themselves to come and seek God, or whether messengers are to go and proclaim God; both are included. To therefore emphasize any of these themes without also emphasizing the missionary dimension is to overlook a crucial component in the meaning of the Old Testament. With such neglect we often fail to see how the Old Testament has a missionary message or can provide the biblical basis for missions today.

The Lord

Gen. 1–2 has two Hebrew terms for God. In Gen. 1 it is stated that Elohim created the heavens and the earth.[4] Gen. 2 states that Yahweh Elohim made the earth and heavens. In trying to explain why these two terms, Elohim and Yahweh, are used in the Hebrew Scriptures, more confusion than enlightenment has been generated. One source of confusion has been repeated attempts to explain these terms etymologically. Much research, for example, has gone into discovering the etymological roots of these words, whether in Hebrew or cognate languages, but with little apparent success. Theologians remain just as uncertain as ever about the historical derivations of these terms.

A greater source of confusion, however, has been the historical-critical method used by modern theologians as the only acceptable foundation from which to interpret the text of the Old Testament. This method asserts that each of the two terms represent a separate historical source or tradition in the Old Testament as it currently stands. These separate accounts of the creation, for example, were later combined to form the single creation account of Genesis. Consequently, according to this approach, there is an "E" strand (standing for Elohim), a "J" strand (standing for Yahweh or Jehovah), plus other strands that purportedly can be detected and extrapolated from the Old Testament text.[5]

When the two terms for God, Elohim and Yahweh, are interpreted functionally however, we see that they do not point to different historical traditions or sources which were later combined to form the Old Testament text. Rather, they represent two different functions of Deity which are combined in the one God of Israel.[6] That is, these are two functions that God performs (more precisely reveals) that are his alone.

Elohim represents the "High God" concept found in so many cultures around the world. In the ancient Near East no god was higher in status or position than Elohim. On the other hand, in the worldview of the time, this high position did not necessarily guarantee total power; lower or lesser gods such as Baal of the Canaanites exercised certain powers not reserved to Elohim (Ulf Oldenburg 1969). There-fore, God revealed himself as Yahweh (Exodus 3:14), as the High God who also has all power. That is to say, the term Yahweh represents the "High Lord" concept of deity analogous to the "High God" concept mentioned above.

From the context of the Hebrew Scriptures it appears that the term Yahweh was considered the name of Elohim. But as God's name it also designated his divine power. In this respect, it was entirely appropriate to have translated Yahweh by the Greek term kyrios (lord) in the Septuagint translation of the Old Testament (see Chapter Nine) or by LORD in English.[7]

Werner Foerster and Gottfried Queli (1958) state that kyrios or lord refers to the right to dispose over distinctive spheres of life. For example, a lord as the owner of a slave has the right to use or dispose of that slave in any way so desired. Therefore, for Elohim to be Yahweh means also that the God of Israel may dispose of everything under him in any way he so desires. Since Elohim is creator of all things, he may in turn dispose of all things in his creation as he sees fit.

Therefore, in the two terms for God in Gen. 1–2 we do not see two different traditions of creation being combined to make one biblical account. Rather, in Gen. 1 we see the High God as the creator of heavens and earth. Then in Gen. 2 we see God as the High Lord exercising legitimate power to organize his creation in the way he desires. Man as male and female, for instance, was made a little lower than the angelic host but at the same time was delegated to have authority over creation (Ps. 8:4–6). These two terms are used inter-changeably for God in the Hebrew Scriptures.

(Ps. 89:6–7)
For who in the skies above can compare with the Lord? Who is like the Lord among the heavenly beings? In the council of the holy ones God is greatly feared; he is more awesome than all who surround him.

Both terms are used, not to show different sources underlying the text, but to show God from two perspectives, that he is both "High God" and "High Lord." In the Hebrew, as well as in Greek and

English, there is no one word that combines both perspectives. Two terms, therefore, are needed.

In the previous section we saw where God's existence, monotheism, and creation point to the missionary message of the Old Testament. They contain within them the message from God that all people are to seek him and repent. That God is Lord reinforces this missionary message.

Ps. 86:8–10
Among the gods there is none like you, O Lord; no deeds can compare with yours. All the nations you have made will come and worship before you, O Lord; they will bring glory to your name. For you are great and do marvelous deeds; you alone are God.

The God we proclaim to the nations is more than the High God and Creator. He is the Lord. Not only will the nations seek him as God, they will also worship and glorify him as Lord.

A functional description of the terms Elohim and Yahweh also explains a seemingly insignificant switch in words between Gen. 1 and 2. Gen. 1:1 states that Elohim created the heavens and earth while Gen. 2:4b has Yahweh Elohim, the Lord God, who created the earth and heavens. In other words, the switch in words parallels the difference in perspective that each term brings to the description of God. That is, to emphasize the perspective of Elohim as High God over creation, it is natural to start with the highest point in creation: the heavens. But to emphasize God as Yahweh, the High Lord who organizes creation, it is natural to start with the most visible part of this organizing activity: the earth.

Sin

Genesis 3 begins with the words "Now the serpent..." This serpent is Satan, the devil. No evidence is given supporting the devil's existence; we have only an assertion that he exists. In fact, we look in vain throughout the Scriptures for clear indications of how the devil, in the midst of God's good creation, could come to be. However, from the Scripture's standpoint, it is enough that since sin itself exists (something that few in our post-progressive culture would wish to deny), the source (the devil) should be identified. The origin of the source is unimportant.

What is important is to realize that sin is now the defining characteristic of all human life. It universally affects all. This universality of sin is what Genesis 3–9 describe for us. It is not a pretty picture of the human race: deceit, jealousy, murder, lying, pride, and rebellion against God are all painted there.

In addition to sin we also see God's curse upon all his creation (Gen. 3:14–19), the "being sold under sin" just as a slave is sold from one slave owner to another (Rom 7:14). The serpent first was cursed above all animals and would henceforth crawl on its belly. Next Adam and Eve would suffer the consequences of their disobedience. To be sure, there is the promise that the woman's seed shall bruise the serpent's head (Gen. 3:15), but in the end nothing is said about lifting the curse. Even today its effects are still felt among all humans. There are still pains to suffer in childbirth, crops to plant and harvest, work to do day and night. Worse of all there is death to endure.

Sin as portrayed in Gen. 3 is individual and personal; it was just the serpent tempting Eve with forbidden fruit, and later Adam, as Eve gave him the forbidden fruit to eat. Later on it was Cain, after he slew his brother Abel, who mockingly asked "Am I my brother's keeper?" (Gen. 4:9). The Lord did not answer this question but impressed on Cain his own personal responsibility for his deed.

From Gen. 6–9, another level of sin is given. From the individual level of earlier chapters we move to the societal level, a level where we are more likely to use the term evil in describing the human condition. This is where the collective sins of society's members become a mindset, institutionalized, and then enculturated into the very fiber of the social network that holds individuals, societies, and nations together.

Gen. 6:11–12

Now the earth was corrupt in God's sight and was full of violence. God saw how corrupt the earth had become, for all the people on earth had corrupted their ways.

The Lord destroyed that world with a flood, saving only Noah and his family. However, after the flood, as the world's population increased once more, nothing really changed. In Gen. 11 we see men wanting to build a tower as a way of subverting God's command to inhabit all the earth. In punishment and as a way of enforcing his command, God sent a confusion of languages upon them and the unity of all humans was broken up into competing, even warring, nations.

This universality of sin and its total effect on life from the individual to the societal to the whole world forms additional hermeneutic pointers pointing to the missionary message running throughout the Old Testament.

The Nations

After listing a great number of names, Gen. 10 ends with this summary. "These are the clans of Noah's sons, according to their lines of descent, within their nations. From these the nations spread out over the earth after the flood" (Gen. 10:32).

We must remember that exegetically the word "nation" in this verse does not refer to the nation-state of modern times. The Hebrew word in this verse means a body or group of people bound together by such common identities as language, religious belief, and geographical location. A modern equivalent for this Hebrew word in today's English would be ethnic group or tribe. (However, the latter word is going out of favor as being more derogatory than neutral when used to refer to people.)

Now the list of nations or ethnic groups in Gen. 11 does not rate very high in significance in modern books on theology. Very few even mention Gen. 11. Gen. 12, the account of the tower of Babel, is mentioned more out of quaintness than anything else.

This lack of interest derives from the Enlightenment of the seventeenth and eighteenth centuries with its de-emphasis on the social nature of human existence and its emphasis on individual autonomy. Since that time the individual and not the social group has become the hermeneutic for selecting what is theologically significant for the interpretation of Scripture.

In liberal theology existentialism, with its emphasis on the religious needs of the individual, is taken as the norm for selection. For a short time just before and after 1900, social progress, a form of Christian socialism, was the popular hermeneutic in liberal theology for interpreting the Bible. This was the social gospel emphasizing the welfare of society and nation over personal conversion. But this turned out to be an aberration.

Before long, the individual of existentialism, not the social group became paramount. Even evangelical theology has not escaped this impact, for there the emphasis has been on personal piety and individual decision to become Christian.

In either case, the table or list of clans, languages, and nations in Gen. 10 and the account of how this condition of the human race came to be as recorded in Gen. 11, has more often than not been passed off as having little modern theological import.

This hermeneutic of the individual, whether evangelical or liberal, has further been strengthened over much of the past 200 years by political ideology and events. The view of the world emerging from these was that the world is composed not of ethnic groups but of individuals. Ethnicity is bad, individuality is good. Our evangelism, therefore, should be to the individual, not to the group.

The "melting pot" ideal of the American social experiment is an example. This is where tribes, ethnic groups, castes, and social classes from around the world are to "melt" together to form the modern American nation. What is to emerge is a new citizenry whose loyalties are no longer to the tribe, clan, or ethnic group but to the state as Americans.

The United States of America has not been the only nation to have experimented with this ideal. Modern empires also have. In the twentieth century Nazism, Fascism, and Marxism-Leninism have pursued the ideal in one cruel way or another. Even the United Nations, while not an empire, still hopes to minimize the social and cultural distance between nations, tribes, and peoples by providing a non-nationalistic forum for discussing and solving international problems.

For most of the twentieth century, the world empires did manage to keep ethnicity under control. But the cost was high. Such a feat required huge standing armies to maintain internal peace by suppressing ethnic feelings, while at the same time enforcing loyalty to the state. In the end the goal became unattainable.

Nazism, for example, was unable to terminate the Jews and other ethnic undesirables during its short reign in Germany. The former Union of Soviet Socialist Republics, or Russia, was unable to keep control over a dozen or more satellite republics, and in the end as Russia disintegrated, each republic began to declare its independence.

The former Yugoslavian state became another example as it violently broke up into warring groups defined mainly by religion. For decades ethnic rivalries that were once kept at bay by Communist ideology in the end burst forth into violence to right old but not forgotten wrongs, to remember old grudges, to settle old scores of hatred, to renew the vicious cycle of vengeance and death, and ultimately to put into execution "ethnic cleansing," a particularly vicious way of reversing the ethnic mix enforced by a communist regime in hopes of achieving the melting pot ideal for society.

Even in the United States the melting pot ideal is coming apart. For example, many now wish to be hyphenated Americans, as in Polish-American or African-American. Quotas in government and labor are encouraged in order to achieve racial balance. In schools and colleges multiculturalism, preserving and reinforcing the ethnic mosaic of America, has become an educational goal for America's future citizens.

And finally, since the end of the Vietnam war in 1975, we must notice the new waves of immigrants from Asia. At first these refugees from the Vietnam war were scattered throughout America in hopes that this would speed up their assimilation into American society. But as with African-Americans, it has been impossible for Asians to "melt" in with the dominant Caucasian population, leading Asians in the end to settle together in their own communities.

In other words, a comforting view of a world melted together to form one happy family has come to an abrupt end. In its place are the ethnoi, ethnic groups, living not as integrated but as separate communities. Ethnicity, after years of submersion in the wake of other ideals, is on the rise once more in the United States and around the world.

The implications of this rise is impacting the church as well. The church must now adjust to include cultural pluralism in her view of society. If the church is to continue to have influence in the traditional Christian societies of Europe and the Americas into the future, Christians must now learn to communicate cross-culturally, whether in the kitchen or across the backyard fence, to individuals who are members of other ethnic groups.

Theologically, it appears, the effects of the Tower of Babel in Gen. 10–11 shall not be denied to God for very long as world history rolls along. Ever so frequently, the fact that this world is still composed of bickering, warring ethnic groups comes crashing in on our consciousness.

The time has come to realize the significance of the nations in Gen. 10–11 for the interpreting and obeying of the Old Testament in our age. Indeed ethnicity is a universal spanning both space and time. Along with sin, and because of sin, the universality of ethnicity constitutes what C. Walter Kaiser, Jr. (1978) has termed the original missionary mandate of the Bible. It is an additional hermeneutical pointer that points to the missionary message of the Old Testament.

Hermeneutically, therefore, ethnicity and not individualism establishes the context wherein the Old Testament is to be interpreted in our age, for it is ethnicity and not individualism that forms the arena of missionary evangelism. God's salvation is to be brought to the nations, tribes, peoples, and languages (Rev. 7:9) of the world, whether in the neighborhoods of America's urban centers or across vast oceans.

This hermeneutic of the Old Testament (indeed of the whole Bible), I believe, will better prepare the church theologically for evangelism in the ever increasingly pluralistic world of the twenty-first century.

Questions For Discussion

1. How does Gen. 1–11 "set the stage" for the missionary message of the Bible (both Old and New Testament)?

2. What insights does a functional analysis of the terms Elohim (God) and Yahweh (Lord) have for the missionary interpretation of the Old Testament?

3. Why do you think that the nations of Gen. 10 have played little or no role in theology? How do you think this neglect has hindered missionary outreach from the church?

4. Why must "the nations" of the Scriptures play an important role in evangelism and missions today?

Endnotes

1. Gen. 1–11 is important in theology, especially in a theology of mission. Unfortunately, as Walter C. Kaiser, Jr. (1978:71) remarks, "this block of Biblical material has rarely been treated in its unified contribution to theology."

2. For an extensive discussion of the doctrine of monotheism as derived from the opening chapters of Genesis, but without any mention of the doctrine's missiological ramifications, see Ronald B. Mayers (1984).

3. An equivalent to this is the two descriptions of light in physics. Light may be characterized as either particles or as waves. Experiments, moreover, may be set up to support either description. Consequently a scientist may explain light in either way depending on his or her scientific goal at the moment.

4. Elohim is morphologically the plural of El, god, in the Hebrew language. Both words, with the plural form used more often than the singular, are used to refer to God; there is no apparent difference in signification in this case between the plural and singular forms. For this reason, therefore, we use only the plural form Elohim in this section.

5. The historical-critical method became popular in theological studies in the 1800s when historical explanations were the prevailing method in scientific investigation. For example, in the social sciences of the time, scholars such as Lewis Henry Morgan, Edward B. Taylor, and others used evolution to show a historical progression from the primitive or savage tribe to modern civilization. Karl Marx and Friedrich Engels used the same historical method which later formed the basis for the historical and economic determinism of communism. At the same time, following the same trend and in order to be "scientific" also, theologians investigated the biblical text to historically and critically determine its evolution into its present form. However, the historical method soon ran its course in the social sciences (including, by the latter part of the 20th Century, Marxism and communism as well) and was replaced by such ahistorical investigative methods as functionalism and structuralism where components are defined and explained in terms of their current functions and contributions (i.e., their "meaning") within a system. It

is indeed unfortunate that theology did not follow this change as well and drop its historical critical approach to the biblical text. If it had, the missionary message of the Old Testament would be much clearer to the church today and the task of fulfilling the Great Commission no doubt that much easier and further along.

6. For a more detailed discussion of this approach to the functions of the divine names in the history of Israel, see Donald Slager (1992).

7. The translators of the Septuagint, in other words, translated Yahweh functionally and not as a name. This is true of English as well: Lord in many English translations of the Old Testament is a functional equivalent of the Hebrew term. For a recent survey of the problems and solutions in translating the Hebrew terms of Elohim and Yahweh, see Donald Slager (1992).

CHAPTER FIVE

The Election Of Israel

"Who was born first, Buddha or Jesus?" shouted the Thai trucker above the noise of his truck as we bounced along a dusty backroad of northern Thailand. This was not the first time I had heard this folk Buddhist apologetic against Christianity, but it certainly was the most inconvenient.

To many Buddhists in Thailand this question—and its obvious answer (Buddha was born in 543 B.C.)—is a powerful defense against the evangelistic efforts of Christian missions. A brief look at the Thai language and social structure reveals why.

The Thai language, unlike English or Greek, has no ready-made words for brother or sister. Only basic words exist for older sibling and younger sibling, either of which may be a brother or sister. This linguistic fact means that sociologically, interpersonal relationships are often built on whether a person is older or younger. Socially an older person is accorded more respect and honor. The younger is expected to defer to the status of the older.

In their contact with Christian missionaries over the past 400 years, Thai Buddhists have extended and adapted these sociolinguistic facts into an apologetic in behalf of their own religion. In this view Buddhism is the older religion; Christianity is the younger. Being in the role of the "older sibling" (we are now in the twenty-fifth century of the Buddhist era), Buddhism should be revered more. Christianity, being in the role of the "younger sibling," should defer to the status of the older religion.

The conclusion is clear. To convert to Christianity is not proper, for it is equivalent to showing more respect to a younger sibling. Furthermore, it is implied, if a person does not want to be placed in an inferior position in society—as in the role of a younger sibling— (s)he should remain Buddhist.

The Call Of Abraham

Under more convenient circumstances I would have countered the Thai trucker by asking him a question. "Who was born first, Abraham or Buddha?"

Indeed, not long after studying the Thai language and beginning my missionary service in Thailand, I learned how important the difference between older and younger is in Thai society. Consequently if it were important to Thai thinking that the older deserves more respect, then it was important for me—in order to make my message creditable—to select someone from the Bible who was born before Buddha and therefore deserving great respect as well.

Abraham was the obvious choice.

He was the choice for two reasons. First, Abraham was born 1500 years before Buddha. Second, since few in Thailand have ever heard of Abraham, his name associated with that of Buddha would cause puzzlement, a puzzlement which would require an explanation of who Abraham was. This in turn would afford an opportunity to explain that the salvation God offers through Jesus Christ alone did not begin with the birth of Jesus Christ or of Christianity, but that it began long before when God called Abraham out of Ur of Chaldees and made a covenant with him.

The Lord had said to Abram,

Gen. 12:1–3
"Leave your country, your people and your father's
    household and go to the land I will show you.
I will make you into a great nation and I will bless you;
I will make your name great, and you will be a blessing.
I will bless those who bless you,
    and whoever curses you I will curse;
and all peoples on earth will be blessed through you."

This covenant contains three parts. First, there is the promise of land for Abraham and his descendants (see Gen. 15). Second, Abraham's descendants would form a great nation. And third, Abraham would be the source of blessing to all peoples of the earth.

God's Covenant With Abraham

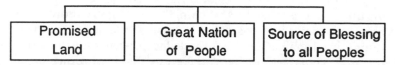

Promised Land	Great Nation of People	Source of Blessing to all Peoples

It is the universality of the third part that makes the choice of Abraham an effective counterargument to the above Buddhist apologetic. Not only was Abraham born before Buddha, but the promise of blessing to all peoples also came long before.

But there is more. As with the Great Commission (see Chapter One), this third part of the promise refers to something more ancient than even Abraham. There is, first of all, the earth, a reference to creation. The universality of this promise draws its own universality from God as Creator. Indeed, since Israel does not yet exist, this can only be the God who created the heavens and earth of Gen. 1:1; there is simply no other universal God.

This third part of the promise to Abraham also refers back to the breakup of the human race into nations (Genesis 10–11). In the Hebrew Scriptures, in the chapters of Genesis 10–12, two words are used to described this breakup.

One word is goi, a body or social group of people and is translated as "nation."[1] The other word is mishah'oh, a clan, lineage, a people. Both words are used, for example, to sum up Genesis ten.

Gen. 10:32
These are the clans (mishah'oh) of Noah's sons, according to their lines of descent, within their nations (goi). From these the nations (goi) spread out over the earth after the flood.

The term mishah'oh is sometimes translated as family. However, this Hebrew word refers to a social unit larger than a nuclear or extended family. It is more properly a lineage or clan. The difference between lineage and clan is this. The former refers to traceable, relatively near biological kinship.

The latter may be extended to include distant biological kinship, even fictive kinship. For example, the social structure of a group, for example, may include clans named after animals, such as the Monkey Clan. However, it is unlikely that there would be a Monkey Lineage as this would imply biological descent.

Exegetically the promise of blessing in Gen. 12:3 is to the mishah'oh, peoples, of the earth. But in Gen. 22:18, when the Lord repeated the same three-part promise to Abraham, the word goi, nations, is used. When the promise was passed on to Isaac, Abraham's son, the term nations is used again (Gen. 26:4). But to Jacob, Isaac's son, the promise was stated using the term peoples. Because these two words are used interchangeably throughout these examples, the differences between their meanings should not be stressed. Rather, their different meanings should be viewed functionally as complementary; i.e., the different reference of each filling in what is lacking in the other.

Hermeneutically, in other words, both mishah'oh and goi together communicate that God's blessing through Abraham is for every size of group, from the (smaller) lineage to the (larger) nation. No people group, no matter how small or large, is to be overlooked or bypassed in being blessed through Abraham.

Some question exists as to whether the Hebrew word for blessing in Gen. 12:3, since it is a verb in this promise, should be translated as a passive ("all the peoples on earth will be blessed") or as a reflexive ("will bless themselves"). The Hebrew verb is in the niphal construction which may be translated either way. Normally, however, the passive meaning is secondary to the reflexive.[2] Students of the Hebrew language are divided on whether Gen. 12:3 should be translated according to the majority reflexive usage of the niphal construction, or according to its minority usage as a passive.

Linguistically, either reading is possible. Semantically, however, the passive reading seems more plausible according to the context, while the reflexive reading is problematic. This is because it is difficult to know what it really means for peoples of the earth to bless themselves because of Abraham. Several interpretations are possible. Does it mean that the peoples of the earth will find blessing as Abraham did? Does it refer to the peoples (clans, lineages) who bless Abraham, indicating they will likewise be blessed? Does this Hebrew verb in the niphal construction somehow refer to both reflexive and passive meanings at the same time?[3]

On the other hand, the meaning of the passive "be blessed" is singularly clear and straightforward at several points of exegesis. In this context it is clear that God is the one blessing both Abraham and those who bless Abraham. Therefore, as God is the agent who is blessing, he will be the one to also bless the peoples of the earth through Abraham, and not the peoples blessing themselves. The passive reading here, in other words, maintains the agency of God, as the one who blesses, in a way that the reflexive reading cannot.

Grammatically it is not uncommon that in such an instance as this, a minor usage can override what otherwise is a normal usage, thus resulting in an interpretation that is more readily understandable. The passive "to be blessed" in Gen. 12:3, even though it is a minor usage of the niphal verbal construction in Biblical Hebrew, is singularly understood in a way that the reflexive meaning cannot match.

In this light it is not difficult to see how the passive has become the hermeneutic of this verse and the preferred translation of many. The Greek translators of the Hebrew Bible in the third century before Christ, resulting in the Septuagint, used a Greek verb in the passive to translate this verse. It is the passive reading of the promise, as combined from Gen. 12:3 and Gen. 22:18, that the Apostle Peter quotes in Acts 3:25—"Through your offspring all peoples on earth will be blessed."

The Blessing

The blessing that comes to the nations through Abraham also refers to something more ancient. Its reference is backward to the curse universally placed on creation because of sin (Gen. 3:14–19). That is, theologically the promise of blessing stands in opposition to the curse. The blessing from God is the antidote for the curse in a world of sin. It is to offset the effects of the curse. As the curse is universal in its effects (Rom. 5:12–21) so is the blessing to be universal as a cure. To Peter in Acts 3:26, this blessing comes from God's servant, the Messiah, who came first to the Jews in order to turn them from their wicked ways.

That all peoples of the earth shall be blessed plays another important theological role at this point in the Scriptures. In calling Abraham, the focus has considerably narrowed from the nations of Gen. 10–11 to just the descendants of Abraham. It appears that from here on through the Bible the focus of God's attention will be only on the Jewish people. But the promise that all shall be blessed counters this narrowing down of the narrative; it maintains, even in the midst of a particular emphasis upon one people, the universality of the Scriptures already seen in Genesis chapters 1–11.

Gen. 12:3 keeps the universality of the Scriptures alive as the narrative narrows to focus on Abraham and his descendants. Now, by combining universality with this narrowing process, the promise in Gen. 12:3 does something else quite significant. For the first time in Scripture, purpose is attached to the theme of universalism.

Monotheism no longer exists as a theme for its own sake alone. The universality of the Scriptures is no longer a directionless concept. Now there is a focus and a purpose for both. Abraham and his descendants exist so that all other peoples may be blessed. From here on through the Old Testament, through the intertestament period and into the New Testament church, the themes of monotheism, universalism, and purpose develop into a missionary message—a missionary hermeneutic—for all of God's people.

A Kingdom of Priests

In the call of Abraham God elected Israel. But with election comes responsibility. God's call does not come without a job to do or a purpose. The first responsibility, as we have just seen in Gen. 12:3, is to be the channel through whom God could bless all nations. A second responsibility is seen after the escape from the army of the Egyptian Pharoah. After passing through the Red Sea, Moses led the people of Israel through the desert to Mount Sinai. Moses went up onto the mountain to receive these words from the Lord to tell to the people of Israel.

> Exodus 19:4–6
> You yourselves have seen what I did to Egypt, and how I carried you on eagles' wings and brought you to myself. Now if you obey me fully and keep my covenant, then out of all nations you will be my treasured possession. Although the whole earth is mine, you will be for me a kingdom of priests and a holy nation.

In these verses three descriptions point to the special election of Israel. The term "treasured possession" points to Israel as highly prized in God's sight, more so than any other nation. The next two terms, a "kingdom of priests" and a "holy nation," refer to the purposes of Israel in being God's treasured possession.

Of the three descriptions, however, one has caught the imagination with regard to the missionary message of the Old Testament. This is the description that Israel will be a kingdom of priests for God. This expression appears particularly rich in association with the ultimate purpose of Israel among the nations of earth.

The description that Israel is a kingdom of priests for God is suggestive for a missionary understanding of the Old Testament because of the work that a priest does. This work has two sides. A priest 1) serves God and 2) serves before God in behalf of others. In the Old Testament Law a priest sacrifices in behalf of the people. In the New Testament Jesus, who is our high priest, offered himself to God as the sacrifice to obtain with his own blood our eternal redemption (Heb. 9:11–14).

Now, in being a kingdom of priests, the purpose of Israel is to serve God. But this raises a question from the other side: in behalf of whom does Israel serve? Israel serves, it is answered, in behalf of the nations as a priest functions in society (Brevard S. Childs 1974). But in what way? It requires Israel to be committed to extend God's presence throughout the world (John I. Durham 1987).

Yet, as we look through the Scriptures, we see that this expression with one exception is not developed in exactly this way. Isaiah referred to Israel being a kingdom of priests, but from the perspective that after the return from captivity Israel would be supported like priests; that is, from the donations of others. In this case the donations would come from the nations (Isa. 61:6). In the New Testament the saved are similarly referred to as a holy priesthood (1 Pet. 2:5), and in Revelation the redeemed are called priests of God who shall serve him in heaven (Rev. 1:6, 5:10, 20:6).

In the Scriptures the emphasis on being a priesthood for God is clearly on the first task mentioned above, serving God, and not on the second. For example, it is difficult to imagine in behalf of whom the saints will be serving before God once in heaven. Yet, lurking in the background (and since we have not yet attained our heavenly reward), as a question demanding an answer, is the suggestion that to be a priest for God is also to serve in behalf of others. In the case of Israel then, which is our first concern here, if an answer is to be given as seems to be required, Israel is to serve in behalf of the nations.

What was to be the nature of Israel's service to the nations of the world? Moses did not answer this question directly in Exodus 19:4–6. In one respect the question had already been answered in Gen. 12:3. So Moses left only the suggestion of service written in the Law. Nevertheless, this suggestion of priestly service among the nations throughout the earth provides another element which ultimately developed into the missionary message of the Old Testament.

That message is this. Monotheism and universalism are not to exist for their own sake alone among God's people. The call to priestly service assures that. The purpose of God's people is to serve the nations, for it is through his people that the nations will come to know of Abraham and the blessing that comes to them because of him. Indeed this was Paul's understanding and, more importantly, obedience, in being a priest in God's service.

Romans 15:15–16
I have written you quite boldly on some points, as if to remind you of them again, because of the grace God gave me to be a minister of Christ Jesus to the Gentiles with the priestly duty of proclaiming the gospel of God...

Paul's priestly duties went beyond service in prayer and praise to God alone. His duties included service before others who had never before heard the Good News about Jesus Christ.

This section should not conclude without a brief discussion of the venerable Protestant doctrine of the priesthood of all believers. This doctrine was formulated from texts mentioned in this section in reaction to the Roman Catholic division of the church into clergy (called priests) and laity.

The doctrine of the priesthood of all believers was and is a valid correction of this division. However, in the minds of most Protestants, it seems, the understanding and application of the doctrine stop at this juncture. No further thought is given to the implications the doctrine may have with regards to the missionary outreach of the church today.

The ramification of this doctrine for missions is the same as that outlined above. Christians, as a holy priesthood, are to serve God. But there is another side to the priesthood of Christians. We are to serve the nations who do not know God. This service is realized in fulfilling the Great Commission in today's world. The task of the Great Commission is the task of all Christians, not just those who are called, as the Apostles Paul and Barnabas (Acts 13:1-2) were. The whole church must be involved in releasing and sending those who are called (Acts 13:3).

Questions For Discussion

1. Why is the passive reading of Gen. 12:3 ("all peoples shall be blessed through" Abraham) a better interpretation than the reflexive ("all peoples shall bless themselves")?

2. Why is the blessing of Gen.12:3 so important to the universalism of Gen. 1–11 in a theology of missions?

3. Why is evangelism a priestly duty of the evangelist? Before whom is the duty performed?

Endnotes

1. For simplicity the Hebrew terms are transliterated in their singular form only.

2. This is quoted from the 1909 edition of Gesenius' Hebrew Grammar.

3. See Gordon J. Wenham (1987) for a discussion of these possibilities.

At Mount Sinai

"How many 'thou shalt nots' are there in Christianity?" the Thai villager asked. His was a common question I had heard many times before. His purpose was to compare his list of prohibitions or commandments in Buddhism with those of Christianity. Comparing the merits of different religions is a favorite pastime of many in Thailand.

Buddhism has five precepts which all adherents are to follow: do not steal, do not lie, do not murder, do not commit adultery, do not become intoxicated. If these rules are followed, one may live a life of merit and good works.

In response to the above question, some answer that Christianity has the Decalogue, the Ten Commandments given by God to Moses on Mt. Sinai (Exod. 20:1–17).[1] John J. Davis (1986:207) states that a major purpose of the Ten Commandments, and of the whole Mosaic Law, was to restrain wrong behavior in order to protect the integrity of the moral, social, and religious institutions of Israel.

This of course is the traditional interpretation of the Law. In fact, this is probably an important function of religious law in general, whether we speak of the five precepts of Buddhism or the Ten Commandments of Moses.

But the Ten Commandments include more than just assuring good behavior. These commands contain a missionary dimension often overlooked in interpreting and understanding this part of the Law of Moses. This dimension provides an additional foundation for the missionary message of the Old Testament, thus enabling later generations in Israel (in a continuation of the preceding chapter) to understand and fulfill their priestly purpose in serving other nations of the earth. This dimension is still valid in the interpretation and application of the Law by the church today in missionary evangelism.

Monotheism

In the Exodus narrative structure surrounding the giving of the Law on Mount Sinai, the Ten Commandments follow almost immediately Moses' proclamation that Israel is the prized possession of God and is to be a kingdom of priests and a holy nation. In fact, the Ten Commandments begin a long section of instructions that finishes at the end of Exodus 23. It is not surprising, given their importance and pivotal role in Israel's history, that they are placed first.[2]

We are not concerned with all ten commandments in our search for a theological basis for the missionary understanding of the Old Testament. Not all are immediately applicable to this task. But it is probably of more than passing significance that the introduction to the Decalogue and the first two commandments are.

Exodus 20:1–5
And God spoke all these words: "I am the Lord your God, who brought you out of Egypt, out of the land of slavery. You shall have no other gods before me. You shall not make for yourself an idol in the form of anything in heaven above or on the earth beneath or in the waters below. You shall not bow down to them or worship them..."

Again, in terms of narrative structure, the introduction to the Decalogue and the first two commandments form a single unit. The introduction is a positive assertion that the Lord, the God of Israel, exists. The two commands that immediately follow are negative restatements of the positive assertion of the introduction.

In language a negative restatement can serve two functions. First, negation can function as a reinforcement of a positive statement. A negative statement can often be more forceful. To have no other gods and not to make an idol forcefully communicates the assertion that God exists, in a way that a positive statement cannot.

Second, a negation will function to eliminate loopholes in understanding and application. A positive statement, since it does not explicitly forbid something, may be interpreted to say that its silence therefore allows the issue in question. God exists, but without a negative restatement this could be interpreted to mean that it is allowable to make an image of God, because an image or idol is not explicitly forbidden. The command not to make an idol eliminates such faulty hermeneutics.

The first two (negative) commands of the Decalogue, therefore, delimit the assertion that God is, in a direction that was only implied earlier. Specifically, it is in these commandments that the implied monotheism of Gen. 1-11 is forcefully made explicit. That God exists now means that only he is God; there is no other. The religion of Israel from this time onward is to be unambiguously monotheistic.

In this respect the first two commandments of the Decalogue parallel the themes of existence and the universality of God that we noted from Gen. 1:1 and the creation accounts that follow. From this perspective, each of these two commandments deserve a more detailed analysis with respect to the basis for a missionary understanding of the Old Testament.

No Other Gods

The first commandment "You shall have no other gods before me" thematically follows the words "In the beginning God..." of Gen. 1:1 as a negative restatement. It restricts the interpretation of God's existence to monotheism. Since God is creator there shall be no, nor can there be, any other god. This negative reinforcement of monotheism is repeated several times in the Scriptures (see Exod. 22:20, 23:13, 34:14, Deut. 5:7, Ps. 81:9). There must be no other gods in addition to him in Israel's life and belief.

This commandment, however, does not deny the existence of other gods, nor does it deny the possibility of polytheism. What it does deny is that either additional gods or polytheism are options for Israel. Other nations may have a multiplicity of gods in their pantheon, but such is not for Israel. The Apostle Paul drew on this observation to make a point about idols for the church at Corinth

1 Cor. 8:4-6

...We know that an idol is nothing at all in the world and there is no God but one. For even if there are so-called gods, whether in heaven or on earth (as indeed there are many "gods" and many "lords"), yet for us there is but one God, the Father, from whom all things came and for whom we live...

It is in this context that we should consider again the term Yahweh, the Lord, for the God of Israel. The introduction to the Decalogue starts with "I am Yahweh, the Lord, your God." The shema of Deut. 6:4 reads, "Yahweh, the Lord, our God, Yahweh is one." In this case, as earlier, the translation of Yahweh as Lord is entirely appropriate, for it captures another dimension of God's uniqueness that often escapes those of us who live in modern, secular society.

There is indeed a host of spiritual beings, other gods and lords, both real and imagined. In the Old Testament this host is variously termed as the great assembly of the gods (Ps. 82:1–8), the heavenly beings and council of holy ones (Ps. 89:6–7), the heavenly host (Ps. 148:2). Angelic hosts include the elders, spirits, and the living creatures of heaven who exist to worship God always (Rev. 4:4–11).

The host of spiritual beings also include the demons (Ps. 106:37). The New Testament speaks of spirits and demons, the principalities and powers of this dark world, spiritual forces of evil in the heavenly realms (Eph. 6:12), the stoicheion or ruling spirits of the world (Col. 2:20, TEV), the host of spiritual beings that people of secular society exclude from their worldview (Paul Heibert 1982).

Over this vast array of spiritual beings, both in subjection and in rebellion, God alone is Yahweh, the Lord of hosts (Ps. 24:10). No other god or lord is over or higher than Yahweh. Just as God stands in absolute oneness over his creation, so does he stand in absolute oneness above and over all spiritual beings, for he is Yahweh alone; no god or lord shares this authority and reign with him. He is the Lord who alone has the authority to dispose of his hosts as he desires. It is he alone who allows and restrains Satan (Job 1:6–12). It is he alone whom the demons fear (James 2:19). Not only is God universally one above his creation but he is also universally the one Yahweh (the Lord) over all spirits, demons, and heavenly hosts.

The teaching that the Lord God is one (monotheism) does not deny the existence of such gods and lords, whether real or "so-called" (to use Paul's designation of 1 Cor. 8:5–6).

Nor does the name Yahweh deny their existence. What the name asserts is that God alone is the Lord over all these spiritual beings as well.

You Shall Not Make An Idol

The second commandment "You shall not make for yourself an idol" thematically follows the creation accounts of Gen. 1–2 as a negative reinforcement of the universality of God over his creation. To make an idol, even of the Lord God, destroys his universality.

This correspondence between the second commandment, creation, and the universality of God may not be immediately apparent. The correspondence is built on the nature of idolatry and what an idol actually stands for or in place of. As already seen, the Apostle Paul told the Christians at Corinth that an idol is nothing. A few sentences later, under instruction about the Lord's Supper, Paul told what really lay behind idolatry and its practice.

1 Cor. 10:19–20
Do I mean then that a sacrifice offered to an idol is anything, or that an idol is anything? No, but the sacrifices of pagans are offered to demons, not to God, and I do not want you to be participants with demons.

An idol stood for (possibly even was housing) a spiritual, demonic power. It was not an object of worship itself; its purpose was to suggest the presence of a god (John I. Durham 1987).

In other words, idolatry was similar to what anthropologists today call animism. Animism may be defined as 1) a belief in spiritual beings such as gods, demons, and ghosts,[3] and as 2) a belief that these spiritual beings are in control of the operations of the phenomenal world, at least in control of that part of the world considered important for human existence and survival (David Filbeck 1985).

Another aspect of animism is derived directly from this two-part definition. Animism is a territorial religion (C. Peter Wagner 1989). A spirit or spirits are in control of how nature operates within a particular piece of land only, and beyond the boundaries of that land the spirit or spirits are no longer in control. Other spirits are in control. As a person, for example, passes from one territory to another, he leaves the oversight of one spirit to come under the rule of an equal spirit in the new territory.

This territorial aspect is readily seen in idolatry. An idol is an object physically placed in a location, which may be a house, a field, a high place, or even a whole nation. Its power and oversight is restricted to the boundaries of the location. Beyond those boundaries other idols are in power. Once having moved into a different location, worship and obeisance is due to the idol of that location. In short, there is no universality in idolatry or animism.[4]

From the above discussion we can begin to understand the theological significance of the second commandment, "You shall not make for yourself an idol." This law was given to safeguard the universality of God in Israel's life and worship. Indeed, the only way to protect this universality was to forbid the making of idols. An idol, even of the Lord God, would conceptually and in worship confine God to just the land that Israel was to possess. Only in the absence of a visible form could God in spirit and truth be praised and worshiped universally in every land and nation as God of heaven and earth and all things residing therein.

From the above we can also understand the missionary significance of the second commandment, for in safeguarding the universality of God over all creation, it also protected the missionary message implicit in this universalism. The God who revealed himself in the pages of the Old Testament is not the god or idol of a local area. He is Lord of all the earth.

To summarize: the first two commandments of the Decalogue do not add any new elements, as we saw from Gen. 12:3, for the development of the missionary message of the Old Testament. Rather, these two commandments exist to protect what has been revealed; God exists and he reigns universally over his creation.[5] Within the total structure of the Scriptures, therefore, we see that these two commandments (that there shall be no other God in addition to the Lord and no idol shall be made) function to guide the development of the missionary message of the Old Testament.

Early on, unfortunately, Israel did not fully follow the reinforcements of these two commandments. Israel soon turned to idolatry, at which times the people of Israel became territorially bound. The Land of Promise, reinforced by idolatry, became the most important part of the three-part promise given to Abraham. The other two parts, a holy nation and a channel of blessing to other nations, took second and third place and became all but lost in the overwhelming need to secure the territorial borders of the promised land from surrounding enemies.

To break this effect of idolatry—to restore the other parts of the promise to their rightful place—took a great deal of effort. But we are getting ahead of our story.

Questions For Discussion

1. Why is an unambiguous monotheism essential as a theological base to world missions?

2. Summarize how the first two commandments of the Decalogue reinforce the theological base underlying the missionary message of the Old Testament.

3. Because of monotheism, how should the missionary evangelist deal with the god(s) and lord(s) of another culture where (s)he has been sent?

4. In terms of the missionary interpretation of the Old Testament, explain why God strictly forbade idolatry in Israel.

Endnotes

1. It is natural to respond in this manner even though two of the ten are not prohibitions (remember the Sabbath and honor one's parents). But it is much better to say that Christianity has no such prohibitions! However, this should not be construed, as some might charge (cf. Walter C. Kaiser, Jr. 1983:145), as antinomianism. For in Christianity there are two positive commands which we are to obey: love God with all of our heart, soul, and mind, and to love our neighbor as ourselves (Matt. 22:37–38), for love fulfills all prohibitions established by religion (Rom. 13:10).

2. When we read through the accounts of the Patriarchs and on into Exodus and the giving of the Law, we get a feeling of moving away from the universalism of Genesis 1–11 to the particularism of Israel, especially in the giving of the Law on Mt. Sinai, and we must wait until the time of the kingdom and prophets before we see the theme of universalism emerge once more in Israel. Consequently, it could be argued, we should pass over the Law of Moses in the search for a theological basis in the Old Testament for evangelizing the nations, for there is no universalism here. However, the case is otherwise. We still find the theme of universalism in the Law, though perhaps not in the way or with the categories we are accustomed to seeing. Far from emphasizing particularism in Israel at the expense of the universal reign of God over his creation, these categories, as we shall see, strengthen and maintain from a different perspective the universalism already observed.

3. Under this definition some anthropologists, including William Smalley and Eugene Nida (1959), define Christianity as an animistic religion because of the teaching that God is Spirit, we are the dwelling place of God in the spirit, and so forth.

4. In many animistic societies we do find what anthropologists call the "high god" concept. However, in most instances this high god is not normally associated with the operations of nature so he is viewed differently from demons and other spirits. Few if any taboos are associated with the god and he goes largely forgotten as people cope with daily life (David Filbeck 1985). Where a high god has become significant in a culture or society, it has often been due to missionaries and their preaching that this God is the God of the Bible who universally reigns over his creation.

5. It is in the area of animism that Protestant theology of missions will differ from that of Roman Catholic theology. In Roman Catholicism animistic practices and beliefs, especially those of the first generation of converts, are often allowed and even incorporated into the practices of the church thus resulting in what many have criticized as Christopaganism. It is hoped, of course, that through education future generations will no longer adhere to such (Christopaganistic) practices. On the other side, Protestant mission practice has generally demanded a clean break from animism even on the part of the first generation of believers. A major reason for this insistence is that any animistic residue in the worship of God is theologically in conflict with God's universality and if not checked will result in something less than a wholehearted worship of God as Lord over all areas of life, and often will result in the ultimate rejection of God and returning to worshiping the demons and spirits of one's local territory.

CHAPTER SEVEN

Into the Promised Land

Israel's entry into the Promised Land opens with the story of Rahab, a prostitute of Jericho who welcomed and hid the twelve spies sent out by Joshua (Josh. 2). She quickly gave her support to Israel's claim to take over the land.

Two reasons for this conversion were given. First was the fear instilled in the hearts of her fellow citizens upon hearing of the victories Israel had won over nearby tribes and nations on the way out of Egypt to Canaan. The second was the God who was leading the people of Israel and who could do such mighty acts. Who was this God? Rahab herself speaks.

Joshua 2:11
When we heard of [the victories], our hearts sank and everyone's courage failed because of you, for the Lord your God is God in heaven above and on the earth below.

To these victories may also be added the earlier reports of what had happened to Pharoah and Egypt during the time of the plagues. The purpose of the plagues was twofold: 1) to show how powerful God was so that 2) God's power and name might be proclaimed in all the earth (Exod. 9:16).

Rahab, in faraway Jericho, had certainly heard these mighty acts of the Lord proclaimed. On the basis of the universality of God, the God in heaven and on earth, Rahab converted to Israel's side and believed in Yahweh, the Lord. Her new status in Israel, moreover, was recognized by New Testament writers. The writer of Hebrews counted her as one of the faithful heroes of the past (Heb. 11:31). James said she was considered righteous because of what she did in helping

the spies (James 2:25). The name Rahab is included in the genealogy
of Jesus Christ (Matt. 1:5) and is presumed by many to be the Jericho
prostitute. In many respects the conversion of Rahab represented a
positive theological beginning for Israel in the Promised Land.

Unfortunately, however, this was not to last. As we read the Old
Testament books of Joshua, Judges, and the opening chapters of First
Samuel we get the feeling of a steady deterioration in Israel's faith and
obedience. After the high point of the giving of the Decalogue in
Exodus 20, the way pointed "downhill" spiritually and theologically
for the people of Israel.

Yet, despite a spiritual downward spiral, this period of Israel's
history is still significant for the development of the missionary
interpretation of the Old Testament. What developed during this
time made lasting contributions to how the Old Testament in later
generations was understood and proclaimed among the other ethnic
groups of the earth.

Idolatry

The decline in Israel's spirituality and obedience had its beginning in the idolatry of the original inhabitants of Canaan. On first
entering the Promised Land the Lord had instructed the children of
Israel through Moses to drive out the Hittites, Girgashites, Amorites,
Canaanites, Perizzites, Hivites, and Jebusites.

Exod. 23:33
Do not let them live in your land, or they will cause you to sin
against me, because the worship of their gods will certainly be a
snare to you.

Israel was to make no treaty with any of them nor show them any
mercy.

Exod. 34:15
Be careful not to make a treaty with those who live in the land; for
when they prostitute themselves to their gods and sacrifice to
them, they will invite you and you will eat their sacrifices.

They were to be destroyed (Deut. 7:1–2). Specifically the Lord
ordered the Israelites to break down their altars, smash their sacred

stones, cut down their Asherah poles, and burn their idols in the fire. For the Israelites were a people holy to the Lord God (Deut. 7:5–6).

After Moses' death Joshua took over the leadership of Israel. In their first battle at Jericho they completely destroyed the city. Every living thing, men and women, young and old, cattle, sheep, and donkeys, all were killed by the sword (Josh. 6:21).

Throughout Joshua's life this procedure was repeated over much of the Promised Land. At Ai the Israelites killed all those in the city (Josh. 8:24). The city of Makkedah was totally destroyed with everyone in it (Josh. 10:28). From there Joshua moved south and destroyed five cities "leaving no survivors" (Josh. 10:29–42). Next Joshua moved to the north and took all the royal cities there, putting every inhabitant to the sword (Josh. 11:14).

The command of the Lord in Deuteronomy to destroy the inhabitants of Canaan has long been difficult for many to accept. Marcion (ca. 60–ca. 160) rejected the Old Testament on this account. He claimed that the God of the Old Testament was cruel, and Jesus came to reveal a totally different God of love. In more modern times some have also rejected the Old Testament for the same reason. For some people, no hermeneutic would justify such action or give any meaning to us today. The Old Testament at this point, it is claimed, is simply too "primitive," when compared with modern sensibilities, to be creditable.

However, more than modern sensibilities, or even Israel's spirituality and obedience, are at stake here. For in the case of idolatry (as we shall see more fully below), it is ultimately the missionary message of the Old Testament—God's desire for his name to be proclaimed in all the earth—that is at stake.

Therefore, we must not let our feelings divorce the Scriptures at this point from what God commanded Joshua to do in driving out the original inhabitants of Canaan.

However, this task had not been completed by the end of Joshua's life. Just before he died Joshua warned the Israelites of the remaining nations that had not been driven out but still lived in the Promised land.

Josh. 23:7–8
Do not associate with these nations that remain among you; do not invoke the names of their gods or swear by them. You must not serve them or bow down to them. But you are to hold fast to the Lord your God, as you have until now.

Joshua asked them to make a decision: serve the gods of idolatry or serve the Lord (Josh. 24:15). The Israelites promised to serve the Lord. Joshua said,

Josh. 24:23
Now then...throw away the foreign gods that are among you and yield your hearts to the Lord, the God of Israel.

But the Israelites did not obey Joshua's instruction. After Joshua died the Israelites forsook the Lord and began to serve the male and female fertility idols of Baal and the Ashtoreths (Judges 2:12–13). They took daughters from surrounding nations (who worshiped these idols) in marriage and gave their daughters in turn. They also served the gods of other nations (Judges 3:6).

This sequence happened often among the Israelites in the years following Joshua's death. And whenever it occurred, the Lord God was no longer the only one in their devotion; they now served several gods. Nor was the Lord worshiped as being universal over his creation; now territorial idols required sacrifices.

To the original inhabitants of the land these spirits or demons assured balance in nature: just enough rain, not too much or too little, not too many insects which would destroy crops, and so on (cf. David Filbeck 1964, 1985). But nature was not always in balance. Drought or too much rain occurred, insects would reproduce in overabundance, and other calamities would happen. During such times sacrifices would have to be made to the spirits of the land to regain the balance in nature that would assure an adequate supply of food and the well-being of the inhabitants.

A biblical illustration of this type of animistic belief is found in the destruction of the northern kingdom of Israel by Assyria in 721 B.C. After the Israelites were deported, groups of other nationalities were resettled in the former northern kingdom. These people did not know the Lord and so did not worship him. Lions came among them killing some. This was reported to the king of Assyria:

2 Kings 17:26
...The people you deported and resettled in the towns of Samaria do not know what the god of that country requires. He has sent lions among them, which are killing them off, because the people do not know what he requires.

An Israelite priest was sent to teach the way of the Lord, but in the end the people set up idols in the land. Such animistic beliefs influenced the Israelites early on.

Even though many of the original inhabitants of the land had been driven off, the spirits or gods of the land remained. The tug of animistic beliefs was strong, and unless dealt with in a radical way, such as smashing and destroying idols, the Israelites would soon succumb.[1]

More significantly, though, we find no biblical record of anyone outside of Israel, such as Rahab earlier, converting to worship the Lord, the God of heaven and earth. In times of worshiping idols the Israelites proved to be no different from the neighboring ethnic groups. They had only local, territorial gods to offer and not the Lord of heaven and earth.

All this resulted from idolatry in Israel. Whenever idols—more properly the demons that the idols represented—were served and worshiped, God's covenant with Abraham was subverted and the purpose for Israel to be a blessing and a kingdom of priests for the nations disintegrated. It is small wonder, then, why the prohibition against idols was repeated so many times in the Old Testament, or why the Israelites were warned about the nations in Canaan who worshiped idols. Otherwise the missionary message of the Old Testament would surely be lost, thus aborting God's will for his people in bringing his salvation to the ends of the earth.

A modern day descendant of idolatry, the new paganism (animism), has the same effect. In this day of religious pluralism this recent reincarnation of animism in modern western society is clamoring for equal attention and status with Christianity. Its potential for aborting the missionary message of the Old Testament, indeed of the whole Bible, is equally as great as idolatry was in Old Testament times.

Of course, the new paganism is not similar in form to the idolatry of Old Testament times. For example, this paganism is more akin to eastern mysticism, emphasizing pantheism and believing in process; i.e., humans are "gods-in-the-making." Old Testament idolatry, on the other hand, was territorial, polytheistic, and required bloody sacrifices.

Yet they are nearly identical in their results: since in idolatry there are many gods, each one in control over a specific piece of land, and in the new paganism God is diffused throughout all of creation (in fact is creation), God is no longer one nor is he universal over all creation. In his place other gods (whether idols, self, or a process) are worshiped. There ceases to be any basis for proclaiming God's name and power to the world (Exod. 9:16).

The Monarchy

During the time of the Judges (ca. 1375 B.C.–1075 B.C.) idolatry fueled chaos and uncertainty in Israel. Because of worshiping idols the Israelites often became divided, with part of the people worshiping the Lord while others worshiped the idols of the land. During such times of little unity Israel became ripe for attack, capture, and enslavement by other nations. When the oppression from these attacks became unendurable, the Israelites would call on God for deliverance. A deliverer, called a judge, would mobilize Israel under the Lordship of God to drive out the oppressors. As long as the judge lived, Israel remained free. But when the judge died Israel would fall once more into idolatry.

This cycle of events—idolatry, oppression, deliverance only to revert to idolatry once more—repeated itself some twelve times during the time of the judges. Toward the end the moral and social conditions of Israel had deteriorated considerably.

Each person did as he saw fit (Judges 17:6, 21:25). One man from the hill country of Ephraim, for example, made idols and installed one of his sons as a priest (Judges 17:5). Later when men from the tribe of Dan formed a raiding party to capture land for the whole tribe, they took over these idols and installed priests of their own (Judges 18).

In another instance, in the territory where the descendants of Benjamin settled, homosexuals came to a house where a traveler from Ephraim was invited to spend the night. They insisted on having sex with him (Judges 19:22). The owner of the house refused, but offered the traveler's concubine instead. The homosexuals abused the concubine, and the next morning the traveler found her dead. He carried the body home, took a knife, and cut the corpse into twelve parts, sending a part to each of the twelve tribes of Israel. This gruesome act galvanized Israel. An army marched to punish the Benjamites (Judges 20). A great number of Benjamites, including women and children, and their animals were destroyed.

To replenish the tribe of Benjamin, for now they had no women for marriage and children, another raiding party was formed. This party of 12,000 men raided the town of Jabesh Gilead killing all married men and women. Four hundred virgins were taken back to the men of Benjamin for wives. Yet this number was not enough. A second raiding party was formed to raid the inhabitants of Shiloh for more young girls.

Such deterioration and chaos was attributed to the fact that Israel had no king (Judges 21:25). So during the time of Samuel, the last of the judges, Israelites called for a king to rule over them (1 Sam. 8:5). They viewed their tribal league, which had formed a loose confederation of clans for over three centuries (John Bright 1953), as a political weakness and not as a moral or theological problem. The solution, they reasoned, was to unite around a king. A king would provide the political unity and stability needed to bring law and order out of chaos. Israel would also be like the other nations, having a king to lead them into battle.

Samuel attempted to dissuade the Israelites from having a king. A king would rule as a dictator according to his own whim, Samuel warned, and not to the wishes of the people. But the people refused to listen. For one thing, the alternative then open to them was worse. Samuel had appointed his own sons to succeed him as judges over Israel. But his sons were corrupt and the people saw no hope in them for justice and fairness when they took over from their father in judging Israel.

Upon instruction from the Lord, therefore, Samuel appointed Israel's first king, a modest man named Saul from the tribe of Benjamin. Saul, however, soon lost his modesty and became despotic. In the end he also lost his throne to David of the tribe of Judah. David was able to consolidate all of Israel into one kingdom and pass it on to his son Solomon. Solomon led the kingdom of Israel to even greater glory. Out of all the glories of Solomon's Israel, however, none was greater than the magnificent temple to God built in the recently captured city of Jerusalem.

The establishment of a monarchy seemingly contradicted God's original plan for Israel. God planned for Israel to be a kingdom of priests and a blessing to the nations. God was to be their king. No man, even a judge with the popularity of Gideon (Judges 8:22–23), was to be king over Israel. When the Israelites called for a king, therefore, they rejected God as their king (1 Sam. 8:7) and their appointed role among the nations of the earth. Yet, in the end, God (re)directed this demand for a king, making it a contribution in accomplishing his own desire to include the nations in his salvation.

This (re)direction was based on the Law of Moses which had already made allowance for a king (Deut. 17:14–20). Israel's king was not to be like the kings who ruled over the nations. Israel's king, for example, was not to be considered divine or a god; such a king would indeed be a contradiction to God's plan. Rather, a king over Israel was to be selected from among the people and rule according to the law God had given. A king could not consider himself better than his fellow citizens.

God promised that the throne of David would be established and that a descendant of his would reign forever (2 Sam. 7:16). Three centuries later Isaiah took up the same refrain and wrote that a son shall reign on David's throne and over his kingdom forever (Isa. 9:7). The prophet Micah also wrote that out of Bethlehem (David's birthplace) a ruler shall appear who will rule over Israel (Mic. 5:2). This descendant came to be interpreted as the promised Messiah and his reign as the Kingdom of God on earth.

The Messiah and God's kingdom, however, were not always understood to include God's planning for nations other than Israel. Indeed some people grievously misunderstood the plan. The Messiah, for example, was sometimes considered a divine warrior who would drive out foreign invaders, and the Davidic kingdom in all of its power and might would then be restored and all nations would come to Jerusalem to pay homage to Israel's Messiah.[2]

Worship

Idolatry, because of its animistic roots, focused attention on the land that Israel had come to possess. The establishment of the monarchy reinforced this attention. Now, the need arose for secured borders and a standing army for national defense. In other words, because of idolatry and the monarchy, a "narrowing down" in attention focused on only one part of the covenant given to Abraham: the land that was promised as an inheritance.

But this narrowing down process did not mean that the universal dimension of the covenant (that all nations shall be blessed because of Abraham) was lacking during this time. In sharp contrast to the effects of idolatry and the monarchy, this universal aspect was alive and well in Israel's worship of God.

Indeed, perhaps the most significant contribution of this period with respect to the missionary understanding of the Old Testament was the recording of Israel's poetry preserving for us in the midst of turmoil (wars, apostasy, disunity, oppression, and exile) the "bottom line" on how God is to be viewed, praised, and worshiped. God is not a local deity restricted to one geographical area or nation. Moreover he is greater than what any monarchical power or dynasty can ever hope to display for our understanding. Even in the midst of turmoil his love and purpose for our lives still shine through. Truly he is the Lord, the God of all we see and ever hope to imagine (Eph. 3:20).

Israel's poetry is found throughout the Old Testament. The greatest concentration, of course, is in the Psalms, the longest book in the Bible. The Psalms are a collection of hymns of praise and petition to God for help, at other times for vengeance or justice, and to exhort fellow worshipers of the Lord, the God of Israel. We turn to the Psalms, therefore, to illustrate how Israel's worship of God made significant contributions to the missionary interpretation of the Old Testament.

The Psalms were not all written by David although many were. Psalms were composed throughout the monarchical period (1000 B.C.–587 B.C.) and beyond into the exile and post-exile period (587 B.C.–400 B.C.). It might seem, therefore, since we are progressing though the Old Testament period by period to show the development of a missionary understanding of the Old Testament, that we need to be careful about the early or late dating of the Psalms. That is, since at this point we are still in the early monarchical period of David and Solomon, we should focus only on the Psalms written during this time.

However, I believe that the dating of Psalms in this respect is a minor problem if indeed it should be considered a problem at all. The Psalms, whether early or late, reflect a tradition of worship and praise handed down from early times. The song that Israel sang when delivered from the Egyptian Pharoah and his army is an early example (Exod. 15:1–21). It ended with the refrain from Miriam, Moses' sister.

"Sing to the Lord, for he is highly exalted.
The horse and its rider he has hurled into the sea."

Hannah, the mother of Samuel before the age of the kings, is another example.

1 Sam. 2:1–2
My heart rejoices in the Lord; in the Lord my horn is lifted high.
My mouth boasts over my enemies,
   for I delight in your deliverance.
There is no one holy like the Lord; there is no one besides you;
   there is no Rock like our God.

The Psalms, therefore, reflect and expand on this long tradition
of communal and individual meditations on God and how he should
be worshiped. Dating the Psalms, then, is not important. What is
important is their content, for the content characterizes for us the
universality of God and establishes an important theological foundation for the missionary hermeneutic of the Old Testament.

Old Testament scholars have attempted to classify the Psalms
into various types. While such classification schemes have been
insightful, not one has been successful in gaining the allegiance of all
scholars. Therefore it is not my purpose to propose yet another way
of classifying the Psalms into types. Rather my purpose is to focus on
the theme of universalism found throughout the Psalms regardless of
type. For in the midst of narrowly focusing in on the land and the
nation, as seen in idolatry and the monarchy, God at the same time
was being praised in universal terms.

We have seen that from the opening chapters of Genesis God is
depicted as universal over all his creation. He is the Lord, the God in
heaven and on earth. We find the same description of God in the
Psalms, only more so. Here we find a full-blown universalism, a
universal description of God in multidimensional terms. Indeed, as
seen in the Psalms God is described with such a variety of terms that
no systemization seems possible. Only by listing the terms and
descriptions, perhaps subsuming them under a few general categories, can we come anywhere close to an adequate coverage of the
universality of God.

God, for example, is the "Lord most high" (Ps. 7:17), whose name
is "majestic in all the earth" (Ps. 8:1). The heavens declare his glory to
the ends of the earth (Ps. 19:1–4). He is exalted among the nations and
in the earth (Ps. 46:10). He is the awesome Lord, the Great King over
all the earth (Ps. 47:2). God is to be praised from the rising of the sun
to where it sets (Ps. 113:3).

Being high and exalted above all things, no god is as great as God
(Ps. 77:13). He is "God of gods" (Ps. 136:2); he is more awesome than

all the spiritual beings that surround him (Ps. 89:7). Among the gods there is none like him (Ps. 86:8). He is to be feared above all gods, for the other gods are nothing but idols (Ps. 96:4–5).

Being high and exalted God rules from "sea to sea, from the River to the ends of the earth" (Ps. 72:8). He rules all peoples justly and guides the nations of the earth (Ps. 67:4). He has set his throne in heaven and his kingdom rules over all (Ps. 103:19). Indeed, may the whole earth be filled with his glory. Amen and Amen (Ps. 72:19).

The universality of God extends throughout eternity. "The Lord is King for ever and ever" (Ps. 10:16). He rules forever by his power (Ps. 66:7). He is God from everlasting to everlasting (Ps. 90:2). His kingdom is everlasting and his dominion endures through all generations (Ps. 145:13).

The universality of God is seen through the vastness of his creation and the complexities of the operations of nature he set in motion. By his word the heavens and their starry hosts were made (Ps. 33:6). He is the maker of heaven and earth, the seas and everything in them (Ps. 146:6). The Lord does what he pleases in the heavens and the earth, in the seas and their depths. He makes the clouds rise from the ends of the earth; he sends lightning with the rain and brings out the wind from his storehouses (Ps. 135:6–7). He covers the sky with clouds supplying the earth with rain. He makes grass grow on the hills and provides food for the cattle and the young ravens. The Lord is great and mighty in power; his understanding has no limit (Ps. 147:5–9).

God's power is universal, making the earth tremble and quake, shaking the foundations of the mountains (Ps. 18:7). God the mighty one speaks and summons the earth from the rising of the sun to where it sets (Ps. 50:1). His judgments are likewise universal, for he summons the heavens above and the earth for judgment (Ps. 50:4). He punishes the nations (Ps. 59:5). He judges the gods and the earth (Ps. 82:1, 8). He will crush the rulers of the whole earth (Ps. 110:6).

So what is to be done when God is praised and worshiped universally with such a variety of terms and descriptions? We are to "proclaim among the nations what he has done" (Ps. 9:11). We are to sing of him among the nations (Ps. 108:3). We are to exalt and praise God as King for ever and ever; we are to tell of his mighty works, of the power of his awesome works and proclaim his great deeds. We are to celebrate his abundant goodness and joyfully sing of his righteousness (Ps. 145:1–7). Indeed, all nations are to praise the Lord, all peoples are to extol him, for great is his love toward us (Ps. 117).

Just In Praise Of God

The Hungarian lay pastor leaned over to give me some instruction before I spoke. The year was 1974 and the Cold War between
communism and the West was still very much on. I had traveled to
Budapest, the capital of Hungary, to glimpse firsthand how Christians lived behind the Iron Curtain. With two college students from
Canada and the United States I had found my way to this evangelical
congregation meeting in the upper storey of an unmarked building
somewhere in the middle of the city. I was immediately invited to
briefly address the congregation.

"Just say a few words in praise of God" the pastor whispered. I
nodded in agreement. "Just a few words in praise of God" he
repeated. I nodded again. "Just in praise of God" he emphasized a
third time.

I got the message. In the congregation of two hundred or more
people before me, surely government agents were there to record
anything that might sound antigovernment or anticommunist. I
suddenly realized that I too was in a vulnerable position because I had
just arrived from Thailand, a staunch anticommunist country and a
major staging area for U.S. warplanes to bomb North Vietnam, an ally
of Hungary.

I stood up to speak. I told the stories of individuals in my
missionary ministry who had turned from sacrificing animals to
demons to serving the living God. After each story I offered praise to
God for his mercy and love.

After I sat down I reflected on the condition to which God's
church and the witness of his people in Eastern Europe, after 1000
years of Christian history, had been reduced. Church buildings could
no longer be built. There were no training institutes and only a few
pastors. Evangelistic teams or crusades were forbidden. They had no
Christian radio or television programs, no literature (we ourselves
had smuggled literature in for the leaders of the congregation), and
no tract distribution in public.

In short, all they had left was worship, singing, and speaking
praises to God. But as events unfolded in communism during the
following twenty years, they had enough! The praise of Christians
outlasted the communist empire, enabling the church, not only in
Hungary but also throughout Eastern Europe and Russia, to rise
again in power and witness to the astonishment of the whole world.

This is a modern day illustration of what occurred in Israel.
Israel's monarchy, for example, lasted only 120 years. Upon

Solomon's death the Israelites split into northern and southern kingdoms, each with its own monarchy. Within 200 and 300 years respectively, these two kingdoms also disappeared. There were many reasons for their downfall. But according to the biblical historians of the time, the fall was attributable to idolatry, for idolatry summed up all that was evil in society.

What survived the disintegration of two kingdoms and the monarchy was Israel's worship of God in universal terms. Indeed, it was the recognition and worship of God as Lord in heaven and earth and as judge of the nations that carried Israel through rough times in the five centuries leading up and into the exile. This was especially true after Solomon's temple was destroyed and the Israelites began to meet in synagogues for instruction and worship.

The survival of Israel's worship also paved the way for the missionary interpretation of the Old Testament. As Israelites now moved out into the world at large their hymns of praise reminded them that the Lord was not their God alone, but he was also the Lord of all the peoples and lands they saw and where they lived. They took delight in declaring his works of creation and salvation to all who would listen. At last they were fulfilling their election of being a kingdom of priests and a blessing to all peoples.

The New Testament church likewise took Israel's worship as a mandate to proclaim God as Father and Jesus as Lord to the ends of the earth. The praise of God and his Son as Lord of all contributed to the church's (missionary) hermeneutic of the Old Testament Scriptures. The church, moreover, took it one step further. The praise of God in universal terms was combined with the Davidic kingdom to make a new song of praise to the Lamb of God.

Rev. 5:9–10

...You are worthy to take the scroll and to open its seals, because you were slain, and with your blood you purchased men for God from every tribe and language and people and nation. You have made them to be a kingdom and priests to serve our God, and they will reign on the earth.

God's kingdom is now extended to include peoples from all tribes, languages, and nations. It is no longer confined to Israel but is universal in scope and time. All peoples, and not just the people of Israel, may serve as priests before God.

This presents a lesson for the church today. How the church praises and worships God plays an important role in how the church understands and acts out her role in the world. When we recognize and worship God as Lord reigning universally over his creation, we can see, and more crucially obey, the missionary imperative of the Scriptures to bring God's salvation to the nations, even at the ends of the earth. The Kingdom of God ceases to be ours alone; it is to be extended to peoples of all tribes, languages, and nations. All of us in the church are priests to serve in behalf of others before God. The church becomes the new Israel through whom the nations of the earth are blessed.

The earth is the Lord's (Ps. 24:1); it is his harvest. When God is praised and worshiped as the Lord of the harvest (Matt. 9:38), the church sees again how truly white the fields are for harvesting. Missionaries, laborers for the Lord, will go forth from the church to harvest the earth for the Lord, filling the earth with his glory.

Eph. 3:21
...to him be glory in the church and in Christ Jesus throughout all generations, for ever and ever! Amen.

Questions For Discussion

1. In what ways are idolatry of Old Testament times and the "new paganism" of today similar? How do both undermine the missionary message of the Old Testament?

2. Why was it easy for idolatry to become associated with the monarchy in Israel? How did this association undermine the missionary purpose that God had for his people?

3. How did Israel's worship of God "save the day" with regard to the missionary purpose that God had for his people?

4. Discuss the cause-effect link that exists between worship and the missionary outreach of a church.

5. Does your worship of God compel you to evangelize people of ethnic groups other than your own? If not, can you give an analysis of the reasons why?

Endnotes

1. We may compare this with the way evangelism is done in animistic societies today. Upon conversion, an animist must destroy, often by burning, spirit paraphernalia. This radically demonstrates a total break from an animistic past.

It is the experience of missionaries in such societies that if every item associated with spirits is not destroyed, and one or a few survive, the converted animist will not remain in his or her new faith but will revert back to animistic practice in times of crop planting and sickness.

2. Later in the New Testament the Davidic Kingdom became an integral part in the missionary hermeneutic and understanding of the Old Testament on the part of the early church. The Messiah, as David's son, came to be the savior for all peoples (John 3:16–17). He is the promised blessing to all nations (Acts 3:25–26); in him all the Gentiles or nations shall place their hope (Rom. 15:12). The Good News about the kingdom shall be preached to all nations testifying to the reign of the Messiah (Matt. 24:14). This preaching shall continue until the full number of Gentiles (the nations) has come in (Luke 21:24, Rom. 11:25). At the end of the ages the kingdom which is this world will become the Kingdom of the Christ forever (Rev. 11:15), being handed over to God the Father (1 Cor. 15:24).

CHAPTER EIGHT

A Theological Tension

"Bai sold his daughter into prostitution," the young Thai preacher told me. I was shocked and saddened, because years earlier Bai had come to belief in Jesus Christ through the witness of a Christian uncle, and I had baptized him. But Bai was in bad health and so had been unable to advance economically. His only asset was a daughter, his only child.

Northern Thai society, where Bai lived, is matrilocal in residence. That is, in marriage the bride stays at home with her parents and her husband moves in as the son-in-law of the house. At first the son-in-law serves as a laborer in his wife's family but, as the parents of the wife become older, he eventually takes over as the main supporter of the extended family. As the parents grow feeble, the son-in-law assumes leadership in the family.

Bai's daughter was married and the son-in-law, according to the matrilocal custom, moved in to work for the family. Soon, however, tension developed between Bai and the son-in-law. Bai accused him of being lazy and not working hard enough to support the family. The tension grew into a conflict and before long the son-in-law packed up his personal belongings and left. It was divorce, northern Thai style.

This financial loss was a heavy blow to Bai. He was physically unable to work to support his family, and now the family's son-in-law, the only source of income for the family, was gone. As Bai surveyed his bleak future, only one alternative seemed open. His daughter was still young, and he could get a good price by selling her into prostitution. The money would be enough to build a new house, and her monthly income would support him and his wife quite well.

The Tension In Israel

Israel's monarchy had several bad side effects (especially when it became linked with idolatry) on the covenant God made with Abraham that he would have land, descendants, and be a blessing for the nations.

One side effect was a heightened ethnocentrism in Israel. Anthropologists tell us that every tribe or nation is affected with ethnocentrism, a feeling of superiority over other groups.

Israel no doubt was affected in the same way. But with the establishment of the monarchy they possessed a visible symbol of ethnocentric pride. Not only were they now "like the other nations, having a king to lead them into battle," but with the military victories won by David (2 Sam. 8) and the renown gained through Solomon (1 Kings 10), national pride became the order of the day for Israel.

A second side effect was the increased institutionalization of Israel's religion. From the Law given on Mt. Sinai some institutionalization had already occurred. They had, for example, the high priest, the priests, the Levites, the tabernacle, and the festivals. But with the monarchy a centralization set in, culminating in Solomon's temple. Service at the temple elevated the status and power of the priests. The temple being close to the royal palace increased considerably the power and prestige of the high priest (2 Chron. 29:20–22).

The institutionalization of Israel's religious life changed the role of the priests and Levites from that of being servants to that of being served. They, along with the king's functionaries, became the elite of Israel's society. They soon began to exercise their influence in corrupt ways. In the end, this institutionalization elevated Mt. Sinai and the Law above the Promise given to Abraham (Gal. 4:21–31). The covenant of being a blessing to the nations got lost in a maze of temple ceremonies and a welter of Levitical and priestly regulations.

All of the above factors produced a tension in Israel's understanding of the Abrahamic covenant during the monarchical era (1000 B.C.–587 B.C.). On the one hand, there was, as we have seen in the previous chapter, the worship of God in universal terms. On the other, the monarchy placed an undue emphasis on the land at the expense of the universalism of the covenant. While this emphasis was not crucial by itself (God redirected the monarchy to be a prototype of his universal kingdom), it still raised the question of what indeed was the most important part of the threefold promise God gave to Abraham. Was it now the land, being a holy people, or its universal nature of being the source by which all nations could be blessed? Worship of the Lord as the God above all gods emphasized universalism. The monarchy, now heightened by ethnocentrism, the institutionalization of Israel's religious life, and buttressed by idolatry, emphasized the land.

This emphasis ultimately wreaked havoc on the Promised Land and all but buried from sight the purpose that God had for his people in being a blessing to the nations.

A Divided Kingdom

Soon after the death of Solomon (ca. 926 B.C.), Israel divided into two kingdoms, each with its own monarchy. The immediate cause for the division was the heavy taxation that Solomon had imposed on the people of Israel to support all of his policies and projects which, while bringing international fame to Solomon and Israel, nevertheless burdened the people greatly. The temple, which took seventeen years to complete, cost enormous sums to furnish and decorate.

And then Solomon had an international policy of making treaties by marrying royal women from surrounding nations (1 Kings 11:1–3). After establishing diplomatic relations with a nation, for example, taking a foreign royal daughter in marriage assured peaceful relations with her home nation. Seven hundred of these marriages occurred, plus three hundred concubines. Maintaining and financing such a large royal harem in and around Jerusalem required a tremendous amount of taxes each year.

When Solomon's son, Rehoboam, succeeded to the throne, therefore, Israelites of the tribes living north of Jerusalem asked for tax relief. Rehoboam, on the advice of younger and inexperienced advisers, refused. The tribes then revolted and separated, retaining the name Israel. What remained of David's original kingdom became known as Judah.

Yet a deeper reason than taxation was behind the division into the two kingdoms of Israel and Judah. Idolatry was the root cause of the downfall of the united kingdom. This is the testimony of Scripture (1 Kings 11:4–8).

Solomon, contrary to his father David, first introduced idols into the kingdom's religious life. After the northern tribes separated from Judah, Jeroboam, their new king, followed the same example. He made two golden calves placing one in Bethel, at the southern edge of the new kingdom, and the other in Dan, at the northern edge.

The introduction of idolatry into the north was to provide political legitimacy to the new regime and to ensure political loyalty from the people. These were the gods, Jeroboam exclaimed, that had brought the Israelites out of Egypt (1 Kings 12:25–33). Otherwise, it was feared, the people would return to Jerusalem and the Davidic monarchy. Because of this need for political legitimacy and loyalty, the kings of the north did not "turn away from the sins of Jeroboam, the son of Nebat" (1 Kings 13:34; 2 Kings 13:11); indeed, all Israelites persisted in the sins of Jeroboam (2 Kings 17:22).

Idolatry had several harmful effects in the two kingdoms of Israel and Judah. We have already seen in previous chapters the potential effect of idolatry on the universalism of the Old Testament and how, if idolatry were left unchecked in Israel's history, it would ultimately undermine the missionary message of the Old Testament. But idolatry has an even more pernicious side to which the historians of the Old Testament turn our attention.

Solomon married many foreign women of royal status. Upon bringing a new wife to Jerusalem he would build a place of sacrifice and worship for the idol of his new wife. When he was old, his wives led him astray into worshiping these idols and offering sacrifices to them. Unfortunately these were not harmless idols that quaintly decorated the hillsides of Judah surrounding Jerusalem and required only picturesque ceremonies in times of worship. They were the idols Ashtoreth (from Sidon), Molech (from the Ammonites), and Chemosh (from Moab). The Hebrew Scriptures call them the "shaqquts," detestable gods (NIV), of these nations (I Kings 11:5–7).

It is difficult to translate, without resorting to crude language, the repulsiveness to which this Hebrew word referred.[1] The word appears first of all to have been a euphemism for feces, manure, garbage, and so on. For example, in Nahum 3:6 the prophet warns Ninevah that the Lord will "pelt you with filth," i.e., the city will become as someone smeared with manure, a sight people will gape at and feel contempt for.

In the Septuagint this term is often translated by the Greek word "bdelygma," which as a verb may refer to feeling nausea or being sick at one's stomach,[2] much as one feels from the stench rising from a pile of feces, manure, or garbage. In other words, these terms refer to something that is repulsive to the point of nausea and vomiting.

Another dimension of the Hebrew term shaqquts is shame or embarrassment due to bodily waste and excrement. Relieving oneself of waste is a private matter under normal living conditions. Without extraordinary conditions, such as sickness or injury, to relieve oneself in urination or defecation in public is a matter of shame, contempt, and repulsion on the part of others. It is crude, even an abomination, to be so insensitive as to relieve oneself for all to see in public.

This then is the feeling of revulsion that the historians and writers of the Old Testament Scriptures wish us to have regarding the idolatry that Solomon allowed to be introduced into Israel. To be sure, these accounts such as 1 Kings 11 were written some 300 years later right after Israel's (Judah's) defeat and deportation to Babylon, but in looking back it could be seen that what Solomon allowed was enough to make one nauseous and was as repulsive as the stench from manure and bodily waste is to the human nose.[3]

We must also understand that it was not the actual idol or image which was so grotesque that it caused nausea just to look upon it. No doubt these idols were artistically done according to the tastes of the times, eliciting praise and satisfaction at the artistry and skill of the idol makers. The artistic craftsmanship of these images probably at first commended them to Solomon. They were innocuous in appearance and perhaps added a decorative enhancement to the Judean hillsides.

Also, we should understand from the writing of Israel's history at this point, it appears that only the idols, and not the repulsive practices, were at first introduced by Solomon. Only toward the end of his life did the evil practices begin, and it was after his death and well into the reigns of both Israel's and Judah's kings that the more repugnant aspects of idolatry became prevalent. In any event, what eventually became utterly nauseating to later historians in Judah had its beginning with Solomon.

What the historians of the Old Testament consequently wanted readers to abhor were the practices of worship and sacrifice required in the religious ceremonies performed around these idols, for the practices and ceremonies were anything but innocuous or harmless in the worship they evoked in their worshipers. Upon investigation we see that these practices were indeed as repulsive as the stench that rises from bodily excrement.

Sacred Prostitution

The most prevalent practice in the worship of idols in both Israel and Judah was sacred prostitution (1 Kings 14:24). This included both men and women who offered their bodies for sex at shrines and in places of worship. Not only was this heterosexual prostitution, but it appears that homosexual prostitution was included as well. Sacred prostitution was animistic in purpose. It was to simulate the operations of nature in producing food; in this case cereal grain which was the main food staple of the area. Sacred prostitution was thus thought to enhance and assure the fertility of the soil for growing grain. As sexual intercourse is the source of new life, intercourse with a sacred prostitute would ritually transfer fertility and life to nature and the soil. As life is produced by sexual intercourse, so the soil would now produce grain.

Apparently idolatry and prostitution were at first not combined in Israel. But after the division into two kingdoms, they were. In Judah, for example, during the reign of Solomon's son, Rehoboam, sacred prostitution occurred in the land. In the north the prophet Hosea condemned the sacred prostitution practiced in Israel (Hos. 4:14).

In this combination of idolatry with sex, a powerful force was now unleashed upon the peoples of Judah and Israel. Psychologists, for example, tell us that sexual relations bond one human to another (Donald M. Joy 1985). And once bonding has occurred as in marriage, a new sexual liaison with another individual as in adultery can break the old bond, creating in its wake a new bonding. We are also told that just as sexual relations can bond one to another, so sexual promiscuity may become addictive (Grant Martin 1990, Mark R. Laaser 1992).

In fact it does not need to be sexual promiscuity alone. Pornography, voyeurism, and masochism, can also become addictive. Sexual addiction in whatever form, as with any other addiction, is difficult to break if indeed it is ever broken, for one is addicted, not to an individual as in bonding, but to physical excitement or a "high" as in drugs. If such an addiction is to be broken, it probably must be done as in the Alcoholic Anonymous program. Just as one is always an alcoholic but thankfully a recovering alcoholic, so must a person who is promiscuously addicted continually consider him- or herself a recovering addict. Otherwise a false sense of security ensues and the person may very well fall back into addiction, whether it is drugs, alcohol, or sexual promiscuity.

Sexual promiscuity, especially if widespread (as it became in sacred prostitution in Israel and Judah) and justified by an animistic belief system, is not just a matter of sex between "consenting adults" as western society would understand it. Social consequences are also widespread, as can be seen in the practical effects of sacred prostitution on the societies of Israel from 926 B.C. to 721 B.C. and of Judah from the same date to 587 B.C.

For example, sacred or ritual prostitution would be a calendrical ceremony (Mischa Titiev 1960) in an animistic belief system. That is, at the beginning of each calendar growing season sacred prostitution, perhaps at a local shrine, would be performed in order to infuse nature and the soil with fertility. But given the addictive powers of sexual promiscuity, sacred prostitution was no doubt performed throughout the year by many, perhaps justified as a means of maintaining fertility.

Another harmful side effect was the giving of sons and daughters to become temple prostitutes (Deut. 23:17). To do this required, beginning at a young age, the sexualization of children to serve as prostitutes. That is, the sexual role of a temple prostitute was promoted in Israel's society. In a family, for example, parents allowed and perhaps encouraged a child to become a prostitute at a shrine; prestige and probably no little monetary return for the family resulted from dedicating a child to serve in this capacity. With the blessing of both society and family, it therefore became easy to influence and direct children into prostitution thus assuring, as older prostitutes became unattractive, a continual supply of new and fresh prostitutes.[4]

The social consequences of sacred prostitution can be seen in a comparison with the effects of adultery. As adultery can break the bond of marriage, and bond a marriage partner with an outside person, so the sacred prostitution of idolatry broke Israel's bond with the Lord and physically and emotionally rebound them to the idols imported from surrounding nations. A "spirit of prostitution" had led them astray (Hos. 4:12); they had become "unfaithful to" God (Hos. 5:4). And on the physical level, once sexually addicted, there was little hope that the people would give up such easy access to sexual promiscuity.[5] It happened as Hosea pronounced:

Hosea 4:10–12
They will eat but not have enough; they will engage in prostitution but not increase, because they have deserted the Lord to give themselves to prostitution...They consult a wooden idol and are answered by a stick of wood...

Ezekiel built on the insatiableness of sexual addiction to show how Israel was never satisfied in her idolatrous worship.

Ezekiel 16:28–29
You engaged in prostitution with the Assyrians too, because you were insatiable; and even after that, you still were not satisfied. Then you increased your promiscuity to include Babylonia, a land of merchants, but even with this you were not satisfied.

All the above underscores why the Lord condemned idolatry as adultery (Jer. 13:25–27). This was no metaphoric condemnation of idolatry based on some spiritual analogy with adultery. Idolatry involved actual sexual promiscuity in acts of animistic worship.[6]

Jer. 14:27
Your adulteries and lustful neighings, your shameless prostitution! I have seen your detestable acts on the hills and in the fields. Woe to you, O Jerusalem! How long will you be unclean?

Ezek. 16:23–24
Woe! Woe to you, declares the Sovereign Lord. In addition to all your other wickedness, you built a mound for yourself and made a lofty shrine in every public square. At the head of every street you built your lofty shrines and degraded your beauty, offering your body with increasing promiscuity to anyone who passed by.

After discussing the above it is difficult not to bring attention to the extent western societies (the traditional Christian societies of the world) have similarly become openly promiscuous, both heterosexually and homosexually, in recent decades. The theological significance of the Old Testament prophets in this regard, I believe, is twofold.

First we must not become so inured to its prevalence that we become desensitized and unable to perceive what this is doing to society. We must remember it was not idolatry (images made from wood and other materials) that caused Israel's and Judah's downfall. It was the sexual promiscuity that the idols required, and which, more insidiously, idolatry as a religious belief system justified. Sexual promiscuity, after all, was an act of worship, and the more "worship" a person engaged in, the more powerful or efficacious religion became. Sexual promiscuity in western society, with the possibility of a few exceptions, is thankfully separated from religion.

Nevertheless, and this is our second theologically significant point, as God's people today we must recognize the destructive force sexual promiscuity has on society and be willing as the prophets of old were to denounce it. It may be that we must also use crude and shocking terms, as Ezekiel did, to describe the repugnance that sexual promiscuity really is.

Human Sacrifice

A second practice that merited the description of shaqquts, a nauseating repulsion, in the idolatry of both Israel and Judah was human sacrifice (Hos. 13:2). Solomon built shrines for the gods Chemosh and Molech on a hill east of Jerusalem, the Mount of Olives in the New Testament (1 Kings 11:7). Both gods required human sacrifice of children (Lev. 18:21, 2 Kings 3:27). A child was sacrificed by being made to "pass through the fire" (2 Kings 16:3, KJV), a euphemism for burning a child in sacrifice (Deut. 12:31, NIV). Presumably a child was killed first in a ritual sacrifice (compare Abraham's preparation for sacrificing Isaac in Gen. 22) and then burned as an offering to the god. Both sons and daughters were sacrificed (2 Kings 17:17).

The sacrifice of a child was a critical ceremony (Mischa Titiev 1960); i.e., in times of crisis or emergency one's own child was sacrificed to a god. When the king of Moab, for example, who paid tribute to Israel (2 Kings 3:4), attempted to rebel, the kings of Judah and Israel joined forces to put down the rebellion. As the alliance was besieging the city where the king of Moab had barricaded himself along with a force of 700 warriors, the king took one last desperate action to prevent total defeat. He sacrificed his firstborn son, who was to succeed him as king, upon the wall of the city he was defending (2 Kings 3:27). This increased the fury of the Moabites in the battle against the alliance, causing both Israel and Judah to stop the siege and return to their own land.

The allegory of the unfaithful wife (Jerusalem has been unfaithful to the Lord because of idols and their attendant shaqquts or abominations) in Ezekiel 16 sheds more light on the critical nature of human sacrifice.

Ezek. 16:20

And you took your sons and daughters whom you bore to me and sacrificed them as food to the idols...

In the original Hebrew language of this verse the term translated as food in the New International Version is the verb "to eat." That is, children were sacrificed for the idol (more properly the god or demon of an idol) to eat. In this verse it is better to maintain the verb "eat" than to restructure it into the noun "food," for the verb better corresponds to what is actually thought in animism when a bloody sacrifice is made to a spirit or demon.

In animism two basic reasons explain why a sacrifice is made. The first is when a taboo of a spirit has been broken and the offended spirit is punishing the offender by causing sickness or some other calamity. This punishment is often described as the demon "eating" the person (in this instance the English verb "to devour" is a closer correspondence). A sacrifice, then, is to "feed" the spirit so that it will stop "eating" or punishing the offender and take away the calamity.

A second reason is when nature is not functioning normally; e.g., a crop is dying or there is a drought. When this happens it is often thought a spirit is "hungry" and has let this be known by disrupting nature's processes. A sacrifice is then made to "feed" the spirit and to restore nature back to its normal operation.

The gods or demons of Israel's idols were a particularly vicious lot. Both historians and anthropologists have found human sacrifice to be a rarity in the world's cultures. Only a few societies have been found that have ever practiced it. Israel of the monarchical era was one of them. Child sacrifice was probably done only rarely in Israel and Judah during the monarchical period. Nevertheless, when it did occur, it was so gruesome and sickening that their heathen neighbors were shocked that the Israelites would kill and burn the bodies of children in sacrifice to the demons (Ezek. 16:20–52).

In this regard, of all the kings of both Israel and Judah, two stand out as being among the most terrible—Ahaz in Israel and Manasseh in Judah. Significantly both engaged in sacrificing their own children to idols (2 Kings 16:3, 21:6). Human sacrifice was not performed by kings only, of course. People in both kingdoms were guilty of this nauseating, repulsive practice comparable to the repugnant stench of feces and manure.

Israel and Judah engaged in other practices of idolatry: divination, sorcery, witchcraft, casting spells, being a medium, consulting the dead. These all contributed to the downfall of both kingdoms. But none of these other practices merited the description of shaqquts. Only sacred prostitution and human sacrifice rate the designation of being despicable abominations.

Conclusion

The tension produced by political division and idolatry was not a creative one for Israel, where the pull of one side influences the other to achieve a better synthesis. But with the monarchy, Israel's energy was turned inward to building up and securing the land in their possession while the role of being a blessing to the nations steadily eroded. Before it was over, the tension that evolved developed into a theological dilemma for the people of Israel. Resolving this dilemma, while painful as we shall see, provided yet another contribution to the missionary interpretation of the Old Testament. Indeed, without what Israel went through during this time, there very well might not have been a missionary hermeneutic of the Old Testament.

Questions For Discussion

1. In an earlier chapter we observed that idolatry undermined the missionary message of the Old Testament because idolatry was a territorial and not a universal belief. In this chapter we observed that sacred prostitution was associated with idolatry in Israel. Discuss how sacred prostitution further undermined the missionary message of the Old Testament.

2. Paul said that covetousness is idolatry (Col. 3:5). Aside from their implications regarding the development of a missionary hermeneutic of the Old Testament, do you see any relationship between a) sacred prostitution and the child sacrifice of idolatry in Israel and b) the sexual promiscuity and abortions often driven by covetousness in American society? Does the prophetic denunciation in the former give us the biblical precedent for the denunciation of the latter in society, whether it is American or some other society?

3. Christians are in danger of becoming desensitized to sexual promiscuity and abortion in American society. Discuss how this desensitization can work to undermine the missionary understanding of the Scriptures and the mission outreach of churches into other ethnic groups.

4. Discuss how purity of life and a high value on life are essential prerequisites in the church for the missionary understanding of the Scriptures and mission outreach from churches to the ends of the earth.

Endnotes

1. Crude language is just what Ezekiel resorted to in describing one aspect of "shaqquts," sacred prostitution (see below). "Yet [Judah] became more and more promiscuous as she recalled the days of her youth, when she was a prostitute in Egypt. There she lusted after her lovers, whose genitals were like those of donkeys and whose emission was like that of horses. So you longed for the lewdness of your youth, when in Egypt your bosom was caressed and your young breasts fondled." (Ezek. 23:19–21)

2. A Greek-English Lexicon compiled by Henry George Liddell and Robert Scott (1976). Three other Hebrew words are similar in meaning to "shaqquts," which are often translated with the English word abomination. They are "to-ebah," "ba-ash," and "piggul." These words also include a semantic component of stench that may cause a person to become nauseated.

3. The Apostle Paul no doubt had the same comparison in mind when he wrote that he considered all things as "skyballa," garbage, manure, in order to gain Christ (Phil. 3:8).

4. This same process is seen among the village peasant families of northern Thailand today. Sociologically a daughter is responsible for the financial welfare of the family, especially as the parents grow older. The traditional way of fulfilling this obligation is for the daughter to marry and bring in a son-in-law to farm and work for wages which are turned over to take care of the extended family. Another way, one that produces more money quicker, is to sell a daughter into prostitution. To do this, however, it is necessary to sexualize a daughter as she grows up to accept being sold as a prostitute as a legitimate way of fulfilling her financial obligation to the family.

5. A modern day counterpart of this practice is when cult leaders employ the power of sexual relations with cult members, both male and female, to bond members to the cult. Pimps will also often rape women as a way of bonding the women to them and to their new profession as prostitutes. In both cases, once sexual relations have begun, it is difficult to rescue members from cults, or prostitutes from their behavior.

6. Perhaps a modern day example of the repugnance felt by the Old Testament prophets toward sacred prostitution would be the feeling of revulsion that many people experience upon learning of the anonymous stall for anal sex in the homosexual bath house or the small cot in a brothel on which a prostitute serves a steady stream of men.

CHAPTER NINE

From Tension To Theological Dilemma

Wong's wife died leaving him a widower with seven children, two of whom were yet quite young. He found fellowship with Christians of a nearby church in the northern Thai resettlement village where he lived and soon became a Christian himself. But his newfound belief in Jesus Christ seemed to have created more problems than solutions for his life.

For starters, none of his grown sons followed him into his Christian faith; they remained outside the fellowship of the church seeking their own friends among non-Christians. Before long they married non-Christian girls. He felt alienated from his sons. He was also illiterate. Since so much of Christian worship and growth revolved around reading from the Scriptures and singing from a hymnbook, he felt more cut off than included in the worship and preaching services of the church.

Wong's biggest problem, however, was opium. In fact, since becoming a Christian, opium had become a big dilemma in his life. When his wife died he began taking opium to alleviate his sorrow and loneliness. But now he knew that taking opium was not only wrong but also a sin before God, and he had to stop taking it. Yet he was addicted to it. Breaking the habit would not be easy. If he did not or could not break the habit, however, he knew that opium would ultimately destroy his Christian life and fellowship in the church.

Wong's dilemma was not unlike that which faced the descendants of Abraham in the Promised Land. Because of the sins and abominations resulting from idolatry which occurred in Israel and Judah during the monarchical era, God thundered condemnation upon the two nations, threatening to utterly destroy both. God sent prophets to warn them of his anger (2 Kings 17:13). Listen to these threats of destruction on both Israel and Judah.

Amos 3:14-15
"On the day I punish Israel for her sins, I will destroy the altars of Bethel; the horns of the altar will be cut off and fall to the ground. I will tear down the winter house along with the summer house; the houses adorned with ivory will be destroyed and the mansions will be demolished," declares the Lord.

Isaiah 3:8-9
Jerusalem staggers, Judah is falling; their words and deeds are against the Lord, defying his glorious presence...Woe to them! They have brought disaster upon themselves.

These threats of destruction, however, created a dilemma. If God had truly called and elected Israel, then why all the threats? Surely God had called Abraham and had elected Israel to be a kingdom of priests. Surely he would not now relent on his call and allow his people to be destroyed.

Repent!

Now the prophets whom God sent also proclaimed the solution to this dilemma. The answer was repentance.

2 Kings 17:13
...Turn from your evil ways. Observe my commands and decrees, in accordance with the entire Law that I commanded your fathers to obey and that I delivered to you through my servants the prophets.

This began with Elijah and his confrontations with Ahab and the false prophets of Baal (1 Kings 18:17). But Ahab was too intimidated by his queen Jezebel to listen.

1 Kings 21:25-26
There was never a man like Ahab, who sold himself to do evil in the eyes of the Lord, urged on by Jezebel his wife. He behaved in the vilest manner by going after idols...

When Elijah confronted him over the murder of Naboth, Ahab "fasted...and laid around meekly" (1 Kings 21:27). He gained reprieve from the Lord after humbling himself, but in the end he still died a horrible death.

Elisha received Elijah's spirit of prophecy and sparked a revival in Israel. He anointed Jehu to wipe out Ahab's descendants, to kill Jezebel and to eliminate the worship of Baal in Israel (2 Kings 9, 10). But Jehu failed to complete his mission and bring Israel back to the Lord. He still walked in the sins of Jeroboam worshiping the golden calves which had led Israel into sin. God also sent Amos and Hosea to the northern kingdom of Israel calling for repentance.

Hosea 14:1–3

Return, O Israel, to the Lord your God. Your sins have been your downfall! Take words with you and return to the Lord. Say to him: "Forgive all our sins and receive us graciously, that we may offer the fruit of our lips. Assyria cannot save us..."

But Israel did not repent. And Assyria brutally deported Israel out of the Promised Land never again to return (ca. 721 B.C.). Isaiah and Micah, prophets of Judah, were observing what was happening to Israel. They too thundered God's condemnation upon Israel. But they did not stop there, for they saw the same abominations in Judah and, based upon what God had done to Israel, warned that the same punishment waited for Judah as well. Later, Jeremiah joined the choruses of condemnations and warned Judah of impending destruction.

Jeremiah 4:5–6

"Announce in Judah and proclaim in Jerusalem and say: 'Sound the trumpet throughout the land!' Cry aloud and say: 'Gather together! Let us flee to the fortified cities!' Raise the signal to go to Zion! Flee for safety without delay! For I am bringing disaster from the north, even terrible destruction."

Jeremiah also called for repentance (Jer. 7:3), as did Ezekiel (Ezek. 14:6). But as with Israel earlier, Judah would not listen (Jer. 25:7).

During this time in Judah there arose the phenomenon of the false or lying prophet claiming to be from the Lord (Richard De Ridder 1976). The false prophet declared "Peace, peace when there is no peace" (Jer. 6:14). They gave false hopes speaking visions from their own minds (Jer. 23:16). They would not prophesy about the destruction the Lord had foretold for that would be a disgrace; rather, the (false) prophet prophesied that there would be plenty of wine and beer for the people (Micah 2:6–11).

These prophets were false because they were powerless to turn back the anger of the Lord until his purposes were fully accomplished; in that day of fulfillment all would know that the Lord had not sent those prophets nor had he ever even spoken to them (Jer. 23:20–21). The false prophet Hananiah, for example, prophesied that the Lord would break the yoke of Babylon, and Jerusalem would not be destroyed (Jer. 28) even though Jeremiah had prophesied otherwise (Jer. 25:9–11). To Hananiah's false prophecy, Jeremiah sarcastically answered "Amen! May the Lord do so! May the Lord fulfill the words you have prophesied..." (Jer. 28:6).

Already by this time Babylon had plundered the temple and taken off the golden vessels, deporting many prominent people in retaliation for king Jehoiakim's rebellion. These things, too, had already been prophesied by the Lord's true prophets (2 Chron. 36:5–7).

In anticipation of the conclusion we want to draw from this period of Judah's history, these false prophets were false in yet another way. For, as God was directing events to accomplish the purpose of his heart (Isa. 46:9–10, Jer. 23:20), they stood in the way of the universalism of the covenant God had given to Abraham: all nations shall be blessed because of him. In opposition to this they wanted Judah to survive for her sake alone. They were false prophets because at this point in time they were blocking the development of the missionary hermeneutic of the whole Old Testament record. As we shall shortly see, what God was doing through Babylon worked to achieve the missionary understanding of the Old Testament that he wants his people to have even today.

God's Three-Fold Plan

The prophets' call for Judah to repent was not heeded. Another solution to Judah's theological dilemma was called for. This was God's three-fold plan for a stubborn people (Jer. 5:23). The outline of this plan had its beginnings in the prophetic writings of Isaiah and Micah. More details were added through Jeremiah and Ezekiel, receiving its finishing touches in Malachi, the final writing of the Old Testament. When the Old Testament closes we see that all the components for the missionary understanding of the Old Testament were at last in place.

The first part of this plan called for destruction. But what was to be destroyed? Everything, Isaiah said. Food, water, the hero, warrior, judge, prophet, soothsayer, elders, captains, men of rank, counselor, skilled craftsman, the enchanter (Isa. 3:1–3). The cities were to lie in ruin, houses to be left desolated, fields ruined and ravaged (Isa. 6:11). The land, the Promised Land, the one geographical location on this earth that belonged to the chosen people of God, was to be utterly destroyed.[1]

The most significant aspect of this part of the plan was that the Lord of hosts, the God of Israel, would cause all this destruction (Isa. 10:13). He would raise up his servant Nebuchadnezzar, king of Babylon, to completely destroy Judah making the inhabitants serve Babylon for seventy years (Jer. 25:8–11). But even more astonishing was what would occur next. After the seventy years were over, God would turn around and punish Babylon for the evil deeds it did upon God's people (Jer. 25:14). God would overthrow Babylon as Sodom and Gomorrah had been overthrown (Isa. 13:19).

That it was Israel's God who was plucking up a mighty empire such as Babylon to be his servant to punish Judah, and then to punish Babylon in response, demonstrated that the Lord was no longer just the God of Abraham, Isaac, and Jacob, of David and Solomon, of Israel and Judah. Indeed, if the Lord belonged only to Judah as the false prophets proclaimed, this whole episode which was about to come upon Judah would be anomalous, even absurd. The prophesied calamities would make no sense. But he who was doing this was the righteous judge of all nations (Isa. 34), the Creator of heaven and earth (Isa. 42:5), the first and the last who laid the foundations of the earth (Isa. 48:12–13). He is the Lord from on high who shouts against all those who live on earth and will bring judgment against all mankind (Jer. 25:30–31).

With these insights (once buried from sight by idolatry and the monarchy) now being brought to light, the whole dark future was beginning to make sense.

In short, it was being recognized once more that Israel's God, the cause of this punishment for sin, is indeed greater than Israel, Judah, or even the Promised Land. He is truly the one God, the Lord of hosts, universal over all gods, nations, and lands. The idolatry and monarchy that was hiding the universalism implicit from the beginning in Israel's election was now painfully being stripped away.

God's people were being set free from a narrow piece of real estate in preparation for fulfilling God's purpose and desire for the nations of the earth.

After destruction, the second part of God's three-fold plan called for cleansing, a theme taken up by the prophet Ezekiel. "I will purge you of those who revolt and rebel against me" the Lord said (Ezek. 20:38).

Ezekiel 36:25
I will sprinkle clean water on you, and you will be clean; I will cleanse you from all your impurities and from all your idols.

Ezekiel, from a priestly family, was exiled to Babylon along with king Jehoiachin in 597 B.C. (2 Kings 24:14–17). He had lived through and saw firsthand the hideousness of prostitution and human sacrifice which infected Judean society. His prophecies and visions became a manual for purging the people of God of their vile sins.

This purging, to be conducted by the Lord himself, would rid Judah of all the shaqquts: the nauseating, repulsive practices the Israelites had performed in the Promised Land. Idolaters would be slaughtered (Ezek. 9:6).

All vile images and detestable idols would be removed (Ezek. 11:18). False prophets would be censored (Ezek. 13:3-7). Those who engaged in prostitution, sexual promiscuity, nakedness, and child sacrifices would be stoned (Ezek. 16:36–40). The people of the Covenant would be dispersed to other lands (Ezek. 22:15) and the Promised Land would be desolate (Ezek. 33:28). The shepherds, the political and religious leadership of Judah, would be removed (Ezek. 34:10). In short, the Lord would save them from their uncleanness (Ezek. 36:29). The final chapters of the book of Ezekiel form a vision of the Promised Land and the temple restored and cleansed from all previous impurities.

Destruction and cleansing, however, were not enough. A reorientation regarding the covenant given to Abraham (Gen. 12:1–3) was called for. This reorientation in effect amounted to a reinterpretation, a new hermeneutic, of the covenant. The covenant promised a land, descendants to inhabit the land, and that the nations would be blessed because of Abraham. The first two promises had come true, but unfortunately the main interpretation or orientation at this point focused exclusively on the land. Idolatry and the establishment of a monarchy reinforced this orientation.

Now, with the horrors of war and forceful deportation to other lands, this first orientation or focus on the land was being destroyed. It was time to look ahead. It was the time for a new hermeneutic to focus on the other two parts of God's covenant with Abraham.

This reorientation began early and in earnest with Isaiah. It was a response to the deep dilemma of how to reconcile God's call with the threats of destruction. That is, what was the reason for Israel's existence if Israel was to be destroyed?

A Light To The Gentiles

To Isaiah the solution to the dilemma was simple. Israel must now consider the third part of the Abrahamic covenant as the most important: they were to be the cause of blessing to all the families and nations of the earth. Under this new hermeneutic, Israel was now, as the Lord's servant, to be a light for the Gentiles in order to bring God's salvation to the ends of the earth (Isa. 49:3–6).

Isa. 42:6–7
I, the Lord, have called you in righteousness; I will take hold of your hand. I will keep you and will make you to be a covenant for the people and a light for the Gentiles, to open eyes that are blind, to free captives from prison and to release from the dungeon those who sit in darkness.

God's law would go out and become a light for the nations (Isa. 51:4). Indeed, after the trauma of defeat and deportation, nations and kings would come to Israel's light (Isa. 60:3). Many peoples and powerful nations would come to Jerusalem to seek the Lord; they would take hold of the Jews and say, "let us go with you, because we have heard that God is with you" (Zech. 8:22–23).

Not only were God's people to turn their thinking outward to the Gentiles, to become once more a kingdom of priests in service of the Gentiles, they were also to look inward into their hearts to become once more a holy nation (Exod. 19:6), to have a new heart and a new spirit (Ezek. 36:26). They must have a heart to know the Lord, for only in this way could they be his people and he be their God (Jer. 24:7). They were to be holy and consecrated to the Lord, the God of their fathers (Ezra 8:28). But this holiness, moreover, was not to be for its own sake alone. It too was to serve a universal purpose among the nations so that all nations, and not just Israel alone, might know that the God of Israel is the Lord.

Ezek. 36:22–23
..."This is what the Sovereign Lord says: It is not for your sake, O house of Israel, that I am going to do these things, but for the sake

of my holy name, which you have profaned among the nations where you have gone. I will show the holiness of my great name, which has been profaned among the nations, the name you have profaned among them. Then the nations will know that I am the Lord, declares the Sovereign Lord, when I show myself holy through you before their eyes."

Ezek. 39:7
I will make known my holy name among my people Israel. I will no longer let my holy name be profaned, and the nations will know that I the Lord am the Holy one in Israel.

This was to be no "silent witness," as a light passively shines in the darkness, on the part of God's people. They were actively "to make known among the nations what [God] has done, and proclaim that his name is exalted...let this be known to all the world" (Isa. 12:4–5).

They were to preach good news to the poor (Isa. 61:1). Indeed, of those surviving the traumatic events of the times, God would send some "to the nations...to declare my glory among the nations" (Isa. 66:19).

A New Kingdom

Under this new hermeneutic of the Abrahamic covenant, now directed outward to the nations, was to be included political reorientation as well. With the old kingdom destroyed, there will be a new kingdom, not made by man but by God, and it will be victorious over the kingdoms of this world (Dan. 2:44–45). But it too will have a universal mission to perform. This new kingdom will both draw the nations to itself and send forth the word of the Lord.

Micah 4:1–2
In the last days the mountain of the Lord's temple will be established as chief among the mountains; it will be raised above the hills, and peoples will stream to it. Many nations will come and say, "Come, let us go up to the mountain of the Lord, to the house of the God of Jacob. He will teach us his ways, so that we may walk in his paths." The Law will go out from Zion, the word of the Lord from Jerusalem.

At this point we should take note of the poetic parallelism that Micah used in the quote above. On the one hand, the nations are exhorted to go to the mountain of the Lord (come to Jerusalem), while on the other the Law will go forth from Zion. Now this characteristic is not just for stylistic effects alone. It has a communicative function as well (see Chapter Four). That is to say, there are two ways of learning about God. The world can come to him for instruction (the "centripetal" motion in missions) or his word will go forth to the world (the "centrifugal" motion in missions). Both are equally true in the missionary message of the Old Testament. To emphasize that the Old Testament stresses only the "coming," while hermeneutically attractive, is nevertheless exegetically a misplaced emphasis.

There will also be a new king, for out of Bethlehem "will come... one who will be ruler over Israel" (Micah 5:2).

Isaiah 9:6–7

...He will be called Wonderful Counselor, Mighty God, Everlasting Father, Prince of Peace. Of the increase of his government and peace there will be no end. He will reign on David's throne and over his kingdom, establishing and upholding it with justice and righteousness from that time on and forever. The zeal of the Lord Almighty will accomplish this.

All nations shall rally under his banner or national flag, submitting to his rule and leadership (Isa. 11:10, Rom. 15:12).

In 597 B.C., large numbers of Jews were deported from Judah to Babylon. This was the beginning of seventy years of exile as prophesied by Jeremiah. Another deportation took place in 582 B.C. Around 400 B.C. the Old Testament record itself closes with a prophecy that a messenger, Elijah, would come to prepare the way for the day when the Lord shall come (Mal. 3:1–5, 4:5). It will be a great and dreadful day when the Lord comes, for he will come to judge the sorcerers, adulterers, perjurers, and those whose defraud and oppress the disenfranchised. (It should be remembered that these terms refer to the repulsive abominations that Israel engaged in during the monarchical era.) However, on that great day God shall also pour out his Spirit on all people and everyone who calls on the name of the Lord will be saved (Joel 2:28, 32).

Solutions

Wong, whose conversion story began this chapter, solved the dilemmas that were threatening to destroy his Christian life. He first set himself on a course of gradually reducing the amount of opium he was taking. In six months time he was down to taking only a small amount. He felt he could break off opium completely at that point. He did and suffered few withdrawal symptoms.

In the meantime he listened closely to the preaching in church and how more mature Christians explained the Scriptures. As a result he internalized an understanding, or hermeneutic, of what the Scriptures mean and what Christian faith should mean to others who were not believers. When he had regained strength after cutting off his opium habit, he moved to a mountain village where his two sons had settled. He was the only Christian in the village.

Wong began to witness to fellow villagers about Jesus Christ. Being unable to read and explain the Gospel message directly from the Scriptures, he in effect was proclaiming his own understanding of the Gospel to his neighbors. Before long his explanation—his hermeneutic—of the Christian faith sparked interest in others. Several villagers were baptized. A church was established and a small chapel built.

Today, his children are Christians. He married a woman, also illiterate, to whom he had witnessed and led to belief in Jesus. A younger son graduated from Bible school and returned to pastor the congregation that his father started.

Wong's solution to his dilemmas was a microcosm of what developed among the descendants of Abraham during their long turmoil with the monarchy, idolatry, exile, and return to the Promised Land. What developed was a particular hermeneutic for understanding the Scriptures (the Old Testament) and what they mean to themselves and to surrounding Gentiles in the context of the (intertestament) time. The resulting hermeneutic turned out to be the missionary interpretation of the Old Testament.

At the close of the Old Testament with the prophecies of Malachi, we can look back over the complete Old Testament record and see that all the components for such a missionary interpretation of the Old Testament are now in place. These may be summarized in four points.

1. The understanding and, just as crucially, the worship of God in universal terms are now firmly planted in the hearts and minds of God's people.

2. Reorientation of thinking regarding the Abrahamic covenant proved successful; i.e., the focus has been reoriented from the land to that of being a holy people of God and a source of blessing to the nations.
3. The way to implement being a source of blessing, moreover, is clear—it is to be a light to the Gentiles, making the name of the Lord known throughout the earth.
4. A new king, the Messiah, and his kingdom inspired by the memory of the Davidic kingdom but including also the nations is now growing in expectancy as the next great event from God.

In effect, the theological dilemma of God's election of Israel amidst threats of destruction was solved. Even the threats and destruction could now be seen to have a purpose. Indeed, all aspects of Israel's history now found their proper place in the grand plan—God's mystery—that was emerging from this history, a plan laid out by God at the very foundations of the earth. Now all that was needed was for the proper conclusions to be drawn and the proper hermeneutic to be formulated as to what this record of (Old Testament) events might mean in a post-monarchical and Gentile-dominated era.

As Jews, now the ethnonym for God's chosen people, fanned throughout and even beyond the known world of that time, they found help along the way in formulating and articulating this hermeneutic. With this help it became the message of the Hebrew Scriptures for a new era. It was not long before it reached the ends of the earth.

Questions For Discussion

1. Why do you think the prophetic call for Israel and Judah to repent was unsuccessful?

2. How was the missionary message of the Old Testament demonstrated and reinforced by God using Babylon to punish Judah?

3. Discuss how reorientation (shifting focus from land to world missions) can be accomplished in the church today.

4. Up to this point, how would you summarize the missionary message of the Old Testament?

5. In our modern times do you see God using nations and armies to bring fulfillment to his purpose? Where? What is happening? What new doors for evangelism are opening?

Endnote

1. There is a lesson here for God's people today also. The idea that God's call and election is associated with a piece of real estate on earth, whether it is the acreage where the church building sets or a whole nation, must be rooted out wherever it is found. All of the earth is the Lord's, so how can any part of it be associated with God's call as opposed to any other part? Real estate is not the peculiar possession of God; only people are (Titus 2:14, 1 Pet. 2:9–10). If this is not recognized, the resources of the church turn inward to shore up property, perhaps a whole nation, and the ends of the earth where the Gospel has not yet been proclaimed is neglected.

CHAPTER TEN

God of the Gentiles

The Old Testament book of Numbers reported more than 600,000 men, age twenty and above, who followed Moses out of Egypt (ca. 1441 B.C.). This number did not include women and children or teenage boys under twenty years of age. The total number of Israelites who escaped from Egypt, therefore, could have surpassed 2,000,000 people (John J. Davis 1986).

Over the next five centuries the number of Israelites more than doubled. Joab, David's army commander-in-chief, for example, counted 1,300,000 men in Israel and Judah capable of bearing arms (2 Sam. 24:9). This would point to a total population of some five million people (A. A. Anderson 1989).

For the next five hundred years we could expect another doubling, except for the defeat of both Israel and Judah and the mass deportations of their populations in 721 B.C. for Israel, and 597 B.C. and again in 582 B.C. for Judah. During the deportations a great number undoubtedly were killed or died due to the hardships involved. Also, many from the northern kingdom evidently were quietly assimilated into surrounding non-Jewish populations and were never heard of again as members of the ancient kingdom of Israel, thus further reducing the number of Israelites left in the world.

On the other hand, under peaceful conditions populations do rebound and in a few short generations can regain and even surpass what was lost in a former time. Indeed, after the trauma of the deportation into exile at Babylon was over, Jeremiah urged the Jews to settle and live in peace in their new land, marry, have children, and find spouses for their children. The command was to increase, not to decrease (Jer. 29:4–7).

Moreover, after the fall of Babylon in 538 B.C. to Cyrus, king of Persia, conditions became quite favorable for the Jews. Those who elected could return to Palestine to rebuild the temple and later the city of Jerusalem. More than 50,000 Jews returned (Ezra 2:64–66), including some Israelites from the former northern kingdom of Israel (Neh. 11:3). Many Jews, of course, did not return but chose to stay in Babylon, Persia, and points beyond. During this period many other Jews voluntarily left their Palestinian homeland to seek a better life abroad.

Over the next 450 years the Jews proliferated and spread throughout the world. They were found from Europe in the west to China in the east, from western Africa to India (Richard De Ridder 1976). At the time of Christ it is estimated that the worldwide population of Jews numbered some 8,000,000 people (Salo Wittmayer Baron 1952), or nearly five percent of the world's population.

Two million Jews, not counting Samaritans and Gentiles lived in Palestine. One in ten people in the Roman Empire was a Jew. Furthermore, one in twenty Hellenists was a Jew. This amounted to twenty percent of the population that lived east of Rome around the Mediterranean basin.

What was the cause of this great population increase of the Jewish people in the four centuries before Christ? Biological growth accounts for a lot of it obviously, but not all. Additional growth was due to Gentiles converting to the Jewish belief and way of life and becoming proselytes in the process.

In the Old Testament story of Esther (ca. 476 B.C.), for example, the Jews in the eastern provinces of the Persian empire were in danger of a conspiracy put together by some government officials to exterminate them. But because Esther was a queen, she had access to King Xerxes and was able to save her people. She was also able to issue edicts ordering the execution of all who conspired against the Jews. Seventy-five thousand conspirators were killed in two days. Because of this, "many people of other nationalities became Jews because fear of the Jews had seized them" (Esther 8:17).

These conversions in the book of Esther account for the great number of Jews mentioned for Persia by Salo Wittmayer Baron (1952) and no doubt were ancestors to the Persian Jews mentioned in Acts 2. But these conversions due to "fear of the Jews" in Esther's time were in the early days. Afterwards other reasons came into play as to why non-Jews became proselytes. One reason, as mentioned at the close of the previous chapter, was the missionary understanding of the Old Testament that emerged among Jews and which allowed them to converse with non-Jews about the Hebrew Scriptures in a meaningful way. As time progressed, this understanding or hermeneutic received some unexpected help along the way. To be sure, many Jews during this period were unhappy with the ramifications of this newfound aid in understanding their own Scriptures and tried to offset its influence in various ways. However, in the end, because of this help, the universalism of the Old Testament was able at last to "go international."

Hellenism

In 334 B.C. Alexander the Great succeeded in unifying the various city-states of the Greek peninsula and headed eastward on his adventure of conquering the world of his time. In twelve years he had succeeded in establishing the world's first great empire stretching eastward from Greece all the way to the Indus River. At the end he lay dead in Persia. What he left behind, however, exceeded even his dreams of empire building for there occurred over the next three hundred years after his death what historians call the Hellenization of the world.

Hellenization resulted in peoples and tribes of lands conquered by Alexander the Great adopting, if not everything Greek, at least the most visible portions of the Greek way of life to an extent that peoples from all corners of the empire and every walk of life could recognize in each other something of Alexander's legacy. As Alexander, and his generals after him, spread Greek culture throughout the Mediterranean world and beyond, people liked what they saw and began to imitate it. Of course, adaptation of things Greek occurred so that local varieties of Hellenization developed from place to place around the empire. However, it is the general characteristics of Hellenization that hold our interest here because these aided the Jews in their contact and conversation with the nations as they scattered and settled throughout the Greek empire.

The first characteristic, as Francis Henry Sandbach (1967) suggests, that took hold across the empire was that the small, city-dominated empire was doomed. There would be, for example, no more Babylonian or Persian empires; nor would there be any more a Jerusalem governing its own territory isolated from Gentile influence. In their place there would be the individual having rights and obligations under a universal code of law. There came into effect the "universal person." That is, an individual was now no longer only a native of an ethnic group. He or she was also a "Greek" able to travel anywhere and have the same opportunities under Hellenistic law. The thought-systems of philosophy also suffered as individuals specialized in mathematics, astronomy, medicines, and other sciences. Religion changed from assuring fertility in the soil to an emphasis on personal salvation, especially after death. The gods decreased in importance but still provided a measure of legitimacy for society at large.

Above all was the Greek language, the instrument that became the universal vehicle for disseminating these characteristics throughout the empire. Peoples of other cultures found their own languages inadequate to assimilate and communicate the many new terms and concepts their Greek conquerors and colonists brought with them. It became easier to learn Greek and thereby have access to new ways of thinking and interpreting the world. What emerged, of course, was not the Greek language of the classical era but a common language spoken with different degrees of proficiency.

Because of this common language, exciting new worlds of knowledge became available. Greek literature became accessible throughout the empire. More importantly and certainly more practical, people of all nationalities had a lingua franca through which they could converse with each other, conduct business, and exchange ideas.

The Jews of this time did not escape the influence of Hellenism. In fact, Jews at first generally accepted Hellenization because of the advantages it brought to their lives now dominated by Alexander's empire.[1]

Hellenism had particular advantage for their own religious beliefs and to the way they now perceived their purpose in the world. For the Greek language became a universal or international vehicle by which the Jewish people could at last be a light to the Gentiles. The Greek language, in other words, became the instrument by which the Jews could at last implement their own understanding or hermeneutic of the Hebrew Scriptures among the nations. There were some differences made to this understanding due to the nature of the Greek language and the cultural characteristics mentioned above that accompanied its acquisition. But for the most part these proved positive and beneficial to the task at hand. Indeed, Hellenization became the chief aid in Jewish propaganda of this time (Salo Wittmayer Baron 1952).

But propaganda or personal witness soon became inadequate. What was really needed was a translation of the Hebrew Scriptures into the Greek language.

The Septuagint

The first impetus for a Greek translation of the Hebrew Scriptures came out of the Egyptian city of Alexandria. Within a century after Alexander the Great established this city in 332 B.C., the Jewish population swelled to one million. As new generations were born they remembered less and less of the Hebrew of their forefathers. At first they probably had Greek "targums," oral translations of the Hebrew, made for the Hellenized Jews of Alexandria. Later, around 250 B.C. and due to official urgings it seems (Elias Bickerman 1962), the Pentateuch or first five books of the Old Testament were translated into the koine or spoken language of Greek.

Over the next two centuries the rest of the Old Testament was similarly translated into Greek. The complete translation became known as the Septuagint, a term derived from the Greek word for seventy. Legend has it that seventy (others say seventy-two) scholars were called in to translate the Hebrew Scriptures into Greek. When they had finished and compared notes, it was rumored, they found exact word-for-word correspondence in each of their translations, a sign many believed was an indicator that the Septuagint had been inspired by God in the same way the original Hebrew Scriptures had been.

Even though the Septuagint was first made for edifying the Jews who lived at Alexandria and in other places,[2] it soon exceeded this original purpose in an unexpected way. This translation became the main instrument which Jews used in explaining their faith to non-Jews and upon which many non-Jews became proselytes. As a written piece of Greek literature, the Septuagint gave power and authority to the Jewish evangelist.

With the hermeneutic that had developed over their long history, the Jewish teacher could succinctly explain what such a massive and ancient document meant to the non-Jew and how he or she should respond to it. In fact the translation was used so much in this evangelistic manner that Philo, a Jewish Hellenist who lived during the time of Christ, could exclaim that the Septuagint was made to enlighten the Gentiles (Salo Wittmayer Baron 1952). Indeed, by the time the New Testament church was established in the book of Acts, the Septuagint had become a missionary translation of the Old Testament for bringing God's salvation to the ends of the earth.[3]

Space allows only one example from the Septuagint to show why it gained the reputation of being a missionary translation. This sample is the translation of the Shema into Greek.

Deut. 6:4
Hear, O Israel: The Lord our God [is] one Lord.

Shema is a Hebrew term meaning "to hear" and has become a specific theological term so that, whenever the term is spoken or written, it refers to this verse. The Shema is considered the main memory verse of Judaism, much as John 3:16 is for Christians. By 200 B.C., for example, each faithful Jew was to repeat, preferably audibly, this verse two or more times a day. Soon other verses were added: Deut. 11:13–21 and Num. 15:37–41. Ideally all 245 words (in Hebrew) of these verses were to be repeated. However, it was the Greek translation of Deut. 6:4 that proved to be an added impetus in Jewish and early church evangelism.

In the above quotation of Deut. 6:4 the verb [is] is enclosed in brackets to show both that this verb is not found in the original Hebrew and that it is necessary in English because of the linguistic requirement of the latter language. (In the older King James Version such words were italicized, but this method was misleading because many thought it was for emphasis instead of showing missing words.) In other words, this verse, after its opening of "Hear, O Israel," reads in the Hebrew like this:

The Lord our God, the Lord, one.

In Hebrew grammar the word "one" in the above sentence, because it is not preceded by the verb "is", functions as an adjective (J. Weingreen 1959); "one" is not an adjective (it is a number) but because of the syntax of the clause it is used to describe God. In linguistics this type of usage may be classified as a topic-comment construction. The following diagram illustrates this type of structure.

Topic   **Comment**

[The Lord our God] the Lord   one

The second part of this structure is, as the grammatical category states, a comment on the first part. Depending on the word or words involved, a comment may give an evaluation, a description, or some other modification of the topic. In Deut. 6:4, the comment "one" describes what the Lord God is like.

Old Testament commentators have noted that the comment of "one" in Deut. 6:4 may be translated or interpreted in various ways.

From the point of view of its syntax the meaning of v. 4 is debatable. For instance, it might be translated: 'Yahweh is our God, Yahweh alone!' But it might also be translated: 'Yahweh, our God, is one Yahweh' (and there are still other possibilities) (Gerhard von Rad 1966).

> The original meaning of the first verse may have been, unlike the pagan gods who have different guises and localities: God is one. At first the main emphasis in the Shema was seen to be in opposition to polytheism: there is only one God, not many gods...later the Hebrew word ehad [one] was also understood to mean "unique"...the supreme being. (Encyclopedia Judaica, Vol. 14, pp. 1372-3)

Upon reading this verse in the context of Israel's exodus out of Egypt and entry into Canaan, it is clear that the immediate understanding was that God stands as one in opposition to the many gods of polytheism or idolatry of both Egypt and Canaan. That is, this understanding would be the explicit meaning of Deut. 6:4. Other senses or meanings are implicit meanings of the verse.[4] An example of the latter is the meaning that there is only one God; i.e., monotheism. In other words, while the Shema specified the Lord as being one, in its entirety it can be interpreted as a proof text for monotheism. In fact, this interpretation became the main hermeneutic of Deut. 6:4 in Hellenistic Judaism and the early church.

Now the Septuagint translation of Deut. 6:4 produced a change in focus because it utilized a different grammatical structure.[5]

Hear O Israel: The Lord our God esti one Lord.

The word esti is the Greek verb meaning "is." That is, instead of using a topic-comment construction as in Hebrew, the Greek translators used a "verb + numeral" which is like the English "[God] is one." However, the Greek translation has an added dimension which is not apparent at all in English and which is implicit in the Hebrew. The Greek verb esti also means "there is...". In the Greek translation of Deut. 6:4, therefore, because of inserting the verb esti, the understanding that first comes to mind is the meaning that "there is one God."

Because of the different grammatical structure in the Septuagint version of Deut. 6:4, there turned out to be a change in focus from "God is one in opposition to polytheism" (in the Hebrew context) to "there is one God universally over all peoples as in monotheism" (in the Hellenistic context).

The Greek, in other words, took what was an implicit meaning of the Hebrew and made it the explicit meaning for Deut. 6:4. Within the context of Hellenism and the universal person it fostered, the change in focus fit in quite well with the Jewish understanding of the Hebrew Scriptures and their purpose as a people of God in the world of Hellenism.

Their purpose was to be a light to the nations. The light they had for all was the revelation of the Shema, that there is one God.[6] And since there is only one God, he is the God of every tribe, tongue, nation, and people to be found in the world. As the Shema was repeated among the Jews in its Greek version, this new focus no doubt became uppermost and soon became a strong impetus to make the one and only God known wherever they wandered on the earth.

It was this sense of one God over all peoples—both Jews and non-Jews—that was in Paul's mind when he argued that all are justified by faith.

Rom. 3:28–30
For we maintain that a man is justified by faith apart from observing the law. Is God the God of Jews only? Is he not the God of Gentiles too? Yes, of Gentiles too, since there is only one God...

The style of language Paul used in Rom. 3:28–30 is revealing. Paul speaks of there being one God in an almost offhanded manner, as though it is an assumption universally accepted and therefore in no need of further argumentation and proof. It is a style suggesting that Paul was appealing to what had become among the Jews a commonly accepted interpretation and application of Deut. 6:4 to justify taking the Gospel to non-Jews as well.[7]

Later on in this epistle to the Romans, Paul again used this same missionary hermeneutic of the Shema, only this time instead of God he used the term Lord (Yahweh).

Rom. 10:12
For there is no difference between Jew and Gentile—the same Lord is Lord of all and richly blesses all who call on him,

It is interesting to observe above in Rom. 3:30 that Paul did not quote verbatim the Septuagint version of Deut. 6:4. Rather, Paul gave a literal translation, with one adjustment to Greek grammar, of the Hebrew: "...since one [is] the God." That is, Paul used an equivalent topic-comment construction in Greek to formally correspond to the topic-comment structure of the Hebrew: the verb [is] is absent in the Greek of Rom. 3:30 (as it is absent in the Hebrew) and the numeral "one" is made to function as a verbal adjective by being placed before the noun.

This adjustment in word order corresponds functionally with the Hebrew describing, in this case, what God is like. However, the context of Rom. 3:29–30 clearly shows that it was the sense of universalism (God over all peoples) and not that God is one as opposed to the many gods of idolatry that was in Paul's mind at the time of dictating this portion of the Roman letter to Tertius (Rom. 16:22).

The other sense of Deut. 6:4, God is one as opposed to the many gods of idolatry, was not forgotten or neglected in the witness of the Jews to their Gentile neighbors. Paul, for example, appealed to this understanding of the Shema in solving a problem of food sacrificed to idols in his first letter to the Corinthians:

1 Cor. 8:4–6
So then, about eating food sacrificed to idols: We know that an idol is nothing at all in the world and that there is no God but one. For even if there are so-called gods, whether in heaven or on earth (as indeed there are many "gods" and many "lords"), yet for us there is but one God...

In this regard it seems that Mark 12:29, 32 and James 2:19, which also quote Deut. 6:4, should similarly be understood in this sense and not in the universal sense of Rom. 3:30.

A Religious Community

Hellenism's influence upon Judaism in the centuries before the opening of the New Testament was more external than internal in its effect (Jacob Bernard Agus 1963). The main role of Hellenism in Judaism, it turned out, was as an instrument in implementing the missionary understanding of the Hebrew Scriptures in the Hellenistic world of that time.

Internally, however, the fundamentals of what defined a Jew survived. Of course, the Promised Land was no longer crucial. Moreover, Solomon's temple, long destroyed but rebuilt by Herod, was perhaps only slightly more crucial in this definition. What arose to take the place of the Promised Land and the temple in Jewish life served not only to define who was a Jew but also to win converts from non-Jews to the God of Abraham, Isaac, and Jacob.

The main reason for this lack of life-changing penetration on the part of Hellenism was that Judaism was more than just a religion; it was above all else a religious community. Wherever Jews were dispersed to, whether voluntarily or by force, they formed themselves into communities. In this manner an individual Jew found a cradle-to-the-grave support for living in the world of Hellenism. In a religious community a child could be raised and socialized into the tenets and rituals of Jewish belief and ceremony. Life's great transitions such as puberty, marriage, birth, children, family, and death could be solemnized and celebrated by community participation. By growing up and maintaining one's identity with such a religious community it became difficult to be led astray by the outside world.

On the other hand, with the security of a religious community standing behind him, a Jew could with freedom and confidence circulate in the outside world in government, travel, business, conversation, work, and trade. With such community support a Jew could also confidently witness in all areas of contact with outsiders that he or she worshiped the God who, because he is one, was the God of non-Jews as well.[8]

Coming together into religious communities for mutual support naturally led to the establishment of central meeting places where such mutual support could be shared. These meeting places became known as synagogues. No historical record exists showing when the synagogue first came into existence. James, the Lord's brother, stated that from the earliest times Moses had been preached in every city in the synagogues (Acts 15:21). Most historians seek to place the beginnings of the synagogue early on in the meetings of exiles along the banks of the Kebar River in Babylonia (Ezek. 1:1, 3). Others, however, place the date even earlier.

Whatever the date, by the time of Christ the synagogue was an established institution in Judaism, not only among Jews of the Dispersion but also in Palestine.

While the synagogue was not meant to take the place of the temple in Jerusalem it quickly grew in popularity because it was able to fulfill several felt needs of the Jews, whether in the Dispersion or in Palestine, that the temple could not hope to meet.

While a few Jews, for instance, could make a yearly pilgrimage to the temple in Jerusalem, the vast majority could expect to make such a pilgrimage only once in a lifetime if at all. Yet there were the daily and weekly needs for mutual support in a hostile or indifferent environment, plus the need for prayer, worship, celebration, and edification in the Law—needs that only a local synagogue could fulfill.

Just as crucial to the growth of the popularity of the synagogue, however, especially in the age of Hellenism, was that if there is truly only one God, whose heaven is his throne and the earth his footstool (Isa. 66:1–2), then prayer and worship of God was possible anywhere whether in Palestine, in a foreign city, or along a river bank (Acts 16:13).

Because Jews in every city formed religious communities and congregated around central meeting places or synagogues, all the essential elements fell into place for the Judaism of the intertestament period to become a missionary religion. There was first of all the message; i.e., the missionary hermeneutic or understanding of the Old Testament. Next, Hellenistic culture and language formed the instrument for communicating this understanding. Now because of Jews congregating together as communities, the strategy existed for converting those who would listen.

We may well imagine the process of missionary outreach used by Jews of this time. A Jew, for example, imbued with knowledge of the Shema that God is one, would become acquainted with a Gentile while traveling as Jonah was, or while at market as the Apostle Paul in Athens (Acts 17:17), or perhaps while working at a trade as Aquila and Priscilla were doing (Acts 18:1–3). Conversation would soon turn to the peculiar belief of the Jews that there is only one God and that the idols of paganism were worthless.

As the Gentile showed greater interest in this teaching, invitations could be offered to attend the synagogue meeting on the Sabbath. There a broader network of acquaintances was created. This included people with different personalities and gifts for explaining the many aspects of Jewish history and Scripture. At times there would be learned rabbis or messengers called apostles (Richard R. De Ridder 1976) from important centers such as Jerusalem or Alexandria who would pass through and teach.

During this time the Gentile would be learning how God is praised and worshiped as well as observing the prayers and rituals as they met together. He would no doubt be impressed by the community spirit and high moral standards of the Jews as they lived together. As time passed, it all added up. As the Gentile assimilated more and more, a time would come when he or she would decide to take on the "yoke of the Law" and become a fellow believer with the Jews.

In short, the Jews sent few if any missionaries (in the later Christian sense) out to evangelize; nevertheless, they gained plenty of converts (Scot McKnight 1990). Little if any aggressive evangelism was initiated by the Jews. Rather, non-Jews converted by becoming incorporated into the Jewish religious community. Indeed, this was life-style evangelism at its best.

Such a "mission strategy" allowed for degrees of conversion and adherence to the Law or Jewish life-style on the part of the non-Jew. This was especially crucial for men. Women, not being subject to the law of circumcision, found it easier to become full-fledged proselytes. But men often found circumcision a stumbling block and only after a long period of time, if at all, would they submit themselves to this surgical rite in order to become proselytes. In the meantime, however, non-Jews could become God fearers (Acts 13:50, 17:4, 17); i.e., submit to various other laws, such as refraining from eating unclean foods, keeping the Sabbath, and synagogue worship. Such an intermediate step in conversion was especially useful if a wife had already become a proselyte but the husband was not ready to be circumcised. This also allowed for children to be born, and the males circumcised, as Jews.

Elias Bickerman (1962) thinks, however, that in early Hellenism people who accepted Judaism by circumcision were rather rare. On the other hand, many Greeks accepted the worship of the Most High God without observing all the prescriptions of the Torah. While Jews generally were open and tolerant toward Gentile converts, it appears that the Jews of Palestine were more eager than the Jews of the Dispersion for (male Gentile) God fearers to complete the process of becoming proselytes and be circumcised.

The role of Jewish apostles (mentioned above), therefore, was to keep the ideal of the Jewish religious community alive throughout the Dispersion. As non-Jews became interested and attached themselves to these communities and their synagogues, the role of the apostolate expanded to include urging and exhorting these non-Jews onward to complete the process and become full-fledged proselytes. The Pharisees from Palestine evidently took this on as a major apostolic function and in their journeys from Jerusalem would go to extraordinary lengths traveling over land and sea to far distant synagogues if there was a chance to push just one such God fearing Gentile into full proselyte status in Judaism. This extreme eagerness was criticized by Jesus Christ because it took a Gentile of innocent faith in the Most High God and turned him or her into a proselyte who was even more legalistic than the Pharisees (Matt. 23:15).

Indeed, to go beyond the simple requirement of faith was against the practice of Jesus, for when Jesus recognized faith in a Gentile (Matt. 8:5–13) he did not require anything else of the Gentile in order to be blessed by God.[9]

It was this precedent of Jesus that Paul and Barnabas followed when they were sent on their first apostolic mission from the church in Antioch of Syria; God fearers and others were accepted on the basis of faith in Jesus Christ (Acts 13–14). To some in the church in Judea, however, the process of conversion was left incomplete. That is, Paul, unlike the Pharisees who also went on apostolic journeys to synagogues around the Roman Empire, did not urge these God fearers to be circumcised and thereby complete the process of becoming saved from Gentile impurities such as idolatry and promiscuity (Acts 15:1). To correct this situation some Jewish extremists in the church went on their own apostolic mission to do what Paul neglected to do and urge these Gentile converts to be circumcised (Acts 15:24).

Success

From their traumatic experience of destruction at the hands of the Babylonians, the Jews developed an understanding or hermeneutic of what their Scriptures meant in their new circumstances of being exiles: God was not theirs alone, he was God of the Gentiles, too. The advent of Hellenism, especially the spread of the Greek language, afforded the instrument for communicating this understanding among the nations of the earth. The Greek translation of the Hebrew Scriptures in the third century before Christ became a powerful tool among the Jews in proclaiming that the God of Israel was also the God of the Parthians, Medes, Elamites, those living in Mesopotamia, Phrygia, Egypt, Rome, etc. (Acts. 2:8–11).

Elias Bickerman (1962:77) states that the religious terminology used in the Greek translation of the Hebrew Scriptures played an important role in making the Scriptures understandable to non-Jews.

Although the ineffable Name [Yahweh] was transliterated in the Greek Bible it was pronounced as kyrios, the Lord.

Likewise, the version omits other appellations of the God of
Israel, such as Adonai, Shaddai, Sabaot, which continued to
be used in Palestine. In their place, the version employs
expressions such as 'the God', 'the Almighty', etc. In this way
the particular God of Abraham, Isaac and Jacob becomes in
Greek the Supreme Being of mankind.

Because of this understanding, therefore, even though there was
no direct command in the Old Testament to do so, it was only a short
next step in urging non-Jews to convert and acknowledge that the
God of the Jews was indeed, as the (Jewish) Apostle Paul wrote, the
"one God, the Father, from whom all things came and for whom we
all live;" (1 Cor. 8:6). Happily the strategy for doing this was at hand.
It was accomplished within the context of a life-style that centered in
the synagogue. Proclaiming that the one God is also the God of the
Gentiles is what the Jews in the centuries between the Old and New
Testaments proceeded to do.

How successful was this life-style evangelism that the Jews
conducted in the years before the opening of the New Testament?
Max I. Dimont (1962:116) estimates that of the Jews in the Roman
Empire only four million were Jews by descent; the rest were converted from non-Jewish populations or were descendants of converts. Frederick Derwacter (1930:116), while giving a lower number
for the total population of Jews in the Roman Empire, nevertheless
exclaims that such population growth was a wonderful increase of
the Jewish people when we consider the little group that came back
from Babylon and founded the Jewish state, or even in comparison
with the Jewish state as we see it at the opening of the Maccabean
wars. No adequate explanation of this great expansion is possible
without taking into account proselytism.

Questions For Discussion

1. Why did the Jews of the Dispersion look with favor upon
Hellenism? How did this help them in witnessing to non-Jews?

2. After reading how the Greek translation of the Hebrew Scriptures helped in making proselytes, discuss the importance of Scripture translation today in proclaiming the Gospel in other nations.

3. After reading about the role of the synagogue and the Jewish
religious community in making proselytes, discuss the role that the
local church and Christian community can play in evangelism.

4. What type of evangelistic strategy does this example and role
suggest for evangelism and missions today?

Endnotes

1. Norman Bentwich (1920:252), for example, writes that "indications are not wanting that at an earlier period the Rabbis looked with favor on the Hellenistic development of Judaism. They applied the verse in Genesis, 'God enlarge Japheth, and he shall dwell in the tents of Shem' (Gen. 9:27) as justification for translating the Scriptures and Jewish tradition into Greek."

2. The rabbis allowed the Shema, the grace after meals, and the eighteen blessings to be recited in Greek. Indeed, outside of Hebrew the rabbis allowed the Scriptures to be translated and read only in the Greek language (Norman Bentwich 1920:253).

3. On the other hand Elias Bickerman (1962:74) leaves open the possibility that the translation of the Septuagint was originally undertaken by the Alexandrine community with the intention of converting the heathen, in addition to enabling the Greek-speaking Jews to read the Scriptures.

4. For a discussion of the difference between explicit and implicit meanings and their roles in translation, see Charles R. Taber (1970).

5. For a technical discussion of the change in focus that may occur in translation, see Jan De Waard and Eugene Nida (1986).

6. The Letter of Aristeas, an anonymous document of the time, referred to the Septuagint stating that it "proved that God is one, manifesting his power in all things and his dominion everywhere" (quote taken from Jacob Bernard Agus 1963:123).

7. Paul, of course, significantly went beyond this Jewish hermeneutic to maintain that justification—becoming right with God—for both Jew and non-Jew is by faith and not by observing the Mosaic Law. In Romans Paul went on to point to Abraham and how he became right before God as justification for this extension. As Abraham believed God, and this belief was counted as righteousness (Rom 4:3ff), so Gentiles can also become right with God by means of faith for, after all, there is only one God and he is God of both Jews and Gentiles.

8. There are indications that on occasion Jews were not well liked by their neighbors (Acts 18:1–2). Jews were considered unsupportive of the wider community religious activities (usually involving idol worship), accused of atheism (not believing in the gods of the community), and of being outspoken about the superiority of their

monotheism. Such dislike no doubt stemmed in part from Jewish confidence, perhaps obnoxiousness, in testifying to this superiority.

9. Roger E. Hedlund (1991:184) states that in Matt. 23:15 Jesus "condemned" the proselytizing efforts of the Pharisees. This I believe, is too strong a statement. Proselytizing the Gentiles was not condemned. This much the Pharisees got hermeneutically correct. What Jesus condemned was the Pharisees going beyond simple faith by requiring Jewish rituals. If a Gentile convert "bought into" this Pharisaical system, he (or she) could end up being more legalistic—a child of hell—than the Pharisees (Joachim Jeremias 1958).

Section III

The Messiah

CHAPTER ELEVEN

New Theological Tensions

The New Testament opens with new theological tensions for the people of God.

The covenant that God had made with Abraham contained three promises: land, descendants who would become a great people, and that other nations would be blessed through Abraham (Gen. 12:1–3). When Abraham's descendants, now the nation of Israel, possessed the land of Canaan and established a monarchy plus adopting idolatry, they faced their first theological tension. These political and religious developments in effect elevated the geographical aspect of the covenant to prime importance over the other two. On the other hand, God revealed that Israel was to be a holy nation (Exod. 19:6) and Israel's prophets, poets, and kings responded by exalting God as universal Lord over all nations and not just over Israel alone.

This was not a creative tension, for in the end idolatry, using the power of sexual promiscuity and addiction, broke Israel's devotion to God as Lord over all creation. At this point the Lord threatened to bring destruction upon Israel. This in turn produced a theological dilemma for Israel: how could God destroy the nation he had called and elected to be his prized possession?

The captivity and exile, first of the northern kingdom of Israel and next of Judah, solved both the tension and dilemma. The land that God had promised was effectively eliminated from consideration as to which of the three aspects of God's covenant with Abraham was the most important. Indeed, the Israelites remaining, now called Jews, saw they could still be God's people without the Promised Land, without a monarchy, and certainly without idolatry.

This development, however, raised a second tension in the history of Israel: of the remaining two aspects of the covenant—descendants who by now had become a great people, or that all peoples would be blessed through Abraham—which should now be considered more important? For a while Hellenism provided an answer: the Jews were to be a light to the Gentiles through Greek culture and translating their Scriptures into the Greek language.

Soon, though, a reaction against Hellenism set in. The Jews felt that if Hellenization continued unabated, the national or ethnic character of the covenant would be lost; there would be no recognizable descendants of Abraham to be a holy nation called and elected by God. Ethnic or racial purity, therefore, was promoted as the more important dimension of God's covenant with the Jews.

Palestinian Reaction

Within two years after Alexander the Great had died in 323 B.C., his newly won empire was divided among several generals, each taking the title of king over his own piece of the empire. Palestine happened to lie between two such territorial divisions.

To the south of Palestine, Egypt was ruled by Ptolemy (son of Lagus); to the north was Syria, ruled by Lysimachus. Palestine and its Jewish population was taken over by Ptolemy and ruled as a part of Egypt for the next 122 years. Under Ptolemy and his successors, Hellenization of Jewish life continued. During this time, for example, the Hebrew Scriptures were translated into Greek, a project initiated in the Egyptian city of Alexandria prior to 250 B.C. As this Hellenization increasingly spread out from Egypt, Jews in Palestine were similarly affected. During this time many of them immigrated to Alexandria and other Greek centers of the empire.

Over this same period of time, however, the rulers of Syria to the north sought on various occasions to take Palestine away from Egypt and make it a part of Syria. Finally, in 198 B.C., Antiochus III succeeded in bringing Palestine under Syrian rule. Antiochus III, as well as his predecessors and successors, followed the same policy of Hellenizing the territory under his control. One method of achieving this was to establish Greek cities at strategic locations throughout the land. The Decapolis of Matt. 4:25, a region southeast of Galilee where several Greek cities had earlier been established, was an example of this policy. From these urban centers, then, Greek language and culture could spread into rural areas and the native population.

When Antiochus III took over Palestine, the Egyptian policy of Hellenizing the Jews was continued. Hellenization would probably have continued unabated in Palestine had not Antiochus III agreed to sponsor Hannibal, the Carthagian general, in fighting Rome (Raymond F. Surburg 1975:28). Hannibal lost and Antiochus III ended up having to pay indemnity equivalent to $30,000,000 to Rome. To pay this amount Antiochus III raised taxes and resorted to robbing temples located in his realm. He robbed the temple of the Jews in Jerusalem. He was killed while robbing a temple in another area of his kingdom. The successors of Antiochus III, however, were still required to pay this exorbitant sum of money. Seleucus IV, who ruled Syria from 187–175 B.C., tried again to rob the temple at Jerusalem. This time the Jews rose up in demonstration and stopped the robbery.

When Seleucus IV died, his brother Antiochus IV took over as ruler over Syria (175-163 B.C.). Antiochus IV was an ambitious king conducting several wars to expand his power and kingdom. He also instituted a luxurious life-style for himself and his royal court. All of this required revenue, and the main source of revenue was taxing his subjects more and more heavily. This aroused the ire of the Jews who in turn sought help and relief from Egypt in stopping Antiochus IV. This infuriated Antiochus IV who in retaliation instructed his army in 168 B.C. to occupy Jerusalem. After the occupation, laws were passed to force the Jews to become completely Hellenized. As a final act of indignity upon Jewish sensitivities, he next turned the temple into a pagan shrine in which pigs were sacrificed to Zeus. All of this, of course, was done in the name of Hellenization.

A fierce reaction against this forced Hellenization arose among the Jews. It started when Mattathias, a priest of the Hasmonean lineage, refused to offer a pig on a pagan altar and instead killed a fellow Jew who was about to make such a sacrifice. He also killed the representative of Antiochus IV who was there to enforce the sacrifice. At this Mattathias along with his five sons fled to the hills and called for volunteers to engage in guerrilla warfare against the army of Antiochus IV.

One son, Judas, immediately took charge of the guerrilla band and scored several victories over the Syrian forces. Judas took the surname Maccabaeus, "the Hammerer." Before long, Mattathias and his sons became known as the Maccabbees.

Among those who joined the Maccabbees were Jews of the Hasidim, a conservative element of significant number that opposed the Hellenistic trends occurring in their society. In 164 B.C., with the help of the Hasidim, Jerusalem was recaptured and Palestine liberated. The temple was purged of pagan abominations and rededicated to God.

However, when Judas wanted to develop a political structure to assure national independence, the Hasidim pulled out of the coalition. To the Hasidim, purity of life was the meaning of the Law, not politics as conducted under the old monarchical system. Consequently Judas aligned himself and the Maccabbees with the more urbane and sophisticated members of Jewish society. With this segment of society as a base of power, even though fewer in number than the Hasidim, the Maccabbees and their descendants, the Hasmoneans, ruled Judea as an independent nation for the next 100 years.

Religious Parties

During the 100 years of Maccabbean and Hasmonean rule, until 63 B.C., the Hellenization of Jewish life was effectively arrested but not "rolled back" to a previous "purer" era of Jewish life in any appreciable way. What had already been accepted from Hellenism up to that point had been so thoroughly assimilated that it was now considered an integral part of Palestinian life and Jewish understanding of the Hebrew Scriptures. What had not been accepted was considered alien and in many instances unscriptural.

These years of national independence were significant in yet another way. They allowed the freedom and opportunity for religious parties or sects to emerge in Palestinian Jewish society. These were not just religious parties alone. They were also political parties, more precisely religio-political or, more correctly in some cases, politico-religious parties. The orientation of the former was that religion was to be the "driving force" of politics while with the latter it was the political structure that religion was to affirm and support. In either case the rationale for the particular relationship advocated between religion and politics was to be found in the Hebrew Scriptures.

The first two parties that emerged during this time developed out of the conservative Hasidim and their more urbane, sophisticated fellow citizens mentioned above. From the former came the Pharisees and out of the latter the Sadducees. No date for the establishment of either party is available. Probably what happened sociologically was that the Maccabbean rule gave opportunity for long-standing attitudes and sentiments to at last become institutionalized into formal, recognizable associations or groups in Palestinian Jewish society. Only a few Jews ever claimed formal membership in or association with a party. On the other hand, most Jews found that their own sentiments rested with one party or the other and so gave moral support to the policies and goals of that party.

To state the matter in our terms: Each religious party represented a particular hermeneutic of the Old Testament with regard to how the Scriptures were to be interpreted, understood, and applied in everyday Jewish life in Palestine some 300 years after the traumatic events of captivity and exile, Hellenization, and the dispersion of kin throughout the known world. In this respect, then, it is not entirely correct to characterize the Pharisees and Sadducees as respectively conservative and urbane or liberal. The matter was more complex than that.

To the Pharisees, for example, the Promised Land, monarchy, and priesthood were not important; they were no longer God's will for Israel during this period of history even though specific commands for such institutions were in the Scriptures. What was important in their place was that Jews fulfill the command of being a kingdom of priests, of becoming a holy and pure race of people in the midst of the Gentiles. To achieve this holiness of life the Pharisees taught that the laws and rituals of the priests serving in the temple should also be practiced by the nonpriestly layman at home (Jacob Neusner 1973:33). To justify this teaching the Pharisees claimed that there was an "oral tradition" (hermeneutic) in addition to the written Torah or Law of Moses, and which was just as true.

> [The Pharisees'] view of the law was that its commandments were to be interpreted in conformity with the standard and interpretation of the rabbis of each generation, and to be made to harmonize with advanced ideas. Therefore, when a precept was outgrown, it was to be given a more acceptable meaning, so that it would harmonize with the truth resulting from God-given reason. The law must be understood according to the interpretation of the teachers who are endowed with God-given reason to do so. When the letter of the law seemed to oppose conscience, it was to be taken, accordingly, in its spirit...The Pharisees generated a ramified system of hermeneutics and found no great difficulty in harmonizing Torah teachings with their advanced ideas or in finding their ideas implied or hinted at in the words of the Torah.[1]

In short, the Pharisees accepted the principle of hermeneutics; the Scriptures needed a hermeneutic for understanding and application in the formation of social and personal life. This principle derived from their association with, and assimilation of, the Hellenism of their time (Jacob Neusner 1973:54).

The Sadducees, on the other hand, rejected the "oral tradition" or hermeneutic of the Pharisees. They did not accept the (Hellenistic) principle that the Scriptures needed to be interpreted to be made relevant. The Scriptures were relevant already in their written form. In this respect the Sadducees were literalists in teaching the Scriptures. Therefore, since the Law had much to say about the land, monarchy, and priesthood, these were the important things for the Jewish nation: the land had to be made secure for national survival, the monarchy had to be preserved, and above all the priesthood had to be maintained. Otherwise, the identifying marks of Judaism would be lost.

Surprisingly, the Jewish masses of Palestine agreed with the Pharisees and not the Sadducees on this theological issue. This is surprising because the Pharisees considered the common folk as sinners (Mark 2:15–16) because they did not keep the priestly or temple rituals at home as the Pharisees did. On the other hand, while differing with the Pharisees in detail and in the extent that this principle was to be followed, Jews in general realized that their ancient Scriptures needed interpretation to be relevant even in the Palestinian homeland. A literal reading and following of the Law was not God's will for an age of Hellenism and international travel.

An illustration of the difference between the Pharisees and Sadducees on the issue of hermeneutics was their respective beliefs on the resurrection (Acts 23:6–8). The Sadducees did not believe in the resurrection because there was no explicit teaching regarding such in the Law, while the Pharisees drew the necessary conclusions from Scripture that there indeed had to be a resurrection of the dead.

On one occasion, for example, the Sadducees sought to trick Jesus into admitting that the Law did not teach the resurrection of the dead (Matt. 22:23–32). They raised the hypothetical question of a widow who had been married to each of seven brothers. The Law of Moses commanded that if a widow had no children from her previous husband, his brother had to take her in marriage to produce offspring for the dead brother. If there is a resurrection, then, so the Sadducees argued, whose wife would she be, for each brother had been married to her? The doctrine of the resurrection, therefore, made the Scriptures self-contradictory. So to resolve this conflict, in the view of the Sadducees, the doctrine of the resurrection had necessarily to be rejected.

Jesus, however, countered this (literalist) argument by saying that there is no marriage in heaven; rather the resurrected shall be like the angels. More crucially, though, Jesus chided the Sadducees for not hermeneutically following through to the obvious conclusion of what the Scriptures teach.

To demonstrate this Jesus referred to the Pentateuch, the portion of Scripture that the Sadducees considered more authoritative, and the account of what God said to Moses at the burning bush (Exod. 3:6): "I am the God of Abraham, the God of Isaac, and the God of Jacob." To be sure there is no explicit statement here revealing that the dead shall be resurrected, but such must be inferred. For example: even though Abraham, Isaac, and Jacob died, God is not the God of the dead—which is a "blatant contradiction" (William L. Lane 1974:430)—but of the living.

In other words, with this passage God "does not identify himself as presently the God of those who have died without hope of resurrection." Abraham, Isaac, and Jacob must therefore have the hope of being resurrected to life.

Moreover, if God is our God as well, we must live even though we too must die. This, therefore, necessitates the resurrection of all so that God may indeed be the God of the living.

Another example was the issue of proselytization. The Sadducees showed little or no interest in proselytizing Gentiles for there was no explicit command in the Scriptures requiring such. To be sure, the Sadducees read the same Scripture that Israel was a light to the Gentiles for the purpose of bringing God's salvation to the ends of the earth (Isa. 49:6), but unlike the Pharisees and the early church this purpose was not interpreted as a command to witness or to evangelize the Gentiles.

The Sadducees recognized that there is one God universally over all nations, but they considered it invalid or unscriptural to reason to the next step that if the Gentiles do not know or recognize God as their God too, then the Jews had the obligation to witness that such is indeed the case (Rom. 3:29–30). The Sadducees felt no obligation to evangelize because there literally was no command to do so. God's Law was for the Jew and the Jewish nation alone. There was no one universal kingdom of God for all peoples.

From these remarks we can see that the Pharisees and the early church of Acts had many things in common: a belief in the resurrection, a feeling of mission to convert the Gentiles, a commitment to the principle that the Scriptures needed interpretation, etc.

Yet, there are New Testament passages that criticize both the Pharisees and Sadducees (Matt. 3:7), something that appears understandable for the Sadducees but less so for the Pharisees. The expla-

nation for criticizing the Pharisees is that, while they employed
hermeneutics to make the Scriptures relevant, they also failed to
allow exegesis to provide a corrective counterbalance. In Matt. 23, for
example, Jesus commended the Pharisees for tithing specific spices,
a practice that was hermeneutically inferable from the text of the
Scriptures (Lev. 27:30), but criticized them for neglecting, from an
exegetical perspective, what was important: justice, mercy, and
faithfulness (Micah 6:8).

In addition to the Pharisees other groups emerged out of the
Hasidim sentiment or hermeneutic of the Hebrew Scriptures. They
too thought that personal piety in order to be a holy nation before God
was the main message of the Scriptures. However, these latter groups
thought that the Pharisees did not go far enough in being holy, for
while the Pharisees remained in society and thereby subject to the
moral pollutions of society, these groups withdrew into a monastic-
like existence into the desert areas of Palestine. There, separated and
isolated from the mainstream of life, they could spend their time in
communal and private worship, studying the Scriptures and practic-
ing the disciplines and rituals of food and dress that entered into
making people holy.

Perhaps the best known group of this type that came into
existence during this time was the Essenes. While some Essenes lived
in Jerusalem and surrounding towns and villages, their favorite place
for living was in the area of the Dead Sea (Raymond F. Surburg
1975:58). In this respect many think that the Essenes and the original
producers of the Dead Sea Scrolls, which date back to 200 B.C., were
of the same group. But this is far from certain because sociologically,
several similar but different monastic-like groups could and probably did come into existence and died out over this 200-year period.

Monastic-like groups require charismatic leaders in order to get
started and continue. This means that when a leader passes from the
scene, the group will disband or another charismatic leader takes
over. But in taking over, the new leader will impress his or her own
distinctive style upon the group, thus changing the group into
something different. Over a period of several generations many
different groups may emerge sharing several similarities. What
probably happened in Palestine, therefore, was that several monastic-
like groups or sects arose in Jewish society, and since they had similar
goals of holy living to achieve, certain similarities and convergencies
among them developed. On the other hand, since isolation from
society was necessary in order to be holy, such groups would also feel

it necessary to be isolated from each other thus opening other avenues for divergencies to develop.

Yet, despite their isolation in the desert these groups still had an influence on Jewish society of their time. This is because they generally forbade marriage as a condition of membership. Consequently few if any children were born and reared to carry on the tradition of the founders of these monastic sects. To survive from one generation to the next, then, these groups had to regularly re-enter society to recruit new members. The fact that they did survive testifies to the sentiments already existing in society at large that the meaning of the Scriptures was for holy living and not for political development. Without such sentiments they would have been unable to recruit new members and survive.

Another group in Jewish society which may be classified as a religious party is the scribes. The scribes had been an occupational group since the days of the monarchy (2 Chron. 24:11, KJV). By the time of the New Testament, however, they had grown in power and influence to the point that they were considered a party along with the Pharisees (Matt. 15:1, KJV). Scribes were also known as lawyers and teachers of the Law of Moses.

With the Pharisees the scribes recognized that interpretation was needed to make the Scriptures relevant. The goal of scribal interpretation was to preserve Jewish distinctives in an age of Hellenism.

The Roman Empire

In 63 B.C., Rome incorporated Palestine as part of its worldwide empire. Hyrcanus II, a descendant of the Maccabees, ruled as ethnarch and high priest over the Jews until 47 B.C. at which time Antipater, an Idumean who had political connections with the Roman emperor, was appointed procurator over Judea. Hyrcanus II was able to retain the position of high priest.

Antipater died in 43 B.C. and after a period of uncertainty and political maneuvering, his son Herod succeeded him. Herod was granted the title of king and because of his long and productive reign, including rebuilding the temple, became known as Herod the Great. From the combination of Rome and the house of Herod, two more religious parties emerged. The first was the Zealots who opposed Roman rule, especially paying taxes to Rome. The hope of the Zealots was to expel the Roman overseers and restore Judea as an independent nation. In 6 B.C., the Zealots were apparently behind a revolt against the Roman occupational forces. The revolt was quickly crushed.

After this the Zealots often resorted to individual acts of terrorism against the Romans and their sympathizers throughout Palestine. They became known as the "dagger men" because of their terrorist acts of suddenly stabbing a Roman or Roman sympathizer to death.

The other party that emerged was the Herodians. They were sympathetic Jews whom Herod the Great formed into a group to promote the legitimization of his rule over the Jews, for Herod was from Idumea and not a Jew by nationality. To be sure, a hundred years earlier the Maccabees had subjugated Idumea and forced all males to be circumcised. Yet, many Jews did not consider the Idumeans to be true Jews. This was especially true of Herod. The purpose of the Herodians, therefore, was to "turn around" this public image of Herod and make him more acceptable to Jews as their ruler.

In this discussion we must not overlook the Samaritans and their claim to legitimacy in worshiping God on Mt. Gerizim in Samaria instead of traveling to worship at the temple at Jerusalem (John 4:21). The Samaritans were descendants of the people that Assyria had settled in the northern kingdom of Israel some 700 years earlier. Their ancestors had learned of the Law of Moses and that it was necessary to worship the Lord according to the custom of the land (2 Kings 17:27-28). In this respect the Samaritans formed still another religious party in the Palestine of New Testament times.

The Samaritans claimed equality with the Jews in that they also accepted the Law and were residing in the Promised Land of the Abrahamic covenant. However, the Jews countered this claim in two ways. First, in addition to the Law or Pentateuch they also had the rest of the Hebrew Scriptures, the historical writings, and the prophets. These Scriptures contained the commandments to establish the monarchy and build the temple in Jerusalem, not in Samaria. Consequently the Jews claimed that the Samaritans, in order to truthfully worship God, should travel to Jerusalem.

Second, since both Israel and Judah had been destroyed, the Promised Land was of minor importance. The important aspect of the covenant now was to be true descendants of Abraham. Because the Samaritans were not pure descendants of Abraham, they had no right to claim equality.

A People Without A Shepherd

From the time of the Maccabbees to the opening of the New Testament, the emphasis in Jewish thinking was on being a holy nation. No longer were the land, monarchy, and priesthood—except in the opinion of a minority—important. The most important thing in Jewish life was to be true descendants of Abraham, called and elected to be a pure and holy race of people before God. But this emphasis raised more questions than answers. What did it mean, for example, to be a pure or holy nation? How could this be accomplished especially in a world dominated by Hellenistic culture and thought?

Unfortunately what emerged was not one answer but several, each competing with the others and clamoring for acceptance as the true solution to the tensions felt throughout Judaism. Were the Jews, for example, to separate from, assimilate with, or adapt Hellenistic culture? If the latter, what could be chosen from Hellenism and what had to be rejected? More crucially, what hermeneutic could the Jews safely use to decide what was good and what was bad in Hellenism?

All of this, furthermore, was compounded by the agitation of some that the geographical aspect, the Promised Land, should be restored as the most important aspect of God's covenant with Abraham's descendants. But in restoration, should it be the splendor of the Davidic kingdom, or should the land become like a vast monastery where only the truly spiritual could withdraw from the world and live holy lives? Or should Israel become only an independent nation with its own political structures among the nations of the world?

And then what about the Gentiles who far outnumbered them, lived in the midst of them, and even ruled over them? Would all these different ethnic groups truly come to Jerusalem, as the prophets of old seemed to have foretold, to submit to Jewish rule?

Given the nature of Judaism, that the Jews were people of the covenant, these were not questions of sociological import alone. They had far-reaching theological ramifications as well. Moreover, each religious party that emerged in Jewish society—Pharisees, Sadducees, Essenes, Zealots, Herodians—proclaimed alternative answers as to how the covenant made with Abraham and his descendants was to be interpreted and applied in the world of that time.

The upshot of all this was that it left Judaism at the beginning of the first century in confusion and with numerous tensions to live with. The people of Palestine were indeed a people without a shepherd (Matt. 9:36). Yet, in the midst of confusion one hope remained. It was the nearly universal consensus that the true answer to these questions—the final alternative—would surely come with the appearance of the Messiah (John 4:25).

Questions For Discussion

1. How did the religious parties of Palestine in New Testament times differ in their hermeneutics of Gen. 12:1–3?

2. How did the parties differ in their application of the Abrahamic covenant for their day and time?

3. Discuss how their differing hermeneutics and applications affected the missionary understanding of the Old Testament.

Endnote

1. Quoted from the article on the "Pharisees" in the *Encyclopedia Judaica*, Vol 13, p. 366.

CHAPTER TWELVE

Reducing the Alternatives

"What is truth?" the former communist insurgent leader asked me. "I want to know."

I could understand his perplexity, even his consternation. He was a Thai village leader from the border area with Laos in northern Thailand and had "bought into" the communist promises for the future. He led his villagers into the jungle to join the communist insurgents and fight the Thai government. However, after several years of hardships the insurgency movement began to fall apart.

First, supplies from China ceased coming across the border from Laos. Before long, he and others experienced shortages needed to carry the revolution forward to success. Next, the villagers began to feel the pangs of hunger and deprivation. Soon he saw that their lives, once filled with hope of revolution, had been reduced to only one alternative. So having no food, medicine, or ammunition, he led his people out of the jungle to a Thai army outpost to give themselves up.

After a short re-education program the Thai army resettled him and his group in a village where there was a dynamic young Christian family. This family witnessed to them and soon invited me to explain more fully the Gospel message of salvation. I arrived not expecting the question the village leader had for me.

The question reminded me of the situation we find at the opening of the New Testament. As we saw at the close of the previous chapter the people of Palestine were in the midst of confusion. Different interpretations offered alternative answers for what it meant to be Jewish, the chosen people of God.

But which interpretation was the truth?

It was a question, as we shall soon see in this chapter, that haunted everyone, right up to the highest levels of Palestinian government.

John The Baptist

Preaching Jewish ethnicity as the meaning of God's covenant with Abraham ultimately proved to have a hollow ring. For as the New Testament opens, we see John the Baptist thundering condemnation at those who were preaching it.

Matt. 3:7–9

But when he saw many of the Pharisees and Sadducees coming to where he was baptizing, he said to them: "You brood of vipers! Who warned you to flee from the coming wrath? Produce fruit in keeping with repentance. And do not think you can say to yourselves, 'We have Abraham as our father.' I tell you that out of these stones God can raise up children for Abraham."

The emphasis on ethnicity proved to be a misleading hermeneutic of the covenant for several reasons. John the Baptist mentioned two of them: the hypocrisy of the Pharisees who preached ritual purity as the mark of Jewish identity but in the end neglected the more important aspects of the Law, and the fact that God could make descendants of Abraham from stones thus bypassing the Jews altogether in creating a people for his own prized possession. It was becoming clear that ethnicity had little if anything to do with being a true descendant of Abraham. Examples of this could be seen in the pious Gentiles whose faith exceeded that of the Jews (Matt. 8:5–13), for surely they were equally acceptable to God (Acts 10:34–35).

Another reason which had also become apparent in the Jewish society of the New Testament concerned the many contradictory ways being presented by the various religious parties as to how Jews might indeed be the people of God in the world. These ranged all the way from close cooperation with the Romans recommended by the Sadducees and Herodians, to expelling the Romans (by violence if necessary) advocated by the Pharisees and Zealots, to complete withdrawal from society and the world as practiced by the more ascetic elements of the Essenes. Truly the coming of the Kingdom of God was in the throes of suffering and violence at the hands of forceful men (Matt. 11:12).

Since the Promised Land was no longer the hermeneutic that "drove" Jewish understanding of the covenant and ethnicity itself was now being questioned, this left only the third part—being a blessing to the nations—as the true meaning and purpose of God's covenant with Abraham and the election of Abraham's descendants to be his people. Indeed, it was just this "reduction" that the Messiah upon his coming confirmed as the true and final hermeneutic of the Old Testament Scriptures—the faith that once for all has been entrusted to the saints (Jude 3).

Rom. 15:8–9
For I tell you that Christ has become a servant of the Jews on behalf of God's truth, to confirm the promises made to the patriarchs so that the Gentiles may glorify God for his mercy...

Jesus Of Nazareth: A Light To The Nations

Soon after John the Baptist appeared in the wastelands of eastern Judea, Jesus of Nazareth came to be baptized by him in the Jordan river. The descent of the Holy Spirit upon Jesus at the time of his baptism was proof to John that Jesus was the Messiah, the Son of God (John 1:32–34). The Spirit compelled Jesus to go into the wastelands for a time of fasting and temptation (Matt. 4:1–17). After emerging from the desert Jesus moved to live in the city of Capernaum of Galilee.

Matthew saw in this move the fulfillment of prophecy.

Matt. 4:15–16, quoted from Isa. 9:1–2
Land of Zebulun and land of Naphtali, the way to the sea, along the Jordan, Galilee of the Gentiles — the people living in darkness have seen a great light; on those living in the land of the shadow of death a light has dawned.

The significance of this prophecy is that it confirmed the hermeneutic and understanding of the Hebrew Scriptures that God's people were to be a light—a blessing—to the nations. Only in this case Matthew reduces the hermeneutic further to Jesus Christ. That is, as it was understood that the meaning of the Abrahamic covenant was now to be a blessing to the nations, so Jesus Christ was the fulfillment of that understanding.

In short, Matthew aligned Jesus of Nazareth with the missionary hermeneutic of the Old Testament and not with any other alternate interpretation current at that time. Luke made the same alignment when he quoted Simeon who proclaimed that the infant Jesus was God's salvation, a light for revelation to the Gentiles (Luke 2:28–32).

The Apostle John followed in making the same alignment, calling Jesus "the true light that gives light to every man" (John 1:9) and explaining that everyone who received him—those who believed in his name—became children of God not by natural descent (born as biological descendants of Abraham) but by being born of God (John 1:12–13). Jesus was not the Messiah of the Jews alone. He was the universal Messiah, as the Scriptures foretold, the Messiah of the Gentiles as well.

It was an alignment, moreover, that Jesus himself confirmed throughout his ministry. "I am the light of the world," Jesus exclaimed (John 8:12). To the Jews' claim of being descendants of Abraham, Jesus said:

John 8:39–41
…"If you were Abraham's children," said Jesus, "then you would do the things Abraham did. As it is, you are determined to kill me, a man who has told you the truth that I heard from God. Abraham did not do such things. You are doing the things your own father does."

The Jews countered that God was their father. But Jesus responded that because of their intention to kill him, the devil was really their father (John 8:44). In other words, biological descent was no longer of any importance in interpreting who belongs to God. One's faith and obedience to God, regardless of ethnic background as in the case of the Roman centurion (Matt. 8:5–13), was the important consideration.

Jesus also confirmed this understanding of the Abrahamic covenant and the Scriptures for his followers. Jesus exhorted his listeners to become "sons of the light" so they would no longer walk in darkness (John 12:36) but would become "the light of the world" (Matt. 5:14). His followers were to continue the missionary hermeneutic of the Old Testament Scriptures: God has made them to be the light of the world in order to bring his salvation to the ends of the earth (Acts 13:47, Isa. 49:6).

After instructing his disciples in the Sermon on the Mount, the crowds who listened exclaimed that Jesus "taught as one who had authority, and not as their teachers of the law" (Matt. 7:29). The instruction in the Sermon was straightforward teaching about right living before God. It was not a constant referral to or quotation from past sages, pitting one's opinion against the other and coming to no certain conclusion about what was the truth for the benefit of listeners. This was the method of the scribes or teachers of the law and it did not have the ring of authority to it (Sherman E. Johnson and George A. Buttrick 1951).

The authority that Jesus displayed in his teaching did not come from his divine personage alone. Actually most of his listeners were still uncertain as to whom he really was.

Was he John the Baptist, Elijah, or one of the prophets (Matt. 16:14)? A few perhaps thought he was the Christ. Rather, his authority in teaching came from his view of the Scriptures. To Jesus the Scriptures were not about the Promised Land, ethnicity, ritual purity, or withdrawal from society as the religious parties variously taught. The meaning of the Scriptures was to "seek first the Kingdom of God and his righteousness" (Matt. 6:33). This was a view or hermeneutic universally applicable to all and not just to the Jews alone. It affirmed what the common people at the time felt was the true application of the Scriptures.

In this respect we must not overlook the contribution that the missionary understanding of the Old Testament Scriptures made in giving authority to the teaching of Jesus. While the religious leaders wrangled over various aspects of the Promised Land and Jewish purity, Jesus aligned himself with the well-known understanding of the Scriptures that the people of God are to be the light of the world, an instrument that God can use to bless the nations.

This was a reduction to the essence of the Hebrew Scriptures which was applicable universally. This hermeneutic of the Scriptures certainly had the ring of truth. In the view of his listeners, therefore, Jesus did not speak with authority because he was the Messiah, for this was still in dispute. It was the universality of his message—the missionary interpretation of the Scriptures—that gave authority to his teaching.

This same missionary hermeneutic of the Old Testament can give Christians today their authority in world evangelization. The Old Testament is not something to be explained away or even made relevant to a post-modern, post-Christian age. Rather the Old Testament is to be the theological foundation for evangelism among all the nations, tribes, and language groups of the world.

This was the hermeneutic of the Old Testament Scriptures that authorized the Apostle Paul to turn from the Jews (because of their disbelief) to evangelize the Gentiles (Acts 13:46–47, Isa. 49:6). When interpreted today in this same manner, we find that the Old Testament still gives authority to the Christian evangelist, indeed to the whole church at large, to be a light to the nations and to enter any nation, even to the very ends of the earth in order to proclaim God's salvation.

Truth

In the trial before Pilate, Pilate asked if it were true that Jesus claimed to be the king of the Jews. Jesus answered by saying that his kingdom is not of this world but from another place. To this answer Pilate responded

John 18:37
"You are a king, then!" said Pilate. Jesus answered, "You are right in saying I am a king. In fact, for this reason I was born, and for this I came into the world, to testify to the truth. Everyone on the side of the truth listens to me."

Pilate picked up on the last statement of Jesus above and asked "What is truth?" If Jesus would give his side of the story then perhaps he could rule in his favor.

Jesus, however, did not respond but remained silent. Jesus did not answer Pilate's question because the answer would have involved all of Jewish understanding of their history and the Scriptures back to the beginning of time.

Even at that moment, the Jews (more precisely leaders representing the differing parties with their various interpretations of this history and the Scriptures) were calling for his death. Indeed, Jesus' death was the only thing they could agree upon, for Jesus had claimed to be the Son of God, a blasphemy punishable by death in the views of the Jewish leaders (Matt. 26:63–66).

In addition to this claim Jesus had also, in his interpretation of Scripture, supported the hermeneutic of none of the religious parties; the Promised Land, ethnicity, and ritual purity were all of minor importance. He proclaimed another hermeneutic, thereby succeeding in offending all religious parties of Jewish society. Furthermore, he claimed that his interpretation of Jewish history and Scripture was the truth.

What was the truth to which Jesus came to bear witness? What was Jesus referring to when he used the term "truth" in John 18:36–

37? The answer must first be set in the context of its time and not interpreted according to western or philosophical definitions or concepts of truth. An example of the latter is Leon Morris (1971:294) as he approvingly quotes Rudolf Bultmann's comment on the meaning of truth in John 18:37–38.

> Bultmann sees "the basic meaning of `truth' in John" as "God's reality, which, since God is Creator, is the only true reality."

Another example is Arthur John Gossey's (1952:769) comment:

> "The truth of which the Johannine Jesus speaks is the true knowledge of God, and it is his mission to bear witness to this" (emphasis in the original).

These comments are true insofar as they go. But they overlook a contextual dimension crucial to the interpretation of the Old Testament, an interpretation that Jesus came to bear witness to as being the truth; i.e., the one hermeneutic for correctly understanding the Old Testament scriptures.

During New Testament times there were several hermeneutics, each one vying for acceptance as the true way for understanding the Old Testament. Which one was the truth? None that any of the religious parties was promoting at the time. Rather, Jesus Christ bore witness to another hermeneutic, one which was based on the promise that through Abraham all nations shall be blessed. That hermeneutic, as stated at the outset of this book, is the missionary message of the Old Testament; namely, God has made his people to be a light to the nations in order to bring his salvation to the ends of the earth (Isa. 49:6, Acts 13:47). This salvation, having come from the Jews (John 4:22), Abraham's descendants, and next taken to the uttermost parts of the earth, is how the nations of the earth are and will be blessed (Gen. 26:4).

Jesus was a witness that this missionary interpretation of the Hebrew Scriptures is the truth. By sending his Son into the world to bear witness to it, it was the one interpretation of the Old Testament that received the very imprimatur of God himself. For while the law was given through Moses, grace and truth—the correct application and interpretation of the law—came through Jesus Christ (John 1:17).

Jesus knew that, after he had returned to the Father (John 16:5), his disciples would face the problem of differing hermeneutics of the Hebrew Scriptures and deciding which would be the truth. For example, even after the resurrection the disciples still misunderstood for they asked if Jesus would now restore the kingdom to Israel (Acts 1:6). Realizing that his disciples were still inadequately prepared to receive the full implications of the truth he came to proclaim, he promised to send the paraclete, the Counselor (John 16:7), to advise them further much as a lawyer would.

John 16:12–14
I have much more to say to you, more than you can now bear. But when he, the Spirit of truth, comes, he will guide you into all truth. He will not speak on his own; he will speak only what he hears, and he will tell you what is yet to come. He will bring glory to me by taking from what is mine and making it known to you.

Jesus in Acts 1:6, in other words, did not bother to explain how the disciples were wrong regarding their understanding of the Scriptures and the Kingdom of God. He left that up to the Holy Spirit to lead them into correct understanding later on (Acts 1:7–8).

The promise to the disciples was not just the truth but "all the truth." What was this "all the truth" that the Holy Spirit would lead the disciples into? The "all" here referred to the interpretation that the Scripture (the Old Testament) was not meant for the Jews alone but is indeed universal in scope encompassing all tribes, tongues, and nations.

For example, the Messiah is the offspring of Abraham (Gen. 22:18) through whom all nations shall be blessed (Acts 3:25). That is, the Messiah is the savior not only of the Jews but also the cosmos, the whole inhabited world (John 3:16–17); his sacrificial death is for the world (John 6:51); the symbols of the Jewish Scriptures, such as the sacrificial lamb (John 1:29), are in fact meant to be interpreted to include the world in their application and not be confined to the benefit of the Jews alone; the Messiah will bring God's other sheep (the Gentiles) into the one fold (John 10:16); all must worship God in spirit and in truth (John 4:23); i.e., God is to be worshiped as God not only of the Jews but of the Gentiles too.

Finally the truth that emerges from this hermeneutic is the theological basis from the Old Testament that mandated giving the Great Commission. In his high priestly prayer for his disciples, Jesus asked the Father to:

John 17:17–19

Sanctify them by the truth; your word is truth. As you sent me into the world, I have sent them into the world. For them I sanctify myself, that they too may be truly sanctified.

By means of the universal hermeneutic of the Old Testament Scriptures the disciples were sanctified—separated, set apart (Acts 13:2)—and sent out to the ends of the earth to proclaim God's salvation to all nations.

Ultimately this universal hermeneutic of the Old Testament Scriptures, through the inspiration of the Holy Spirit, would be canonized as a new covenant, the New Testament Scriptures (Heb. 12:24).[1]

"Is This The Christ?"

When the former communist insurgent leader asked me "What is truth," I admit I gulped. I had not expected such a question in the jungles of northern Thailand close to the Laotian border. To have time to compose myself and an answer, I first asked members of the evangelistic team traveling with me to give their testimonies of why they had accepted Jesus Christ as Lord. As I thought (and I am sure the Holy Spirit was prompting me at this point), I came up with this answer.

I told the leader that the dictum of Mao Tse Tung (the founder and leader of the Communist revolution in China) stating that "power grows out of the barrel of a gun" cannot be the truth. This is a statement that produces murder and death. How can an ideology, such as communism, that kills off potential converts be the truth, I asked. Only a message that offers life, especially eternal life in heaven, to all of every nation, tribe, and language can be the truth.

This is why, I went on to explain, Jesus is the way, the truth, and the life (John 14:6). He is truly the Christ of the living God, for it is only he who offers abundant life—life that lasts eternally—to all whether in America or the jungles of northern Thailand.

Toward the close of his earthly ministry, people were confused regarding whether Jesus of Nazareth was truly the Messiah, or the Christ, in the Greek language (John 7:25–31).

On the one hand, the Jewish authorities were trying to kill Jesus, signifying their conclusion that He was not the Christ. But on the other hand, the authorities were doing nothing to stop him from teaching, which signified that they perhaps knew something about

Jesus' claims to be the Christ that they were not revealing. And then there were the miracles that Jesus did. If Jesus was not the Christ, would the real Messiah perform any more miracles than Jesus? Still others had concluded that Jesus could not be the Christ, for when the Christ would come no one would know where he would be from. Therefore, since people knew that Jesus was from Nazareth, he surely could not be the Christ.

That Jesus of Nazareth was indeed the Christ had been disputed from the beginning. One reason is that when Jesus revealed himself as the Jewish Messiah, his life and ministry did not completely match or fulfill public expectation as to what the Christ would be like or do, once having arrived from God. Consequently there was need to point again and again to the evidences or proofs demonstrating that Jesus was truly the Christ. In the history of Christianity these have become the traditional proofs for the divinity of Jesus showing that he is the Christ, the Son of the living God (Matt. 16:16).

The miracles that Jesus performed play a large role in these proofs. The Apostle John called them signs, for they signified or testified to others who Jesus was.

John 20:30–31
Jesus did many other miraculous signs in the presence of his disciples, which are not recorded in this book. But these are written that you may believe that Jesus is the Christ, the Son of God, and that by believing you may have life in his name.

These miracles were the "works" that testified that God had sent Jesus (John 5:36). But there were other testimonies (John 5:33–47). Jesus, for example, referred to the testimony of John the Baptist who testified that the one coming afterwards (meaning Jesus) is more powerful (Matt. 3:11). Jesus also referred to the testimony of the Father at the time of his baptism: "This is my Son, whom I love; with him I am well pleased" (Matt. 3:17). The Old Testament Scriptures also testified, predicting the place of his birth in Bethlehem, that he would inherit the throne of David, that he would die and be raised from the dead, etc. Moses also wrote about the Messiah in a way that pointed to Jesus.

Deut. 18:15
The Lord your God will raise up for you a prophet like me from among your own brothers. You must listen to him.

Since the beginning of the church, testimonies recorded in the Scriptures, like those above, have been used to demonstrate the deity of Jesus and show that he is the Christ. However, in this demonstration another line of proof that Jesus of Nazareth is the Christ has often been overlooked. Namely, it was only Jesus who confirmed the universal or missionary interpretation, and not the particulars of land and ethnicity, as the true message of the Old Testament Scriptures for the world.

As revealed through the Scriptures, God's desire was to bless the Gentiles through Abraham and his descendants; therefore, God has made his people to be a light to the Gentiles in order to bring his salvation to the ends of the earth. All other "Messiahs" emphasized either the land or Jewish ethnicity as the hermeneutic for understanding the Old Testament.

Jesus warned his followers that there would be false Christs and false prophets who would turn many away from the faith and even betray them; they will perform signs and miracles in order to deceive the elect if possible (Matt. 24:4–26). Those, however, who stand firm until the end will be saved. Now it is significant that Jesus placed this warning of false Christs in connection with proclaiming the Gospel to the nations.

Matt. 24:14
And this gospel of the kingdom will be preached in the whole world as a testimony to all nations, and then the end will come.

In other words, the true Christ of God is he who confirms the missionary message of the Old Testament Scriptures. He who would turn the understanding of God's people away from this message back to an interpretation that emphasizes the land or racial purity is a false Christ and a false prophet.

During and after the time of Jesus there were many who presented themselves as Messiahs to the Jewish people. However, their goal was to be saviors of the Jews and not of the world. The Egyptian mentioned in Acts 21:38, for example, was thought to be one. He led 4,000 people, others say up to 30,000, in A.D. 45 in revolt against the rule of Rome over Palestine.[2] The Jewish revolt against Rome of A.D. 66–70, and the final defeat at Masada three years later, were led by Messianic figures. In A.D. 132–35 Simeon Bar Kochba led a revolt against Rome for building a temple to Jupiter in Jerusalem. He was considered a Messiah. In A.D. 448 a Jew from Crete announced he was Moses and promised to lead the Jews through the sea without ships back to Judea. Several believed him, many of whom were drowned at sea in the attempt.

Certainly Jesus of Nazareth did not fulfill society's expectations for the Messiah. But he did fulfill the missionary interpretation of the Old Testament Scriptures. Indeed, any "narrower" interpretation and fulfillment of the Old Testament would disprove the deity of Jesus as it disproved the messianic claims of all the others who sought to (re)establish the Jewish kingdom or purge Jewish society of foreign and pagan elements as the fundamental message of the Scriptures.

Jesus of Nazareth came to bear witness, indeed to affirm, that the missionary understanding of the Old Testament is the truth. This affirmation that Jesus gave is a powerful proof of his divinity enduring down through the centuries. It is for this reason, along with the others mentioned above, that we may with confidence accept him as the Christ, the Son of God, indeed as God who became flesh and dwelled among us to be the savior of the world (John 1:14).

1 Tim. 3:16
Beyond all question, the mystery of godliness is great: He appeared in a body, was vindicated by the Spirit, was seen by angels, was preached among the nations, was believed on in the world, was taken up in glory.

Questions For Discussion

1. Discuss how the New Testament expression "light of the world" is expanded from your previous understanding of the term and explained by the missionary hermeneutic of the Old Testament.

2. From reading this chapter, how would you now answer the question "what is truth?"

3. Describe the relationship between truth, the Holy Spirit, and the missionary interpretation of the Old Testament.

4. Explain how the missionary interpretation of the Old Testament is another proof of the deity of Jesus of Nazareth.

Endnotes

1. To the Apostle Paul, this universal interpretation of the Old Testament Scriptures is the "truth of the Gospel" (Gal. 2:5), of which the church is the pillar and foundation (1 Tim. 3:15). The church supports and validates this interpretation of the Old Testament throughout time. Paul would not compromise this truth in his confrontation with the Judaizers of Galatia who wanted to require the Gentile Christians to complete the Jewish proselytization process by being circumcised (see Chapter Nine), for "There is neither Jew nor Greek, slave nor free, male nor female, for you are all one in Christ Jesus" Paul exclaimed (Gal. 3:28).

Unfortunately Peter and Barnabas were briefly led astray from this truth of the Gospel (the universalism of the Old Testament) when they withdrew from eating with Gentile Christians because they feared the criticism that would come from the Judaizers (Gal. 2:14). Not only were these two intimidated but the Galatian Christians themselves began to have doubts whether this universal hermeneutic of the Old Testament was the truth. Yet, Paul was confident that they would take no other view (hermeneutic) of the Scriptures (Gal. 5:7–10).

2. Examples are selected from the article "Messianic Movements" in the *Encyclopedia Judaica*, Vol. 11.

Jesus and the Gentiles

"Why have you gone and joined the Jesus religion?" the government official quizzed Sao. "Jesus is the religion of the whites, not Asians."

Sao had just become the first Christian in his tribal village in northern Thailand. Now he was facing a common argument against his decision. He could not be a true Asian if he persisted in being a Christian.

Sao fortunately was not intimidated and even though he was a new Christian, he attempted to answer in the clearest manner he could. The official soon left expressing disappointment over Sao's determination to maintain his faith in Jesus Christ.

Is Jesus meant to be Lord and Savior of others besides those who believe in him—those whom we might call "Gentiles" today? This is a question that even Christians, from laypeople to theologians, have debated. Some of course think not. Surprisingly, there appears to be some support for this position from the words of Jesus himself.

For example, on two occasions Jesus expressed the fact that the Gentiles were not the major focus in his ministry. The first time was when he sent out the twelve disciples to preach on their own. These twelve Jesus sent out with the following instructions: "Do not go among the Gentiles or enter any town of the Samaritans. Go rather to the lost sheep of Israel" (Matt. 10:5–6).

The second event occurred when he told the Canaanite woman (who had asked him to cast a demon from her daughter) that "I was sent only to the lost sheep of Israel" (Matt. 15:24). Therefore, he saw no need to help this non-Jewish woman. It was only after the woman had pleaded and shown her willingness to accept an inferior position to the Jews that Jesus agreed to heal her daughter. "You have great faith," Jesus said to her. "Your request is granted." Her daughter was healed from that very hour (Matt.15:28).

To The Jews First

Earlier generations of Bible scholars saw in these verses a contradiction to the Great Commission and the early church's inclusion of the Gentiles into its ranks of believers (Richard R. DeRidder 1976). The alleged contradiction was sometimes explained by saying that Jesus, being from a Jewish background, at first shared the same negative attitude toward the Gentiles as his compatriots and so did not view his mission as one that included them. But when the Jews rejected him he changed his mind and gave the Great Commission, and later when the church was indeed successful in converting a great many more Gentiles than Jews, the record was revised to show that Jesus' mission on earth was universal in scope and not confined to the Jews.

Such explanations of these verses from the Gospel of Matthew are fortunately no longer popular (Joachim Jeremias 1958). The main reason for their demise is that the verses can readily be reconciled with the Great Commission and the missionary practices of the early church. Indeed, the earliest reconciliation was that of the Apostle Paul. Instead of considering these statements and the Great Commission as Jesus contradicting himself, he saw in Jesus and his behavior in this matter the Scriptural precedent or principle for his own missionary strategy:

Rom 1:16
I am not ashamed of the gospel, because it is the power of God for the salvation of everyone who believes: first for the Jew, then for the Gentile.

Just as Jesus came first to the Jews and included the Gentiles in his ministry on occasion as they called on him for help, so would Paul preach first to the Jews and second to the Gentiles.

But this did not mean that the Gentiles would end up receiving anything less in heavenly reward—or judgment for evil—than the Jews. There is for all humans either judgment for doing evil or heavenly glory for doing good, first to the Jew and also the Gentile (Rom. 2:9–10).

Paul followed this precedent in his missionary journeys where he entered into synagogues to preach first to the Jews (Acts 13ff). Only after the Jews rejected his message did he turn to preaching the Gospel to the Gentiles. He followed this principle to the end of his missionary career.

When at last Paul reached Rome as a prisoner he immediately called for a meeting with the Jewish leaders of the city (Acts 28). Paul explained to them he was a prisoner because of proclaiming Jesus as the Christ. He tried to convince them about Jesus from the Law of Moses and the prophets. But the Jews demurred, upon which Paul announced that from that time on "God's salvation has been sent to the Gentiles, and they will listen!" (Acts 28:28).

Paul And Luke

A deeper yet related problem regarding Jews and Gentiles faced the early church. It was not whether the Gentiles were to be accepted. That issue had already been settled since the beginning of the Dispersion and Jewish contact with Hellenism: non-Jews could indeed be blessed by God and be incorporated into his covenant with Israel. The early church accepted this hermeneutic of the Old Testament Scriptures from its Jewish beginnings and successfully expanded its application over the Roman empire.

The main issue now facing the church was not whether, but how, the Gentiles were to be incorporated into the Kingdom of God. On one side was Paul who maintained that the proselytizing techniques of the Jews as exemplified in the Pharisees, and which Jesus condemned (Matt. 23:15—see Chapter Nine), was contrary to the Gospel of Jesus Christ as exemplified in the life and teaching of Jesus. In essence, Paul proclaimed that faith in God as Father and in Jesus as Lord, a faith that resulted in obedience and righteous living, was the only thing needed.

Circumcision and other Jewish rituals, including such sacred places as the Promised Land and the temple, were no longer important in becoming a child of God. To scripturally back this up, Paul referred to Abraham who, even before he was circumcised, believed God and therefore was counted as a righteous person. In believing on Jesus Christ as Lord, a Gentile could straightforwardly become a descendant of Abraham (Rom. 4:22—25).

On the other side were the Judaizers, Jewish Christians who taught that Gentile believers had to be circumcised in order to be saved (Acts 15:1).

These Christians evidently at first approved of Paul's apostolic missions to Gentile cities in the Roman empire. This was an accepted practice in Judaism, especially by the Pharisees, and had resulted in many proselytes or converts. However, after hearing Paul's report on his first apostolic mission (Acts 14:27), they became alarmed. Paul accepted Gentiles, both God fearers and pagan alike, on the basis of believing in Jesus who can make a person righteous at those points where the Law of Moses could not (Acts 13:26–39). The Judaizers saw that in such preaching, circumcision—and along with it the hermeneutic that ethnic purity is the important aspect of the Abrahamic covenant—was effectively eliminated.

The question, therefore, that came to affect the early church throughout the Book of Acts was this: who was right, Paul or the Judaizers? That the Judaizers were a force to be reckoned with in the early church can be seen in the church council they forced to be held in Jerusalem (Acts 15). At the council the leaders of the Jerusalem church rejected their contention that circumcision was necessary for salvation. The Judaizers were undaunted, however, and followed Paul into Galatia and other areas in hopes of imposing their "gospel of Judaization" on the new Gentile believers (Gal. 1:6–7).

Paul, though, was able to offset the influence and effects of the Judaizers through personal visits (his second apostolic mission to the Gentiles—Acts 16–18) and the letter composed by the church at Jerusalem urging the Gentile Christians not to listen to the Judaizers (Acts 15:23–29).

On his second apostolic journey Paul traveled through Galatia and Asia Minor to the city of Troas (Acts 16:6–10). There he met Luke, a Gentile physician who joined him on his apostolic mission into Macedonia and Europe. Being an apostolic companion of Paul, Luke soon became embroiled in the same Judaizing controversies that plagued Paul throughout his missionary ministry. Only now these controversies came from both Jewish Christians and non-Christian Jews as they opposed Paul and his interpretation of the Hebrew Scriptures that Gentiles may be accepted into the Kingdom of God without circumcision.

The opposition at times turned violent. Paul was stoned, left for dead, brought to court, and even put into prison. Yet, in all of these sufferings, Luke took Paul's side in the controversy. Luke, after all, was a Gentile. He also saw the force of Paul's hermeneutic that if a Gentile male was circumcised he was duty bound to observe all the law, at which time he would also be severed from the grace of God in Christ Jesus (Gal. 5:2–4).

But this left a nagging question. Was Paul really correct in his hermeneutic or interpretation of the Hebrew Scriptures? Could it be the truth when, after being proclaimed in a community, it often caused civic disturbance? No doubt it was embarrassing to explain to Roman officials and noblemen why he, Luke, as an educated Gentile could have joined up with a Jewish rabble-rouser like Paul. Perhaps the Jews and Judaizers were right after all in accusing Paul of distorting the Jewish Scriptures to his own purposes (Acts 24:19–20).

There was only one way to prove once and for all—not only to himself but also to anyone else who might be interested—which side of this issue represented the truth. That way was to go back and investigate the original sources for the Gospel he had first heard from Paul and to learn from eyewitnesses if it were true that Jesus himself had actually taught by word and in action that Gentiles were to be included in God's Kingdom on the basis of faith and not Jewish ritual. If true, then there were indeed true precedents from Jesus' life and teaching for accepting Gentiles in Israel's inheritance on the basis of faith.

Luke soon had his opportunity. Sometime in A.D. 58 he and Paul arrived in Jerusalem (Acts 21:17). As the matter turned out, this was not a happy visit. Paul was arrested and kept in prison for two years, first in Jerusalem and later in the Roman garrison town of Caesarea. On the other hand this allowed ample time to check out all the original sources including perhaps Mary the mother of Jesus, James (the Lord's brother), Peter, and many others from Galilee to Judea regarding Jesus and his interpretation of the Hebrew Scriptures respecting the Gentiles.

Theophilus

Luke was not the only Gentile interested in the question Theophilus, who merited the honorific Excellency, was also interested.

Jewish-Gentile relations in the Roman Empire often turned nasty and when they did, it was all that officials could do to maintain public order and peace. Moreover, a new Jewish sect, the Christians, were now claiming that the Son of the Jewish God had revealed a new interpretation of the Jewish Scriptures that eliminated some requirements for Gentiles who might wish to worship their God. Those who disagreed, even some who claimed belief in the Son, would stir up a whole community against the sect in order to force them out of town. But leaders of the sect claimed that the founder of the sect, Jesus Christ, was truly the Son of God and that the new interpretation of the Scriptures which he revealed did in fact include non-Jews without the old requirements or Law, as one of its foremost leaders explained. Furthermore, they claimed that this new interpretation was the truth.

Indeed, the controversy seemed to hinge on two questions. Was the founder the Son of the Jewish God and did he intend to include non-Jews without the old requirements? If both could be answered in the affirmative, then it would help the Roman officials in adjudicating cases of civil disturbances that sometimes followed whenever an evangelist of the new Christian sect entered a Jewish synagogue or preached in a public square. To provide this added help Luke undertook to write a life of Jesus Christ to his Excellency Theophilus.

Nothing outside his title and name is known about Theophilus. Some Bible scholars have even doubted that he was a real person. Since the name meant "God's friend," perhaps Luke meant to address his Gospel to anyone who was God's friend.

However, it is more likely that Theophilus was a real person and because of the title could have been a Roman government official, perhaps a governor over a province or, even more likely, a high-level deputy. He may have been stationed in Caesarea attached to the office of Felix who was governor (Acts 23:24) and perhaps assigned the duty of overseeing public order and peace among the various ethnic groups of the area. This could have put the arrest and imprisonment of Paul under his charge. It may have been under these circumstances that Luke became acquainted with Theophilus.[1]

Soon after Paul had been transferred to Caesarea, Jewish leaders obtained the services of a lawyer named Tertullus to present their case against Paul before Felix (Acts 24:1–8). Paul was accused of being a troublemaker and of having desecrated the temple in Jerusalem. Paul countered that he was really arrested on account of his belief in the resurrection of the dead.

Felix was well acquainted with Christian doctrine (Acts 24:22) and so realized that the case involved only religious and not secular concerns. But he decided to hold Paul anyway in hopes of receiving a bribe to be set free. In the interval he talked often with Paul and perhaps ordered a deputy to prepare a brief that would detail the exact charges against Paul. A brief could come in handy in deflecting criticism from the Jews over any future release of Paul (should Paul agree to pay a bribe) or sending a summary of the charges to Rome for final adjudication should Paul appeal his case to Caesar.

Theophilus probably was not a Christian. John Nolland (1989:10) writes that the word Excellency was not used in early Christian literature of Christians. On the other hand he probably was sympathetic enough to want to know what Jesus Christ had taught or said regarding the new interpretation.

Theophilus knew about Jesus Christ and the Christians and perhaps had even read accounts of Jesus' life that had previously been written by others. But these were not satisfactory with some being written perhaps only in Aramaic or as fragments of Jesus' life. A more comprehensive account would help him and his superiors in handing down a decision regarding the Jews and Paul.

If the Jews were right, then a decision could be made in favor of the Jews against Paul, who could then be conveniently handed over to the Jews to be tried internally according to Jewish religious law. But if Paul was right; i.e., the founder of the Christian sect was the Son of God and did intend to include non-Jews into the sect without first having to observe Jewish requirements, then Paul was not a trouble-maker and the Jewish leaders must bear the responsibility for causing social disturbances when opposing Paul.

This case, in reality, was turning out to be in answer to the question of an earlier Roman governor, Pilate, about what truth is (John 18:38). Perhaps Theophilus, as he talked with Luke, asked the same question.

An Accurate And Orderly Report

Luke proposed to investigate and write a history on the life of Jesus Christ. But it would be more than a history. It would be more like a deposition submitted to Theophilus to be used in preparing a legal brief for adjudicating Paul's case. The deposition, as Luke promised in the opening verses of his Gospel (Luke 1:1-3), would be both accurate and orderly:

[Luke's] claim to offer a well-ordered account points...to a presentation in which the parts are reported and organized from the perspective of Luke's own coherent understanding of the whole. Luke is implicitly presenting a message and arguing a case, and he organizes his material in relation to the these ends. (John Nolland 1989:xxxi)

Luke's purpose was so that Theophilus could be certain about the information that had been transmitted to him (Luke 1:4).

Bible scholars have noted that Luke 1:1–4 contains the best example of the Greek language to be found in the New Testament. The rest of Luke's Gospel is written in rather ordinary Greek. However, this division of style is to be expected if the Gospel is meant to fulfill a legal function of presenting "just the facts" in order to arrive, by a process of deductive reasoning, at the truth. Luke 1:1–4 would entail a formal introduction using good Greek while the remainder of the Gospel would reflect the common, everyday speech or testimony of those who were witnesses to the events and teaching of Jesus of Nazareth.

What was the "coherent understanding of the whole," to use John Nolland's words above, that Luke was arguing from as he wrote to Theophilus? The Apostle Paul, I believe, gives us a hint when he wrote that Jesus came to confirm the promise which was given to the patriarchs that the Gentiles would also glorify God for his mercy (Rom. 15:8–9).

In other words, it was the missionary interpretation of the Hebrew Scriptures that Jesus Christ came to confirm in both word and deed. It was indeed, as Paul had explained many times (Eph. 3:6), God's purpose from the beginning for his people to be a light to the Gentiles in order to bring his salvation to the ends of the earth and that the Gentiles be included in God's salvation on the same basis as Abraham, which was by belief and not circumcision (Rom. 4:9–10).

Questions For Discussion

1. How much time and energy should the church today spend in Jewish evangelism?

2. Why do you think Luke wrote a Gospel to Theophilus?

3. For what purpose did Luke write an accurate and orderly account of Jesus's life?

Endnote

1. It must be remembered that this discussion on Theopilus, who he was, how he became acquainted with Luke, and why Luke wrote his Gospel to him, perhaps qualifies more as a "historical reconstruction" of the biblical data than an exegesis or even an interpretation (hermeneutic) of the relevant texts. Nevertheless I believe that the discussion gives an accounting of several odds and ends in the life of Paul and his companion Luke that perhaps otherwise would be left unaccounted for.

CHAPTER FOURTEEN

The Gospel According To Luke

Kham, along with several other Christians of his area, was arrested on orders from the Japanese Imperial Army. This was during the early days of World War II in Thailand, and the Japanese Army was trying to consolidate its power by rounding up and incarcerating those who were considered potential enemies.

After his arrest Kham was led before a Japanese Army officer. The officer interrogated him about why he had decided to follow the western or white-man religion of Christianity instead of adhering to an Asian religion. He could not be a true Asian as long as he continued to be a Christian, the officer lectured.

Indeed, the Japanese Imperial Army considered it traitorous to be a Christian under these wartime conditions with western, Christian nations. It would be to his advantage, therefore, to renounce his faith in Jesus immediately. Otherwise, he would have to remain under custody.

After a few days of incarceration, however, Kham and the others were released. The Japanese officer and his assistants had completed their interrogations in Nan Province in the north and returned to more civilized parts of Thailand. A local Thai government official was left in charge of the Christians. The official, knowing that Kham and the others were not traitors or dangerous to Japanese power, told them to quietly return home to their families and continue their lives as usual.

When Kham returned home he continued worshiping God and living as a Christian. The experience, more importantly, confirmed his faith that Jesus was not just for the white race only but for Asians as well. After all, Jesus had promised to be with his followers until the end of the age (Matt. 28:20), and the promise had proved true. He as an Asian was home safe from Japanese harassment.

J. W. Shepard (1971:8) calls the book of Luke the Gospel of universal and free salvation, written for the Gentile as well as for the Jew. But more basic than universalism, I believe, was Luke's writing in defense of the missionary hermeneutic of the Old Testament Scriptures. His research and interviews with eyewitnesses confirmed that Jesus demonstrated his acceptance of the Gentiles. This was an important point for Theophilus as a non-Jew and Roman government official to understand.

Luke wrote that he would give Theophilus an orderly accounting of Jesus' life. John Nolland (1989:10) describes Luke's "orderly" (Luke 1:3), not as a chronological ordering of events as a historian might do, but as an organizing principle. We must remember at the outset, however, that life is much more complex than a single principle around which a life might be organized and lived. The life of our Lord on earth encompassed much more than the correct interpretation of the Old Testament.

Nevertheless, when the Gospel writers recorded his life some years after his death, resurrection, and ascension, each one obviously organized and wrote, under the promised guidance of the Holy Spirit (John 16:13), from a particular perspective on what his life as a whole meant. In this respect only certain events from his life of approximately thirty-three years were selected which were germane in one way or another to the development of each perspective.

Luke, in this regard, used the missionary hermeneutic of the Hebrew Scriptures as the organizational principle in arranging his material on the life of Christ.

Luke's Organizing Principle

Luke demonstrated this organizational principle of his in two ways. First, there was material (events, statements, and so on) from Jesus' life that the other Gospel writers (Matthew, Mark, and John) used in one context but which Luke used in another.

Second, Luke included new material which the other writers did not. Because of these differences it is not necessary to accuse Luke of rearranging material formerly used by others (Matthew, Mark, Ur-Mark, etc.) or to say that he included new material from a so-called "Q," "K," or Proto-Lucan source.

Unfortunately much of modern theological scholarship has been occupied with postulating such constructs as sources for explaining the textual differences found in the four Gospel writers.

However, such textual differences are not to be explained by means of postulating theoretical constructs (these are beyond empirical verification anyway). It becomes more plausible, given how complex life is, to explain them functionally.

For example, Jesus himself no doubt said the same thing in different contexts for different purposes and each writer therefore recorded not only the same saying but also the different context in order to communicate the different purpose (Robert L. Thomas 1986). In the same manner a writer selected from memory (Matthew) or from his investigation (Luke) an event not selected by others for the purpose of communicating a particular point or message. In other words, each textual difference serves a communicative function within the context of the four Gospels.

This concept of communicative function is taken from sociolinguistics, a branch of linguistics investigating how language is used in social interaction and communication. A main postulate of all branches of linguistics is that language is not learned and used diachronically (historically) but synchronically (the present time). Therefore, observable differences are not so used because that is the way language developed over historical time, but because of distinctive functions current at the time of speaking or writing.

In social interaction differences in language usage similarly do not reflect historical development but are meant to communicate different meanings. That is, each difference found in conversation, discourse, or a text is ultimately meaningful or functional. Since differences in the texts of the Gospels do exist, describing the communicative function of a difference, not its alleged historical source and development, should be the task of theology.

We must remember in this regard that we are dealing with texts at a macro-level of analysis. At this level a text must contain a great deal of material (narrative, events, statements), the main function of which is to provide the necessary frame or structure for the text to be a complete unit. Without such materials we would have no text for arriving at an overall meaning or purpose.

Luke's Gospel contains a lot of material, the main purpose of which, in this regard, is to form the frame or setting to show that Jesus indeed confirmed a hermeneutic of the Old Testament that allowed Gentiles entry into God's Kingdom. In the absence of such a setting, we have no structure from which to arrive at an understanding that this was indeed the objective of Luke in writing his life of Christ. In other words, the overall meaning or purpose of Luke's Gospel turns out to be something greater than what its parts (narratives, events, pericopes, etc.) individually and separately suggest.

At Nazareth

With Luke, the communicative function of many textual differences in his Gospel was to demonstrate that Jesus of Nazareth did indeed confirm in both word and deed the missionary hermeneutic of the Hebrew Scriptures thus allowing non-Jews into the Kingdom of God. An early example of this in Luke's Gospel is his account of Jesus' rejection at Nazareth, which occurred at the beginning of Jesus' ministry in Galilee (Luke 4:16–30).

In Luke's account Jesus entered the synagogue and, as was his custom, read from the Scriptures and preached. He read from Isaiah.

Isa. 61:1–2
The Spirit of the Sovereign Lord is on me, because the Lord has anointed me to preach good news to the poor. He has sent me... to proclaim freedom for the captives and recovery of sight for the blind...to proclaim the year of the Lord's favor...

I. Howard Marshall (1978:183) is undoubtedly correct in saying that (exegetically) this text referred to Isaiah and the awareness of his own call to preach good news to the people of Israel. But hermeneutically by New Testament times, this text was understood to also describe the Messiah and his work, once he had come to Israel. Jesus announced as he started preaching that he was the fulfillment of that understanding.

His listeners were amazed at these words that came from his lips. Could it be that Jesus was the Messiah? After all, they had heard the report of miracles he had performed in Capernaum. Now they asked him to perform miracles in Nazareth as he had elsewhere in order to back up his claim of fulfilling a messianic interpretation from the Scriptures. Jesus refused, citing the well-known aphorism of a prophet having no acceptance in his own hometown even if he does perform miracles there.

What comes next in Luke's account is an interpretation of Scripture that offended Jesus' listeners. Jesus cited two examples from the Hebrew Scriptures where non-Israelites, over equally qualified Israelite candidates, received special blessings and benefits from God.

The first was a widow of Zarephath (1 Kings 17:8–16) and the second was Naaman the Syrian (2 Kings 5:1–14).

Luke 4:25–27
I assure you that there were many widows in Israel in Elijah's time, when the sky was shut for three and a half years and there was a severe famine throughout the land. Yet Elijah was not sent to any of them, but to a widow in Zarephath in the region of Sidon. And there were many in Israel with leprosy in the time of Elisha the prophet, yet not one of them was cleansed—only Naaman the Syrian.

The full impact from these two examples was not lost on his Jewish listeners. First, together the two references formed a rebuke to the people of Nazareth that hometown people should not expect any special privileges over outsiders.

Beyond a rebuke, however, these two illustrations had a much wider implication which offended his listeners. Because these examples involved Gentiles, they meant that non-Jews were worthy to be blessed by God, sometimes even before Jews. The implications that Nazareth had no special privileges, and that as Jews they were really no better off before God, infuriated the audience in the synagogue. They forced Jesus out to a cliff hoping to cast him over to his death. But Jesus turned and walked away unharmed.

Matthew and Mark also recorded a visit of Jesus to Nazareth (Matt. 13:54–58, Mark 6:1–6), but each without the material that Luke included (all accounts mentioned that the people there were amazed at Jesus' teaching, only later to be offended).

Two explanations have been offered for this difference between Matthew/Mark and Luke. First is that Jesus made two visits to Nazareth, an earlier one recorded by Luke which included the quote from Isaiah and the examples of the widow of Zarephath and Naaman, and a later visit recorded by Matthew and Mark (Albert Cassel Wieand 1950, J. W. Shepard 1939, R. C. Foster 1966). The second explanation is that there was only one visit and that Luke copied from Matthew/Mark, adding material he found from some other source (I. Howard Marshall 1978).

However, both explanations miss Luke's main objective for recording Jesus' visit to Nazareth, for both fail to explicate the significance of the different material found in Luke. To Luke the examples of the widow of Zarephath and Naaman in the Hebrew

Scriptures confirmed what he had learned from Paul; namely, that God even back in Old Testament times intended to bless people of other nationalities and ethnic groups who would call only on him (Rom. 10:12–13). Furthermore, since Jesus referred to these events in his sermon at Nazareth, it demonstrated that Jesus himself interpreted these events in the same way and thereby was in agreement with including the Gentiles in the blessings God had promised to the descendants of Abraham.

Some time after leaving Nazareth Jesus returned to Capernaum. There a Roman Centurion who had a sick servant sent a number of Jewish elders to him with a request (Luke 7:1–10). They asked Jesus to come and heal the servant. They stated that this Centurion was worthy of help because he loved the Jewish people and built a synagogue for them.

But as Jesus approached the Centurion's house, friends came out to meet Jesus with a message. The Centurion, they said, felt unworthy to come out and receive Jesus. So if Jesus would just say a word of healing (the Centurion would understand since he also ordered people around), that would be sufficient. Jesus was amazed that the Centurion would have this much faith. Most people would want a healer to come and minister personally with the sick person. This was what Jesus' Jewish brethren required. But here was a Gentile who exercised more faith than the Jews. Jesus was not required to be there in person; only his word spoken from afar would be sufficient.

In summary then, these two events in Galilee, Jesus' rejection at Nazareth which occurred early, and healing the Centurion's servant which occurred in the middle period of ministry in Galilee, marked the tone of Jesus' ministry not only in Galilee but also later on in Judea (see following section). This ministry included the Gentiles in the blessings promised to Abraham on the basis of faith and not Jewish requirements of purity. This was a characteristic of Jesus' ministry that Luke wanted Theophilus to understand clearly.

Through Judea And Perea

As the time for the Feast of the Tabernacles came near during the last year of his ministry on earth (John 7:1–10), Jesus traveled from Galilee through Samaria to Judea (Luke 23:5). Over the next six months and after the appearances at the Feast in Jerusalem (John 7–8), Jesus stayed outside of Jerusalem traveling and teaching in the villages and towns of Judea and Perea (Albert Cassel Wieand 1950). While all four Gospel writers refer to this time, Luke differs from the other three by giving details of what Jesus did and said in travels outside the city of Jerusalem.

Indeed, these final six months of Jesus' ministry occupies nearly one-half of Luke's Gospel, from the last eleven verses of chapter nine to the first half of chapter nineteen. The whole section has been termed "Luke's great interpolation" (Carl S. Patton 1915).

During the tour of Judea and Perea, Luke recorded Jesus as repeating much of the teaching he had given earlier in Galilee. But now the teaching occurred in different contexts and with different lesson objectives in mind. Luke also included events in the life of Christ that occurred only in this period but which the other writers do not mention. During this time Jesus taught as he had done in Galilee that non-Jews or Gentiles are to be included in God's Kingdom. Indeed, this is perhaps the most significant aspect of this difference in the text of Luke's Gospel.

Galilee was known as "Galilee of the Gentiles" (Matt. 4:15). The Jews of Galilee were heavily intermixed with Gentile populations, creating of necessity greater contact with and toleration of Gentiles. Galilean Jews also showed greater laxity in observing Jewish purification rites after such interaction. Consequently the Jewish purists of Judea treated Galilean Jews with some contempt.

Under these conditions in "Jewish" Judea (which Theophilus no doubt knew well), for Jesus still to teach that the Gentiles are to be included in God's Kingdom was significant in at least two ways. Not only did the teaching confirm the missionary interpretation of the Hebrew Scriptures for the Jews of Judea, but for Theophilus it also showed that Jesus was consistent and not afraid to stand up for this truth even in the face of an entrenched ethnocentrism and prejudice against Gentiles and especially Roman officials. In Judea it would have been more convenient for Jesus to have soft-pedaled this issue, but he did not. This reconfirmation is apparent in several passages that only Luke wrote.

The first reconfirmation came through the positive and charitable attitude that Jesus showed toward the Samaritans during this time, an attitude that was not expected from a Jew (John 4:9). As Jesus and his disciples left Galilee to travel through Samaria, Jesus wished to stay overnight in a Samaritan village (Luke 9:51–56). But unlike Sychar earlier (John 4:5), this village refused to grant hospitality. The disciples wanted to call down fire from heaven to destroy the village. Jesus rebuked them for this suggestion and led them to another village.

Next came the parable about the Good Samaritan in response to a question from a scribe asking who is one's neighbor (Luke 10:25–37). In this parable, in order to answer the question, Jesus juxtaposed a badly injured Jew with a priest, a Levite, and a Samaritan, all who had the resources to help. But only the Samaritan helped.

The conclusion of the parable was inescapable for the scribe. The priest and Levite, who were geographically and ethnically neighbors, turned out to be no neighbors to the injured Jew while the Samaritan, who was not geographically close and who was ethnically despised, became the neighbor. Of the three only the Samaritan had the "right" to walk on pass the injured Jew; but he did not exercise that right. Jesus then told the Jewish scribe to follow the example of the Samaritan.

On a return trip to Jerusalem, perhaps from an excursion into Perea, Jesus met ten lepers (Luke 17:11–19). At least nine of the men were Jews with one being a non-Jew, a Samaritan. Jesus healed them and told them to go show themselves to a priest. As the ten lepers left only the Samaritan turned back to thank Jesus. Jesus praised the Samaritan, announcing "your faith has made you well." The significance of this last pronouncement within the total context of this event must not be overlooked.

At first Jesus told the lepers to follow an instruction of the Law. Next he declared that the non-Jew was made well by means of his faith. Of equal importance was the basis for the declaration: the non-Jew praised God with a loud voice and fell in worship at the feet of Jesus to thank him.

In other words, this one brief event summed up the missionary hermeneutic of the Hebrew Scriptures (see conclusion of Chapter Nine). This was "theology at work" for it demonstrated Jesus' positive attitude to Samaritans, a non-Jewish population, and on what basis he accepted them: no longer by the Law but by faith. More importantly perhaps for Theophilus, however, was that this simple event confirmed the complete life and apostolic ministry of the prisoner Paul; namely that what Paul preached and wrote regarding the Gentiles being accepted by faith and not by circumcision indeed had a firm precedent in the life and work of Jesus Christ.

On another occasion while Jesus was traveling to Jerusalem, a person asked him if only a few people would be saved (Luke 13:22–30). Jesus did not give a specific answer to the question. Rather, he used the question to answer something more basic: everyone should make every effort to enter by the narrow door, a metaphor of salvation he had used earlier in Galilee in the Sermon on the Mount (Matt. 7:13).

Jesus proceeded to give a parable of a house owner who refused, once having closed the door to his house, to reopen the door to let people in. The people outside protested, however, stating that they had the right to enter because of their association with the owner. They had earlier eaten and drunk with him. But the owner told them to leave because he never did know them.

The parable was easily interpreted as referring to the Jews who opposed Jesus: they shall not be saved. On the other hand, Jesus went on to say:

Luke 13:29–30
People will come from east and west and north and south, and will take their places at the feast in the Kingdom of God. Indeed there are those who are last who will be first, and first who will be last.

This was a clear reference to the Gentiles from the four directions of the earth who shall enter the Kingdom or be saved even before the Jews. Jesus had earlier used the illustration of people coming from the four directions of the earth to refer to the entry of the Gentiles into God's Kingdom. This happened in Galilee when he healed the Centurion's servant (Matt. 8:5–13). While Luke records the same event, he did not include this illustration. Rather, he chose to save its impact in his ordering of Jesus' life for the Judean phase of Jesus' ministry.

However, there was irony in Jesus' answer to the question of how many shall be saved, an irony that perhaps was not lost on Theophilus either. It was this: while the door into heaven is indeed narrow (meaning few will be saved), the door is still wide enough for non-Jews to also enter and be saved.

The Final Week

At the close of the six-month period in Judea and Perea, Jesus returned to Jerusalem in a triumphal entry. This was the final week before the crucifixion. Even during this time of great personal distress, Luke reported to Theophilus, Jesus still taught about the Gentiles being a part of God's Kingdom. Only now the teaching had a more ominous tone.

Throughout the week Jesus engaged in several disputes with the Jewish leaders. In one dispute the leaders wanted to know by what authority Jesus did what he did (Luke 20:1–18). Jesus answered by asking them a question: was John's baptism from God or from men? The leaders were fearful for if they said "from God," then Jesus would ask why they had not obeyed John by being baptized themselves. But if they said "from men," then the people would stone them for the people believed that John was from God. So when they admitted they could not answer this question, Jesus said he would not answer their question either.

Immediately following this, Jesus told a parable (Luke 20:9–19). A man planted a vineyard and rented it out to some sharecroppers. His payment was to be a part of the grapes produced in the vineyard. But when it came time to receive his share of the crop, the tenants refused to give any. The owner sent first one, then two, and finally three servants to receive his share. But each time the sharecroppers would beat or shamefully treat the servant and send him away empty-handed. Finally the owner sent his son, but the sharecroppers killed the son and disposed of his body outside the vineyard. Then Jesus asked his listeners this question.

Luke 20:15–16
...What will the owner of the vineyard do to them? He will come and kill those tenants and give the vineyard to others...

The listeners understood the interpretation of the parable. The story referred to Israel as the people of God, and because Israel had disobeyed the covenant God made with Abraham, the Kingdom would be given to the Gentiles. "May this never be!" the people gasped. Yet, as events were fast unfolding in Jerusalem during this final week, it would surely take place just as Jesus foretold.

Later in private conversation with his disciples, Jesus told of the end of time (Luke 21:5–36). The disciples asked what the sign would be that signaled the end. Jesus replied that the time was near. A great persecution and affliction would soon come upon them. The city of Jerusalem would be surrounded by armies, destroyed, and "trampled upon by Gentiles until the times of the Gentiles are fulfilled" (Luke 21:24).

In summary, the Gentiles would indeed enter the Kingdom that God had established for his people. But unfortunately it would be by means of Israel being broken off from the vine and the Gentiles grafted onto the vine in Israel's place (Rom. 11:13–24).

Yet, as Paul said, this would be only temporary until the "full number of the Gentiles has come in" to the Kingdom; in the end all Israel will be saved (Rom. 11:25–27).

Jesus And The Romans

At the end of the final week and after several trials, the Jewish leaders handed Jesus of Nazareth over to the Romans to be crucified. The crucifixion of Jesus was a crucial point in Luke's Gospel as he wrote to the Roman Excellency Theophilus (Luke 23:26–49). What was Jesus' attitude as a Jew toward the Roman officials who governed his country during his life? What was the church's attitude toward Rome since Rome played a large role in the crucifixion? The answers could become an important part in the adjudication of Paul's case before the Roman government.

Luke structured into his deposition several accounts of Jesus in contact and interaction with Roman officials. These included tax collectors who, while still Jews, were working on contract for the Roman government to collect various types of taxes from the Jewish people. In his Gospel Luke describes Roman officials in favorable terms. This also included the tax collectors especially as they were compared with the Pharisees, scribes, and other Jewish purists. This was an important point to get across to Theophilus as Roman officials in Palestine considered the Pharisees and their kind as the main agitators against Roman rule. In the preaching of John the Baptist, for example, tax collectors came out favorably (Luke 3:12–13). They were not condemned for working for Rome; they were told only not to collect more than required.

Luke recorded the call of Levi the tax collector to be one of Jesus' disciples (Luke 5:27–32), a fact that was sure to attract a favorable response from Theophilus. Luke also recorded the criticism that Jesus received from the Pharisees and Scribes when Jesus later went to Levi's house for a banquet with tax collectors and others. The Pharisees and Scribes considered tax collectors as sinners and anyone associating with them as equally corrupt.

In his answer Jesus did not deny the assertion that the tax collectors were sinners. Nor did he deny righteousness to the Pharisees and Scribes. What he pointed out was that his mission was to sinners, a mission that under the then-current definition would include Roman officials as well. His mission was to call them to repentance as John the Baptist had earlier done.

In another comparison with the religious purists, Luke recorded a parable that Jesus told about a Pharisee and a tax collector who both entered the temple to pray. The Pharisee extolled himself as he prayed—he was not like robbers, evildoers, adulterers, or even the nearby tax collector. The tax collector in his prayer, on the other hand, could not even lift his eyes to heaven but bowed his head in contrition begging God to have mercy on him, a sinner.

Jesus announced that it was the tax collector, even with his Roman connections, and not the Pharisee with his credentials of purity, who returned home having been put right with God through prayer. From this parable Jesus drew an application that was universal for both Jew and non-Jew: "...For everyone who exalts himself will be humbled, and he who humbles himself will be exalted" (Luke 18:14).

Luke also recorded the account of Jesus meeting Zacchaeus, a chief tax collector, which meant Zacchaeus had connections with high Roman officials in Palestine (Luke 19:1–10). Indeed, he was a high official in the regional Roman government, having under him several petty collectors who did the actual work of collecting taxes. Because of Zacchaeus' high status, people no doubt considered him a greater sinner than most other tax collectors. So when Jesus announced he was going to stay with Zacchaeus, the people grumbled. But Zacchaeus immediately protested this stereotyping of his person. To be sure many tax collectors were corrupt, but to prove he was not he offered to give half of his possessions to the poor and to repay back fourfold anyone he may have cheated. Upon hearing this, Jesus pronounced Zacchaeus, even with his high Roman connections, a son of Abraham.

The reason for the pronouncement was his mission: he had come to seek and save what was lost. In other words, it was not status that determined whether a person was lost or not. Rather it was what the person, whether Jew or Roman, did in repentance and showing mercy.

Luke depicted Pilate, the Roman governor who presided over the trial and sentencing of Jesus, in perhaps a more favorable light than what history in general has treated him. When some Jews, for example, told Jesus of the time when Pilate murdered some Galileans as they were making sacrifices (Luke 13:1–9), Luke wrote that Jesus redirected the story to bring a lesson on the need for all to repent; otherwise they too will perish.

During Jesus' trial Luke reported how Pilate told the Jewish leaders three times that he had not found Jesus guilty of anything worthy of death (Luke 23:1–25). During one trial session Pilate sent Jesus over to Herod, the ruler of Galilee where Jesus was from, and Pilate's arch competitor for power and favors from Rome. This act of deference from Pilate to the ruling authority of Herod in this case dissipated the enmity between Pilate and Herod and they became friends.

In Luke's account of the trial, Pilate tried to release Jesus three times. But the crowd wanted Barabbas, an insurrectionist condemned to die. Pilate argued with the crowd and its leaders but to no avail. The crowd grew louder in shouting down Pilate. Pilate soon capitulated and delivered Jesus to the will of the crowd to be crucified.

The Crucifixion

Jesus was led by Roman soldiers to a place of crucifixion outside the city of Jerusalem (Luke 23:26–49). Two criminals were taken to be crucified as well. All three were nailed to crosses and left suspended in agony for six hours. The Jewish leaders sneered at Jesus, the soldiers mocked him, and even one of the criminals hurled insults. The other criminal, however, rebuked the first and then asked Jesus to remember him when he came into his kingdom. Jesus promised the criminal that on that day he would be with him in paradise.

At about the sixth hour, or twelve noon, a darkness came over the land lasting until three in the afternoon. Jesus then called out with a loud voice, "Father, into your hands I commit my spirit." And then Jesus died.

During these six hours the Roman Centurion in charge of the crucifixion watched, wavering back and forth between the taunts of the Jewish leaders and his own growing admiration for Jesus as he hung on the cross. But at the end, as Jesus slipped from life, he gave his verdict. "Surely this was a righteous man" (Luke 23:47). This was a verdict made by a Roman official in opposition to the Jewish leaders.

It was also a verdict that would doubtlessly impact Theophilus' thinking, especially as he contemplated the legal brief he would write. The conclusion to the whole matter was simple.

Jesus was innocent.

But he was more than innocent. He was also right.[1]

The Gentiles are indeed to be included in his kingdom. Therefore, Paul was not guilty of the charges leveled against him.

We do not know, of course, if Theophilus ever used Luke's Gospel to prepare a brief as we have outlined in this chapter. There is, however, one hint as to how this Gospel may have impacted his life in another way. Luke wrote a second document to Theophilus: the Acts of the Apostles, a history of the expansion of the church throughout the Roman Empire up to the time of the imprisonment of Paul at Rome. In this second document Luke addressed Theophilus as simply Theophilus, without the honorific Excellency.

During the first century Christians did not address each other with the honorific Excellency. Perhaps after reading Luke's life of Christ, Theophilus believed and claimed Jesus of Nazareth as his own Lord, too.

Questions For Discussion

1. In what ways do you think the missionary hermeneutic of the Scriptures guided Luke in selecting events and sayings from the life of Christ for inclusion in his Gospel?

2. Read Luke 7:1–10, 36–50 and discuss how these two events formed the precedent for Paul's teaching in Rom. 3:29–30.

3. From Luke's Gospel, in what ways do you see Jesus "living" the missionary hermeneutic of the Old Testament and not just teaching about it?

4. Read Luke 17:11–19 and Rom. 10:12–13 and then explain how the former provides the precedent for the latter in the missionary interpretation of the Scriptures.

Endnote

1. Peter Doble (1993), in a recent review of the relevant literature, rejects the sense of innocence for translating the Greek word dikaios in Luke 23:47. His arguments against this appear sound but only up to a certain point, for the concept of innocence should not be dismissed as a component composing the semantic range of dikaios. This sense was available to Luke and it may have been uppermost in his mind in writing about the Centurion's pronouncement. On the other hand, dikaios certainly had a range of meaning that is difficult if not impossible to match with an English equivalent. It is a range, I believe, that is apparent when the missionary understanding of the Hebrew Scriptures, and for which Paul was in prison, is taken into account. Under this hermeneutic dikaios takes on the broader meaning that Jesus was indeed justified and right in the way he lived his life and treated the Gentiles, and for that reason the sentence of crucifixion was inappropriate and unjust.

Another point of contention in this regard is the difference between Luke and Mark, who had the Centurion pronouncing Jesus as Son of God (there are no definite articles used with this expression in the Greek of Mark 15:39). According to Doble the current explanation for this is that Luke's account is a "redaction" of Mark's. However, it is plausible that the Centurion could have said both and that Luke chose dikaios because this pronouncement fit in better with his purpose in writing his Gospel. That purpose, as I have maintained, was in defense of the missionary hermeneutic of the Hebrew Scriptures. In this regard Mark may be a "redaction" of Luke or of one of Luke's sources. It seems equally plausible that the Centurion said dikaios but Mark, in writing for his audience, chose to translate this term with the expression "Son of God." Exegetically there is only a difference in perspective in translation between the two expressions, for without any definite articles the expression "Son of God" may be considered an attribute of Jesus; i.e., Jesus was a "godly person." At this point we return full circle to the significance of Luke 23:47. That is to say, in the estimation of the Centurion Jesus was truly God-like in the face of an unjust trial and execution on the cross.

CHAPTER FIFTEEN

The Great Commission

I opened the envelope with some curiosity. The return address revealed that the letter came from a well-respected pastor who had recently asked me to preach in his place while he recovered from minor surgery.

I pulled the letter from the envelope and read it. The message urged me to reconsider my decision in going to Thailand as a missionary. My talent for preaching, the pastor argued, was too good to be spent and wasted on some foreign mission field. Let those with less ability go. Since good preaching talent was scarce, I should stay in the United States to become one of "the better preachers."

While the pastor meant well—and his letter was a sincere though exaggerated compliment—I could not follow his advice, especially not after the risen Lord had spoken to me through the Great Commission.

The Resurrection

On the third day counting from the crucifixion, Jesus of Nazareth rose from the dead. When two women first broke the news on that Sunday morning, Jesus' disciples did not believe them, for the words seemed like nonsense (Luke 24:11). Peter and John ran to the tomb to investigate and found it empty. While John believed at that point, Peter walked away wondering what had happened.

Fear seized all the disciples, for if the Jewish leaders and Roman officials learned of this, it could only be concluded that the soldiers had blundered in crucifying Jesus and that somehow he had survived, or the soldiers had been lax in guarding the tomb and the body stolen. In either event the Roman officials would come looking for the disciples. This time the disciples would not be spared but would be interrogated, beaten, and possibly killed in hopes of extracting information from them regarding the location of Jesus or at least his body.

It is not difficult to sympathize with the fearful disciples. The trials, beatings, and crucifixion of Jesus no doubt traumatized them, so much so that some years later this was still remembered vividly, prompting Mark apparently to close his Gospel with the words "They [the women] said nothing to anyone, because they were afraid" (Mark 16:8). (It was only later that an ending was attached to his Gospel which included the Great Commission.)

This fear was not unexpected. The soldiers guarding Jesus' tomb, for example, went to tell only the chief priests about the events surrounding the resurrection: the earthquake, the angel, the stone rolled away, and so forth (Matt. 28:11–15). It was to everyone's advantage to keep this news away from the Roman governor Pilate. So the chief priests bribed the soldiers to spread the rumor that Jesus' disciples came and stole the body away. Should this rumor reach Pilate, the disciples would be in danger. But so would the soldiers for derelict duty. So the chief priests promised that should Pilate hear, they would make things right with him.

On that first resurrection Sunday the disciples locked themselves in a room for fear of the Jewish leaders (John 20:19–29). Jesus suddenly appeared among them and they were overjoyed. But Thomas the Twin was not there. When they later told Thomas they had seen the Lord, he retorted, "Unless I see the nail marks in his hands and put my finger where the nails were, and put my hand into his side, I will not believe."

A week later, in the same house, Jesus appeared again to the disciples, and Thomas was with them. Jesus invited Thomas to put his finger on the nail wounds and his hand into his side. "Stop doubting and believe," Jesus exhorted. Thomas did, and it was a turning point in his life. "My Lord and my God!" exclaimed Thomas.

All Authority

The disciples' recognition of Jesus as Lord and God was the finishing touch on the missionary understanding of the Hebrew Scriptures. Now that Jesus had risen from the dead it had become clear that he was not only the Messiah of the Jews but he was also God and creator of all things (John 1:1–3)—indeed, all things were created by him and for him (Col. 1:16).

Moreover, he sustains the created universe by his powerful word (Heb. 1:2–3). Now Jesus' name must be proclaimed and praised among the nations. His salvation must be taken to the ends of the earth. It will be Jesus who judges the nations in righteousness.

The resurrection also demonstrated that Jesus was Yahweh, the "High Lord" who may order his creation around as he desires (see Chapter Four). God made him "both Lord and Christ," Peter declared (Acts 2:36). "There is but one Lord, Jesus Christ," Paul exclaimed, "through whom all things came and through whom we live" (1 Cor. 8:6). And in reminiscence of the Shema of Deut. 6:4 (see Chapter Nine), since there is only one Lord (Eph. 4:5), he is universally Lord over all, both Jews and Gentiles (Rom. 10:12).

In short, the universal Lordship of Jesus Christ meant that he had the authority to order his little band of disciples to do anything he wanted done anywhere in his creation. And order them he did.

Matt. 28:18-20

...All authority in heaven and on earth has been given to me. Therefore go and make disciples of all nations, baptizing them in the name of the Father and of the Son and of the Holy Spirit, and teaching them to obey everything I have commanded you. And surely I will be with you always, to the very end of the age.

In other words, Jesus received authority to make explicit what all along was implicit in the Old Testament Scriptures. The nations or Gentiles are to be included in God's Kingdom; this much was readily inferred. This was the missionary interpretation of the Scriptures. What was dimly perceived, if at all, was the command to therefore go and make disciples from among the Gentiles. Now these words became the explicit command for his disciples until the end of the age.

Some missiologists claim that the verb "Go!" in Matt. 28:18 above (and also in Mark 16:15) is not a command. The reason cited is that grammatically the Greek word translated "go" is a participle and not a verb in the imperative mood.

Therefore, the argument goes, the word should be translated into English as a verb having an -ing ending; e.g., "going." It is next claimed that the participle in Matt. 28:18 (and Mark 16:15) must be understood not as a command but as a temporal; e.g., "while going." That is to say, the Great Commission must be interpreted to read that while or as the disciples were going to different nations, they were to preach and make disciples. In this translation the command is not to go, but to preach and make disciples.

However, this claim is incorrect exegetically. While formally it is true that in the Greek of Matt. 28:18 (and Mark 16:15) the word go is a participle, this is where the Greek language of the New Testament differs from English. For in Greek a participle can take on the same force as the verb of its context (A. T. Robertson 1934). Since therefore the verb of the Great Commission in both Matthew and Mark is imperative or a command, the participle of going that precedes it is also imperative. In other words, it is just as imperative for disciples to go, as it is to preach and make disciples.

By the authority he received, Jesus sent the Holy Spirit upon the disciples to lead them into all truth (John 16:7–13) and to have power to be his witnesses to the ends of the earth (Acts 1:8). He next called Saul of Tarsus to become an apostle (Acts 9:15) in addition to those he had already chosen (Luke 6:13). Under his authority the Spirit interrupted the service of the fast-growing church at Antioch of Syria to send two of its five ministers (Barnabas and Saul) to the mission field (Acts 13:1–4). Later the Spirit of Jesus exercised authority again to direct Saul, now known as Paul, through Asia Minor and on into Macedonia in order to preach the Gospel in Europe (Acts 16:6–10).

But the "ordering around" of his disciples did not stop here. Jesus also made provision to organize all of his disciples making "some to be apostles, some to be prophets, some to be evangelists, and some to be pastors and teachers" (Eph. 4:11) so that the new Gentile disciples might be taught all things that he himself taught in order to prepare them for works of service in the church.

As Yahweh or Lord, Jesus ordered his band of disciples to baptize the Gentile converts. In one respect this is an unexpected command because there seems to be no immediate Old Testament precedent for baptism, nor is there any Jewish record of baptizing proselytes until A.D. 300. Yet, as T. M. Linsey (1967) states, no scholar doubts that baptism (immersion) was required of Gentile converts to Judaism from early times, for hermeneutically baptism was a "natural" for Gentiles in becoming descendants of Abraham and members of God's holy people.

Immersion in water easily simulated the "rebirthing" process that the Abrahamic covenant seemed to call for. This would be especially significant for female Gentiles. While males had to be circumcised, no comparable ceremony existed for females. Baptism, however, filled this void for women while also making circumcision complete for men.

John the Baptist extended this hermeneutic when he came preaching a baptism of repentance for the forgiveness of sin (Mark 1:4). People streamed from Jerusalem and the Judean countryside to confess their sins and be baptized. In other words, John proclaimed that baptism was no longer just for the Gentile to simulate another birth to become a descendant of Abraham, but it was for the Jew as well to simulate a spiritual renewal born of repentance and confession of sin. Upon repentance, confession, and baptism, there was the assurance of salvation or the forgiveness of sin.

In essence Jesus himself confirmed this hermeneutic when he came to be baptized by John the Baptist. John at first refused to baptize Jesus; to John's thinking it would make more sense for Jesus to baptize him. But Jesus insisted explaining that it is proper even for him to fulfill all righteousness (Matt. 3:15). That baptism played a part in making a person right before God was a matter of understanding what the Old Testament Scriptures meant. No longer was biological descent from Abraham important for being right with God. But a life washed and cleansed from all sin was essential (Ps. 51:2). For Jesus to do any less, even though he was sinless, was to do less than what the Scriptures fully mean.

In this regard, we should not be surprised that Jesus included baptism in the Great Commission. In its own way it summed up for the individual believer, whether Jew or Gentile, what the Old Testament means. To be a child of God by faith, there must be a renewed heart born again of water and the Spirit (John 3:5).

Beyond the new birth, however, baptism simulated the believer's own death, burial, and resurrection to a new life (Rom 6:3–4), just as Christ Jesus himself died, was buried, and raised from the dead according to the interpretation of Scripture from Moses to the prophets by the Lord himself (Luke 24:25–27). This is how the Old Testament was to be understood, Jesus told his disciples (Luke 24:45–46).

Therefore, Jesus ordered that repentance and forgiveness of sins be preached to all nations beginning at Jerusalem (Luke 24:47) so that whoever believes and is baptized shall be saved (Mark 16:16).

From Nation To Nation

God's desire is to include people of other nationalities in addition to the Jews in his salvation. This is clear from the Old Testament Scriptures. But as the Old Testament unfolded, a problem developed. How shall the Gentiles be included? At first God called only Abraham, then Isaac and not Ishmael, and then Jacob and not Esau.

Finally He elected only Israel to be his people. Jesus came and was born a Jew and died as a Jew. Even though his death was viewed as being for the whole world, this interpretation oddly enough was still dependent on Old Testament images and symbolism.

The world of the Bible consisted of tribes, peoples, and nations who spoke different tongues and languages. God was the cause of this condition at the Tower of Babel. He broke up a unified human race into different language and ethnic groups as the punishment for disobedience (Gen. 11:7–9). People at that time sought to contravene God's command by staying in one place and not inhabiting the whole earth.

Ethnicity, therefore, has been built into the fabric of the human race, and this in spite of modern ideology to the contrary. For example, ethnicity played a prominent role in the final disintegration of the Communist Russian empire and the reopening of that vast land mass in Europe and Asia to church renewal and evangelism among previously unreached tribes and peoples.

Jesus came to reconfirm through his life and work this desire of God to (re)include the Gentiles in his salvation. The ultimate reconfirmation of this desire, of course, is the Great Commission. It is as though Jesus himself was saying that the Father's wish is his command.

Theologically the Great Commission—preaching the Gospel in other nations—is necessary if God's desire is to be fulfilled. Otherwise, there would be only one other way, and that would be for the Christ to come time and again to die in and for each ethnic group that has ever existed. But this was not God's original plan. His plan was to send his Son to die in Jerusalem and that only once (Heb. 9:27–28), and then to have that death count for the whole world. The next stage, as is clear from the Great Commission, was to have apostles and evangelists, beginning in Jerusalem, take the news of this universal death for the sins of the world from one nation to another until they reach the ends of the earth.

The thrust of the Great Commission, therefore, is outward, across cultural boundaries into other ethnic groups speaking different languages. This, I believe, is the significance of calling Paul to be an apostle and why the Book of Acts turned out to be more Paul's story than Peter's. From what we know of Paul's background he was much more suited to this thrust than perhaps Peter was. To be sure, Peter was given the promise of being the first to preach the Gospel to the Gentiles (Acts 15:7). Plus Paul was a "Pharisee of the Pharisees," surpassing all his peers in the study of this Jewish sect (Phil. 3:5). Both of these facts, it seems, should have disqualified Paul from being chosen to preach to ethnic groups other than his own.

But Paul's Phariseeism was a veneer, an overlay acquired after having been socialized as both a Jew of the Dispersion (he was born in Tarsus) and a Roman citizen. Some time in his youth he went to study Pharisee doctrine in Jerusalem. In his studies he surpassed his peers not only because he was brilliant but also because he was a convert to Phariseeism. He was not born and reared in a Pharisee environment such as Jerusalem afforded. So he felt a need to prove his Pharisee devotion by doing more. He became "twice as much a son of hell" as the others (Matt. 23:15), or, to use his own words, "the chief of sinners" (1 Tim. 1:15 KJV).

But when this veneer was stripped away upon meeting Jesus on the road to Damascus (Acts 9:1–19), his bicultural background of being both Jew and Roman emerged and became prominent once more. He could be used as a vessel or chosen instrument to carry God's name to the Gentiles and their kings as well as to Israel. He was able to become a Jew to the Jew and a Greek to the Greek, in short to "become all things to all men" in order to save some (1 Cor. 9:19–23).

Even though the Great Commission is given to a fragmented world, it is still based on a universal feature of creation: all human beings regardless of ethnicity are made in the image of God (Gen. 1:27). There is an underlying unity to the diversity of peoples and languages.

As professor David Bidney used to say in his classes in Anthropology at Indiana University, there is a "psychic unity" among all humans. This unity is seen in the universal capacity of humans to understand each other across cultural boundaries, to see analogies of their own life in other ways of living. At a basic level, people of other cultures do indeed share much the same condition of human existence on earth.

That is to say, the Great Commission is based on the assumption that people of all cultures can "come to a knowledge of the truth" and be saved (1 Timothy 2:4), and to know what the perfect and good will of God is in their lives (Rom. 12:1–2). To restate the matter, the Great Commission is based on the ability of people in other cultures and speaking different languages to also "do theology."

One's own ethnic or sociocultural background is essential for an individual to have knowledge. An individual depends on his or her background as a hermeneutic for interpreting and coming to a knowledge of the world. Sociocultural background is also essential for gaining new knowledge, such as the Gospel would be when proclaimed for the first time to an individual. In such cases an individual refers to his or her own background for comparisons and contrasts to see what the Gospel means in the context of being a member of one's own social group. When these are thought through, a decision can be made regarding the Gospel's call to repentance and belief. (For a more extended discussion on the role that sociocultural factors play in the cognitive structure and processes of individuals, see David Filbeck 1985.)

Proclaiming the Gospel from nation to nation, as the Great Commission commands, is to achieve yet another desire of God. This is the "healing of the nations" (Rev. 22:2), undoing the divisive effects of the Tower of Babel and thereby producing a new unity of all humans. But this unity is not based on one language or one culture, but on faith in Jesus Christ (Eph. 2:11–22). This unity allows for and indeed draws upon sociocultural diversity for understanding the richness of the Gospel as well as for communicating the Gospel to the nations (Eph. 3:8).

At one time non-Jews were separated from Christ, excluded from citizenship in Israel and foreigners to the covenants of the promise, without hope and without God. But Christ Jesus himself brought both Jew and non-Jew together, tearing down the (cultural) wall of hostility that was between the two. He made the two one, making of the two a new man, thus establishing peace. He reconciled both through his cross. Therefore, the two are no longer foreigners and strangers to each other but members of the same household of God. Together they are God's people.

Perspectives In The Great Commission

In the forty days between his resurrection and ascension, Jesus taught the disciples many things regarding the Kingdom of God (Acts 1:3). One topic undoubtedly covered was the expansion of the Kingdom throughout the world. Jesus probably reminded the disciples of the Kingdom parables he had earlier taught the people (Matt. 13:31–35). The Kingdom, for example, is like a tiny mustard seed which grows and expands until birds can come and perch. Or the Kingdom is like yeast that is mixed in with flour until it is worked through all the dough. The Kingdom of God, in short, is to expand and spread throughout the earth until it has permeated every area of human life.

During this period Jesus also gave the Great Commission, the disciples' marching orders to expand and spread the Kingdom to the ends of the earth. In fact, the Great Commission was given several times, each time with a different set of words (Roger E. Hedlund 1991). The accounts as recorded in Luke 24:47 and John 20:21–22, for example, were given in Jerusalem on the day of the resurrection. Matt. 28:18–20 was given while in Galilee. And Acts 1:8 was given on the Mount of Olives back in Jerusalem.

Each new set of words, moreover, gave a different perspective on the work that needed to be done with respect to the expansion of the Kingdom. Consequently when it came time for the four Gospel writers to write their biographies of Jesus Christ, each writer chose from the Lord's words that particular perspective in the Great Commission which he wished to emphasize.

From the accounts of the Great Commission given in Matthew (28:18–20), Mark (16:15–16) and Luke (24:46–47, including Acts 1:8), we see three perspectives regarding the work of expanding the Kingdom of God throughout the world.

Make Disciples...Teach. This is Matthew's perspective on the Great Commission task of taking God's salvation to the ends of the earth. His perspective came from the impact that Jesus had made on his life at the time when Jesus called him to be a disciple (Matt. 9:9–13). Matthew was a tax collector, a "sinner" in the view of the Jewish purists. Yet, Jesus as a rabbi called him and over the next three years taught him the truth regarding the Messiah and God's plan for the Gentiles as revealed in the Scriptures. This was, in other words, a method of evangelizing nonbelievers that he could recommend first-hand.

Preach. This is the perspective of both Mark and Luke in their Gospels. This perspective was certainly influenced by what Jesus himself did when he began his ministry.

Mark 1:14 KJV
Now after that John was put in prison, Jesus came into Galilee, preaching the gospel of the kingdom of God.

In fact, preaching was what Jesus said he had come to do.

Luke 4:43–44, KJV
And he said unto [the disciples], I must preach the kingdom of God to other cities also, therefore am I sent. And he preached in the synagogues of Galilee.

The task in this perspective on the Great Commission is to preach. Since this was the method Jesus used upon entering for the first time in Jewish society, it was a method that both Mark and Luke could recommend for future evangelists as they entered non-Jewish societies around the world.

Witnesses. This is a perspective on the Great Commission that Luke used in the Book of Acts. Jesus' disciples are to be his witnesses to the ends of the earth (Acts 1:8). This perspective Jesus himself had earlier taught the disciples.

John 15:26–27 KJV
But when the Comforter is come, whom I will send unto you from the Father, even the Spirit of truth, which proceedeth from the Father, he shall testify of me. And ye also shall bear witness, because ye have been with me from the beginning.

But being witnesses for Jesus Christ also reflected the missionary strategy of the Jews in the Dispersion, which was followed by the Apostles of the early church and which Luke had observed first hand. This was Peter's method, for example, after he had been chosen to be the first one to proclaim the Gospel to a Gentile, the Roman Centurion named Cornelius.

Acts 10:39–42
We are witnesses of everything he did in the country of the Jews and in Jerusalem. They killed him by hanging him on a tree, but God raised him from the dead on the third day and caused him to be seen. He was not seen by all the people, but by witnesses whom God had already chosen—by us who ate and drank with him after he rose from the dead. He commanded us to preach to the people and to testify that he is the one whom God appointed as judge of the living and the dead.

Peter ended his witness by offering an "invitation" to Cornelius and his household: "All the prophets testify about him that everyone who believes in him receives forgiveness of sins through his name." When the Holy Spirit descended on Cornelius and his household, Peter could find no excuse for denying them baptism (Acts 10:46–47).

This method established Christian churches in city after Gentile city beginning in Antioch of Syria (Acts 11:19–26) from where churches began to be established throughout Galatia, Asia Minor, Macedonia, and Achaia. The church at Rome was in all probability established when converts from the first day of Pentecost (Acts 2:1–10), or perhaps Paul's relatives who were Christians even before Paul (Rom. 16:7), returned to Rome and witnessed to others about their new-found faith in Jesus Christ.

Each perspective above brings with it a distinctive contribution to the Great Commission task of being a light to the Gentiles in order to bring God's salvation to the ends of the earth. To make disciples implies an intimate, personal approach to winning the lost to Christ. To preach brings forth the image of boldness, of intruding to make an announcement or proclamation never before made: repent, for the Kingdom of God has come. The announcement is "news" in its literal sense for never before has it been proclaimed. Preaching connotes that the announcement of the kingdom is a proclamation, formal and official. To witness gives the opposite impression of informally telling others what Jesus has done to bring salvation to the world. It is carried on at home, at market, at work, and while traveling and on vacation.

All of this adds up to the various gifts that Christ has given to the church to fulfill the Great Commission in this world. Some have the gift of making disciples, of encouraging, exhorting, and teaching others on a personal basis to know the Lord (Rom. 12:3–8). Others can preach, to proclaim the name of Christ before others in formal settings. Still others have the gift of witnessing about Christ while sitting beside another on a restaurant stool or in an airplane seat.

No one Christian in the church is capable in every gift just mentioned. The Apostle Paul recognized this. This is why he assembled groups or teams of missionaries to travel with him. First came Barnabas and Mark, next Silas and Timothy, and later Luke and Titus. Each was gifted where Paul was not. This wisdom is still employed today in forming missionary teams to carry God's salvation to the ends of the earth. In this way the church uses every possible person and gift in order to save those who are lost.

The Church

When Jesus gave the Great Commission he also instructed his disciples to wait in Jerusalem for the Holy Spirit to give them the power to be his witnesses to the ends of the earth (Acts 1:8). The Holy Spirit descended on the disciples some ten days later on the Day of Pentecost (Acts 2). People from at least fourteen different nations were present in Jerusalem to celebrate this Jewish festival.

Peter preached and on that day 3000 people were baptized. This Pentecost is considered the beginning of the church.

In one respect we have now exceeded the original scope of this book as outlined in the beginning. In Chapter Four we stated that, in order to demonstrate the Old Testament basis to world missions today, we need to discuss the Bible only from Genesis 1 to Acts 1, for in this part we see developing and coming to completion a missionary understanding of the Hebrew Scriptures. The rest of the Bible, from Acts 2 onward, would be referred to in order to show the missionary interpretation of the Old Testament in action and exposition in the New Testament church.

In reality, however, we have not exceeded our scope by including the church and its establishment in this chapter on the Great Commission because the missionary hermeneutic or understanding of the Scriptures that also ultimately brought forth the church preceded the Great Commission.

The prototype of the New Testament church was the Jewish synagogue. The Hebrew Scriptures contained no command to establish the synagogue, but once established it was not questioned. Indeed, the synagogue seemed necessary as Jews were dispersed from Palestine throughout the world. As Jews witnessed to their Gentile neighbors about the one God over all nations, the synagogue became indispensable in incorporating Gentile proselytes into Jewish life and communities.

It is equally remarkable that in the New Testament Scriptures there is no command requiring the church to be established. Rather, as we read the Gospels we see that the establishment of the church—it would indeed be established in due time—is a "given." "Upon this rock I shall build my church," Jesus declared (Matt. 16:18). Its eventual establishment was not questioned, just as the synagogue was not earlier questioned in Judaism even though no instruction in the Old Testament required it.

That the establishment of the church was a "given" in the Gospels is due in large measure to the prior success of synagogues in incorporating proselytes into Judaism. That is to say, in view of the missionary hermeneutic of the Hebrew Scriptures which Jesus Christ confirmed, and which anticipated the Great Commission, it was inevitable that the church would also be established for the task of making disciples of the nations.

When, for example, some Christian Jews of a Dispersion background witnessed to Greeks or non-Jews in Antioch of Syria, and many believed, the church at Jerusalem sent Barnabas to encourage them (Acts 11:19–26). He needed more help, so he traveled to Tarsus to recruit Paul to return to Antioch with him to help teach the new Gentile believers.

They met with the new believers, now called a church, for a whole year and the Gentile disciples were called Christians first at Antioch.

Not long after this, at the close of their first apostolic missionary journey (Acts 13–14), Paul and Barnabas made their return trip by retracing their journey through the Gentile cities of Lystra, Iconium, and Antioch of Pisidia where they had only recently preached. By this time, in addition to the Jews who had believed, Gentiles had also been converted to belief in Jesus Christ. Without any comment on when and how churches in these cities were organized, Luke reported that Paul and Barnabas appointed elders in the churches of each city (Acts 14:23).

In short, it was expected that churches would be organized among believing Jews who (formerly) attended the synagogue, as the Gospel was preached to the Gentiles. A church among and for Gentile believers, to help guide and incorporate these new Gentile disciples in the way of the Lord, was the natural outcome of obeying the Great Commission of Jesus Christ.

Later, in keeping with the outward thrust of the Great Commission, these same churches became the source of additional missionaries for further outreach into other Gentile cities. At Lystra, when Paul revisited the church there, a young man named Timothy joined him (Acts 16:1–3).

Later other men such as Tychicus, Aristarchus, and Epaphras (Col. 4:7–12) would also serve. They would teach the many Gentile converts of Colossea, Laodicea, and other places where Paul would be unable to go and preach.

Questions For Discussion

1. Why is the resurrection of Jesus Christ important in fulfilling the Great Commission in today's pluralistic world?

2. From reflection on the crucifixion of Jesus, why is preaching the Gospel in other nations and ethnic groups necessary?

3. Compare and contrast the different perspectives on evangelism contained in the various accounts of the Great Commission.

4. Why does it appear "natural" that the church should be established when a missionary has gone to preach in another nation?

Section IV

The Wealth of the Nations

CHAPTER SIXTEEN

The Twenty-First Century

What lies behind the Great Commission?

Everything!

The Great Commission is:

- the conclusion to the Old Testament;
- the result of the missionary hermeneutic of the Old Testament;
- the summation of the missionary message of the Old Testament;
- what the Old Testament is meant to mean, the true and final interpretation of the Hebrew Scriptures.

The Great Commission makes the missionary imperative of the Old Testament grammatically real. No longer do we see it theologically, as perhaps through a "glass darkly" (1 Cor. 13:12 KJV). The Great Commission makes the missionary mandate of the Old Testament explicit and clear.

The Great Commission is the capstone of the Old Testament message, the agenda for the church until the end of the age. So what else is there to do but go and preach the Gospel to every human?

More important than what lies behind the Great Commission, therefore, is what lies ahead. Where is the missionary message of the Old Testament as summarized in the Great Commission leading us, the church?

The Priority Of Missions

Since 1792, the beginning of the modern missionary movement, we have seen tremendous growth in the number of missionaries serving at any one time, from a few dozen in 1792 to more than 150,000 in 1992. But as Ralph D. Winter (1992) reported, the missionary movement from 1992 onward faces such an avalanche of retirement that even if 25,000 new missionaries were to be sent out over the subsequent ten-year period we would be barely holding our own in the overall number of missionaries available for the twenty-first century. The church may have reached a plateau in sending out missionaries.[1]

What can be done in getting beyond this plateau? The answer should be apparent. Now that we know what lies behind the Great Commission, we should return to the Old Testament for its mobilizing power in motivating an ever increasing number of personnel for evangelizing the world of the twenty-first century.

It is still God's purpose for his people, the church, to be a light to the nations in order to bring his salvation to the ends of the earth.

Over the past 200 years the church has been planted on every continent of the earth. Yet, as the twenty-first century opens up we see that two-thirds of the world's population remain non-Christian. What is disturbing is that this one-to-three ratio may form a "ceiling" which we will find difficult to break through in the decades to come. Indeed, there are signs that this ratio is actually widening in favor of the non-Christian population. David B. Barrett (1992), in his work on the status of the world Christian movement, states that:

> Each day some 234,200 hitherto unevangelized persons become evangelized. However, unevangelized individuals are increasing every day through birth by 257,800 persons. So, overall, we are losing the battle to evangelize [the non-Christian world] at the rate of 23,600 persons every day.

This increase of the unevangelized over the evangelized is unfortunately projected to continue into the twenty-first century—unless, of course, we utilize once more, as the church of the first century did, the Scriptures of the Old Testament to understand God's perfect will for the nations of the earth. From the Old Testament the church of today can learn that God's desire for his people is still to bring his salvation to the ends of the earth.

From the opening chapters of Genesis we see that sin is the universal condition of humans. Throughout the Old Testament God called his people to be the light of the world and to proclaim his name among the nations.

The purpose of the call, to proclaim the forgiveness of sins throughout the earth, is still operative for his people. Obeying this call and its purpose, therefore, must be first in the agenda of the church.

Evangelizing and winning the lost to Jesus Christ is still the mandate of the whole Bible for the church. Good works—and there are many that the church can perform—are secondary to the priority of proclaiming his salvation, the forgiveness of sin, throughout the world.

Preaching the Gospel to the lost, especially to those who had never before heard the Gospel, was Paul's policy and first priority.

Rom. 15:15–16, 19–20
I have written you quite boldly on some points, as if to remind you of them again, because of the grace God gave me to be a minister of Christ Jesus to the Gentiles with the priestly duty of proclaiming the gospel of God, so that the Gentiles might become an offering acceptable to God, sanctified by the Holy Spirit...So from Jerusalem all the way around to Illyricum, I have fully proclaimed the gospel of Christ. It has always been my ambition to preach the gospel where Christ was not known...

Paul went on in this text to cite Old Testament authority for this policy.

Rom. 15:21, from Isa. 52:15
Rather, as it is written: "Those who were not told about him will see, and those who have not heard will understand."

Isa. 52:13–15 is a text describing the suffering servant of God. The words were therefore interpreted to be a description of the Messiah. In this passage Isaiah said that God's servant would be exalted even though he was disfigured and rejected. Because of the servant's (Messiah's) exaltation, the kings of the earth would then know and understand things about the servant that had never been told before. Hermeneutically to Paul, the exaltation of the Christ was in essence a command to preach the Gospel of Christ in places where Christ had never before been proclaimed.

In other words, only by proclamation can Christ be exalted in previously unreached areas. Missions, or evangelizing the nations, therefore, is still the top priority of the Scriptures, both Old and New Testaments. This is the message that is meant for us to learn from the Old Testament. This message, furthermore, has been concisely summarized for us in the Great Commission.

Pluralism And Evangelism

From Genesis we also learn that the proclamation of God's salvation is to take place within the context of the nations—the ethnic groups, tribes, nations, and peoples of the world—and not in terms of individualism. In other words, evangelism is to take place within the context of pluralism.

Paradoxically the world we live in is becoming more pluralistic even as it becomes "smaller" in a real sense. As peoples of the world draw closer together in real time through instant communication and the jet airplane, we see a reaction. People rush to find ways of maintaining ethnic and cultural distinctives. Even where such distinctives have been suppressed, as soon as the agent of suppression has been removed, cultural and linguistic distinctives (whether old, new or modified) (re)emerge.

The increasing pluralization of society has been alarming to Christians of the West, especially in the United States. To be sure, comfort can be found in living in a more homogeneous society whose culture, values, and laws are more or less based on a Judeo-Christian view of the world. But we must remember that social homogeneity was not the world of the Old Testament nor of the New Testament world when the church was first established. The Biblical world was pluralistic. Indeed, God called Abraham and chose his descendants to be one more ethnic group in an already highly pluralistic earth. God has also established his church to be another people-group among the thousands of peoples already populating the earth.

The world of the twenty-first century will become more pluralistic, not less, even as we draw closer technologically. Ironically it is technology as a common element in pluralism that will enable the world to become more pluralistic. It is part of the "Third Wave" that Alvin Toffler (1980) discusses. Life will become more decentralized than ever before. People will organize their lives into more and more groups and subgroups.

Communication and relationship among these groups will no longer be hierarchically arranged as in the recent past but will be accomplished by networking along lines of special interests—such as status, language, occupation, hobbies—that happen to overlap.

If there is a lesson in this that we can learn from the missionary message of the Old Testament, it is this. We should not decry the pluralism we see taking shape. Rather, we should theologically recognize it for what it is: It is the constraint that God has placed on all humans so that as we seek him we may find him on his terms of faith and not on the all too human traits of power, empire, ideology, politics, cultural superiority, language, and so forth. As the church we must recognize and become obedient once more to the role that the tribes, peoples, and nations play in God's plan and strategy—the mystery of the Gospel (Eph. 6:19)—for the proclamation of salvation throughout the world.

This is not a comforting view of the future. But then the call of God was never meant to be. The call of Abraham, including the existence of his descendants since that time, was and has more often than not been considered an unwelcome intrusion of God into the affairs of the nations. Jesus proclaimed that he came not to bring peace but a sword: there would be division between parent and child, husband and wife, mother-in-law and daughter-in-law. (Matt. 10:34–36).

The church is also considered an unwelcome intruder into the affairs of nations, especially in nations that are secular or whose predominant religions are non-Christian. The missionary, pastor, and evangelist are looked upon as intruders into an otherwise peaceful and functioning society. The church is viewed as a "misfit" in the society. The society already has a religion: Islam, Buddhism, Hinduism, animism. To many, the Gospel and its messengers only bring division to society. But, of course, to those who are called, a new unity is forged that in essence bypasses the dictates of language, custom, and culture. Such unity does not deny their legitimacy or use. Rather, they are used by God through the Great Commission to create a new bond of peace between Him and believer, and believer with believer (Eph. 4:1–4).

From Mission To Missionary Sending Churches

The lesson of pluralism from the Old Testament is not confined to the church of the West or United States. The Old Testament Scriptures have a missionary message for mission churches planted throughout the world as well. As has all too often happened, it has been too easy for churches in non-Christian environments to withdraw into Christian enclaves, even looking to the Scriptures to find support and rationale for isolating themselves from the world at large.

This habit must be broken if all remaining unreached people and ethnic groups are to be evangelized by the year 2000 (Bill and Amy Sterns 1991). It is estimated that one-third of the world, or 1.2 billion people, have never before been evangelized or ever heard of the Gospel of Jesus Christ (David B. Barrett and Todd M. Johnson 1990).

This mass of unevangelized people is further broken down into 12,000 people groups—groups where no churches have been established or where the number of Christians is so few that they are yet unable to impact the group in evangelism in any significant way.

It is also estimated that 100,000 new missionaries and an annual budget of $300 million are needed to enter each of the 12,000 unreached people groups and plant a witnessing church by the year 2000. To accomplish this mission, however, will require personnel and finances from mission churches planted in the nineteenth and twentieth centuries. For example, many of these unreached groups live in close proximity to groups already evangelized and where the church is well established. These churches, if properly motivated, can do their part in evangelizing the unreached.

By turning to the missionary message of the Old Testament and its motivating power for mobilizing the people of God, the habit of isolationism can be broken on the part of mission churches and unreached groups can be evangelized.

The missionary message of the Old Testament must be taught in the mission churches that were established in the nineteenth and twentieth centuries so they can become missionary sending churches in the twenty-first century.

Lois McKinney (1993) sums up the educational task that lies ahead of us quite well.

A major task of missionary education in the twenty-first century will be to bring...disparate disciplinary streams back into the single flow of Mission Dei. The story of what God is doing in the world will flow from the Old Testament, where God reveals himself in history as he prepares the world for the Messiah. It will flow on into the New Testament where Jesus' incarnation, life, death, resurrection, and coming Kingdom are revealed. It will flow from the sending of the Holy Spirit and the beginnings of the church through twenty centuries of history of the church's expansion. It will flow on into the future as it records the histories of the emerging Third-World churches and their missions movements.

Questions For Discussion

1. How does the Old Testament demonstrate the priority of missions for the church today?

2. What is the message of the Old Testament with regard to the pluralism we see in the world?

3. In what ways do you think the Old Testament can motivate and mobilize the church today for world missions?

Endnote

1. David Howard in personal communication, however, remarks that the statistics in this paragraph refer only to the missionaries from the traditional missionary sending countries of North America and Europe. When missionaries from other countries—the "Third World" nations—are included, their number in the future may very well offset any decrease in the number of Euro-American missionaries. This means that instead of a decrease in the number of missionaries in the next century, there could be an even greater number than what we see now.

CHAPTER SEVENTEEN

To God Be The Glory

There is a greater purpose and meaning to the Old Testament and the Great Commission than twenty-first century missions, however. The Apostle Paul summed it up in a stirring doxology to an inspiring passage on missions that he dictated in Ephesians 3.

In this chapter Paul told of a special insight (hermeneutic) he had regarding the mystery of the Christ; i.e., the mission of the Christ on earth. That insight was this: by means of the Gospel the Gentiles are heirs with Israel in the promise of salvation which the Christ came to offer. It is through Jesus Christ and by means of faith in him that Gentiles can claim this inheritance. This insight was termed the "manifold wisdom of God" and is the duty of the church to proclaim (Eph. 3:10).

With proclamation being the duty of the church Paul next prayed that the members of the Ephesian church would be firmly established in the love of Christ in order to understand this insight and to have the power to fulfill the duty that follows to the "measure of the fullness of God" (Eph. 3:19). Paul's prayer was that their proclamation would indeed faithfully match the full extent of God's desire for the Gentiles to be included in his salvation.

At this Paul breaks forth into a doxology of praise to God:

Eph. 3:20–21
Now to him who is able to do immeasurably more than all we ask or imagine, according to his power that is at work within us, to him be glory in the church and in Christ Jesus throughout all generations, for ever and ever! Amen.

Paul associated the inclusion of the Gentiles—ethnic groups other than Jews—into God's Kingdom with giving glory to God, not only through Christ Jesus but also in the church. This relationship is still valid today. In fact, it is operative throughout all generations—for as many generations as this final age shall have. The ethnic groups of this world are to be evangelized with the Good News of Jesus Christ until the end of time.

That evangelizing the lost in our own ethnic group brings glory to God in the local church is clear enough. But local evangelism within one's own ethnic group amounts to only a halfway measure in giving glory to God. It is only by extending outward to evangelize ethnic groups not our own—world mission—that we can complete the full measure of giving glory to God in the church in this generation and for every future generation to come.

The Nations And God's Glory

World missions have unfortunately become a neglected dimension in giving glory to God. In the Scriptures the term glory is a multidimensional concept. The word refers to more than a bright, dazzling light associated with the appearance of God (Acts 7:55).

Actually in this regard the term refers to the presence of God, especially as he exhibits his power for humans to see. When the Tabernacle or Tent of Meeting was finally set up, for example, "the glory of the Lord filled the tabernacle" (Exod. 40:34). The Psalmist states that the "heavens declare the glory of God, the skies proclaim the work of his hands" (Ps. 19:1), and then instructs us to "ascribe the Lord glory and strength" (Ps. 29:1). In this respect Israel was chosen to be God's glory (Isa. 43:7), to be a people for God's renown, praise, and honor (Jer. 13:11). They were to glorify God, praising him for his mighty works and deliverance.

In the New Testament the term glory refers to splendor; e.g., the splendor of Solomon which could not match the beauty of lilies in the field (Matt. 6:28–29), and to praising God (Luke 2:13–14). Jesus used this term to refer to the equality that he shared with the Father in divine status, power, and authority before his incarnation. In his high priestly prayer before his crucifixion, Jesus prayed:

John 17:4–5
I have brought you glory on earth by completing the work you gave me to do. And now, Father, glorify me in your presence with the glory I had with you before the world began.

The Apostle Peter used the term to refer to the resurrection of Jesus Christ (Acts 3:13–15). The writer of Hebrews states that the Son still shares divine equality with the Father, for he is "the radiance of God's glory and the exact representation of his being, sustaining all things by his powerful word" (Heb. 1:3). Finally the term is used to refer to the eternal life that the redeemed shall receive, the "crown of glory that will never fade away" (1 Pet. 5:4).

At this point, however, when glory is discussed, a crucial dimension is often overlooked. The glory of God, the glory that God deserves, is also bound up with the nations (Gentiles). "Declare his glory among the nations," David commanded. "Ascribe to the Lord, O families of nations…ascribe to the Lord the glory due his name" (1 Chron. 16:25, 28–29). His glory is to be proclaimed among the nations of the earth so that the nations may glorify God in turn. Jesus Christ came to confirm the promises made to the patriarchs so that the Gentiles may glorify God for his mercy (Rom. 15:8–9).

When Cornelius and his household, the first Gentiles, believed and received the Holy Spirit (Acts 10:45), the Jewish believers in Jerusalem glorified God for granting the Gentiles repentance unto life (Acts 11:18 KJV). When the non-Jews at Antioch of Pisidia heard that Paul would turn to preaching to the Gentiles in accordance with the interpretation of the Old Testament Scriptures (Acts 13:14), they glorified the word of the Lord (Acts 13:48 KJV).

Indeed, the non-Jews in Antioch who had been appointed to eternal life "honored the word" (NIV) by believing its interpretation which invited them to enjoy the blessing of God's salvation as well.

In the church, whether in its local or universal form, there is more to glorifying God than the words of praise that issue from the lips of Christians in prayers and songs. Glorifying God in full measure today is ultimately bound up with the nations of the world. More precisely, for the church to evangelize the nations through world missions is to give glory to God to the full extent He desires and deserves in the world he has created.

But if the church, again in its local or universal form, is not declaring God's name among the nations—is not promoting world missions as the first priority—the church is not praising God in full measure. This amounts only to a halfway measure of what God expects and deserves in praise and glory. The church is failing, regardless how loud the singing or how long the prayers, to give glory in measures matching the fullness of God.

On the other hand, when missionaries or evangelists enter a previously unreached tribe or people group to preach the Gospel, or a language is reduced to writing and the Scriptures are translated and read, or a Bible study group is organized in an apartment building or neighborhood, more and more glory redounds to God. This is matching in full measure God's desire for the lost in these people groups to be saved.

This glory originates from two sources. First, God's word will produce additional believers who in turn will add their new voices in praising God.

Second, such successes in evangelism create additional praise to God from those who sent the missionaries, evangelists, translators, or the organizers of the Bible study. Together they—the praise from the sending church plus the praise from new believers in previously unreached groups—add up fully to what God deserves and desires in praise and glory in the church. Making sure this happens (that God is glorified to the measure of his fullness) is his purpose for us in the church.

Romans 16:25–27
Now to him who is able to establish you by my gospel and the proclamation of Jesus Christ, according to the revelation of the mystery hidden for long ages past, but now revealed and made known through the prophetic writings by the command of the eternal God, so that all nations might believe and obey him—to the only wise God be glory forever through Jesus Christ! Amen.

The Wealth Of The Nations

Ewan had been suffering from ill health for several years. In fact, her health had recently deteriorated even further. Her husband Phat called me over as I was walking into the village, to tell me about her condition. Phat squatted on his haunches as he began to talk. I squatted beside him to listen.

I along with my family had recently moved to the mountain village of Pha Nam Yoy, Ewan's home village, of the Mal tribe in the northern part of Nan Province in Thailand. We were the first missionaries ever among the Mal.

The Mal speak a Mon-Khmer language. They are a small language group, numbering approximately 6000 people. I had already started learning the language and forming an alphabet. My goal in life was to translate the New Testament into the Mal language. I was also beginning to teach about Jesus Christ in the Mal language to the villagers of Pha Nam Yoy.

Phat explained to me how Ewan had been in poor health for quite some time. She was weak and had problems breathing and getting enough breath to walk any distance or to do any manual labor. So he had to do everything, from her work of carrying water to the heavy field work of cutting brush and planting the yearly rice crop. They had visited several shamans to divine the spirits in hopes of finding a cure. They had sacrificed numerous animals to many spirits. But all to no avail.

Phat announced he was willing to let Ewan become a Christian in hopes of being healed. I explained to him what Ewan had to do to be a Christian. I also told him that healing is ultimately from God but that we would pray and commit her to God's care. I went on to tell him that a greater benefit from faith in Jesus was power over demons. Jesus was more powerful than demons and by trusting daily in him they could conduct their lives without performing expensive and debilitating ceremonies that financially drained them. Another benefit, the greatest of all, was the assurance of eternal life with God because of forgiveness of sin.

Ewan started attending worship service at our house. She would sometimes bring her two children. She explained more of her illness and we prayed for God to heal her. But as she explained more of her symptoms it appeared that something was wrong with her heart, perhaps a leaky valve.

There was no way she could walk the five hours out of her mountain village to the nearest medical clinic for a definitive diagnosis. It appeared it would not be long before she would suffer heart failure and die. We prayed even harder.

One Sunday morning after worship Ewan announced she was ready to be baptized. This posed a problem because she was unable to walk down the mountain to the river to be baptized and then walk back up. So we went to a nearby mountain stream and found a pool that could be deepened. We took turns removing rocks, boulders, and digging away gravel to make the pool deep enough. As Ewan descended into the stream, the cold mountain water nearly took away what little breath she had. I quickly baptized her.

This was Christmas Day, 1963. Ewan did not know it was the day we traditionally celebrate the birth of Christ. She did know, however, that this was the beginning of her new life as a Christian.

Life was not easy for Ewan or the other Christians at Pha Nam Yoy. Opposition and verbal abuse was hurled against them from their neighbors and the village leaders. The main reason was that the Christians no longer observed the taboos of the spirits nor joined with the non-Christian villagers in sacrificing animals to the spirits. The non-Christians were fearful that the spirits, whom they believed protected them from sickness and crop failure, would abandon them, and they would suffer many calamities.The villagers were always trying to force the Christians to recant their newfound faith in Jesus.

Yet in spite of the opposition the Lord added new believers from time to time to the small group that worshiped on Sunday mornings. But each new believer seemed to bring about an increase in the level of opposition against the Christians.

On one occasion, during the New Year festival, the main spirit of the village possessed the shaman and gave out an oracle. The spirit announced that all Christians had to move from the village or be killed. The shaman called Phat and told him he had to divorce Ewan and drive her out of the village.

Phat returned to tell Ewan. She listened and then quietly announced that she would not renounce her faith in Jesus even if Phat decided to cast her out or even kill her. Phat pondered through the night about what to do. Even though he was not a Christian he knew it was not right to cast a frail wife out of her house and from her children. Phat decided to defy the shaman's order.

Other Christians were threatened with their lives. The Christians gathered at my house for a special prayer meeting. We prayed that God would drive out the spirit that had possessed the shaman and given the oracle. After the third day and the third prayer meeting, we noticed that peace had returned to the village. The threats ceased. The shaman was in a friendly mood and no longer our enemy. Phat and Ewan were still together as husband and wife. We recognized that God had answered our prayers. A great spiritual victory had been won.

While the atmosphere was much better for the Christians, we realized that there was still an underlying hostility against the Gospel. It would be only a matter of time before open persecution would break out again. I began to worry about Ewan. Her health was failing even more, and I was afraid she would be unable to endure another round of threats and opposition. But there was no need to worry.

Late one evening I was called to Ewan's house. She had just died. When I arrived Phat told me what had happened.

She had eaten supper and gone behind the bamboo partition to go
to bed. Sometime later Phat looked in to see if she was all right and
noticed she was not breathing. She had died peacefully in her sleep.
    I stayed with Phat and the two children throughout the night.
Singers from the village came and composed chants about Phat's and
Ewan's life together. I sang hymns I had translated and which Ewan
had been learning to sing herself. I preached from the Scriptures and
prayed. At daybreak some men came and wrapped Ewan's body in
a blanket and a bamboo mat. The shaman, now the headman of the
village, came and asked forgiveness from Ewan's spirit for any
offenses he may have committed against her. Then the men tied a long
pole lengthwise to the body, lifted it up, and walked out of Phat's
house heading toward the village burial grounds out in the nearby
jungle.
    At the burial ground the men selected a spot and commenced
digging a shallow grave in the rocky ground. After they had finished
digging they lowered Ewan's body into the ground. I stopped the
proceedings at this point to read Scripture and pray. When I had
finished, one of the men reached into the bamboo mat holding Ewan's
body, pulled out a corner of the blanket in which her body was
wrapped, and tore it about three inches deep into the cloth. The man
told me that this signified that a wife and mother was being buried
and that a household had been torn apart by the death of the mother.
    The men covered the body with dirt and piled brush on top to
discourage animals from digging up the grave. I asked to pray again.
When I was through, the men began climbing in single file up the
mountain side to the trail that led to the village. I lingered a bit longer
at Ewan's grave site. When I turned to leave I looked for the men, but
the dense jungle had already closed them off from eyesight. Their
voices, muffled by a thick canopy of vines and leaves, seemed far
away.
    As I started picking my way through the jungle undergrowth to
rejoin the men ahead of me, a sudden surge of peace and joy
overwhelmed me. For I knew that this place would not be the final
victor over Ewan, but that in a paraphrase of Rev. 20:13 "even the
jungle shall yield up its dead" on that great day when the Lord shall
judge the nations (Matt. 25:32). We would indeed meet again before
the throne of the Lamb who was slain to purchase men for God from
every tribe and language and people and nation (Rev. 5:9).
    John the Revelator saw a vision of the New Jerusalem, the Bride
of the Lamb, coming down from heaven (Rev. 21:1–2). In the New
Jerusalem John declared that:

Rev. 21:24–26

The nations will walk by its light, and the kings of the earth will bring their splendor into it. On no day will its gates ever be shut, for there will be no night there. The glory and honor of the nations will be brought into it.

The Bride, the New Jerusalem, is understood to be the church. The words "splendor" and "glory" and "honor of the nations" reflect an Old Testament view of the wealth of the nations, or Gentiles being brought to Israel (Isa. 60:5). Wealth is a term often translated as glory in the Old Testament (Isa. 66:12 KJV). John used an Old Testament backdrop to describe what will be brought into the church and ultimately into heaven itself. It is the wealth of the nations.

But wealth here does not mean material possessions or riches in terms of gold, silver, or precious stones. It is a metaphor, more precisely metonymy. A metonymy is a figure of speech that stands for something else. In this case wealth refers to the people of the nations, like Ewan above of the Mal tribe in northern Thailand. As far as I know, Ewan was the first from her tribe to have died in the Lord (Rev. 14:13) and to add her voice in the Mal language with countless others from every nation, tribe, people, and language in singing praises to the Lamb (Rev. 7:9–10). She is part of the wealth of the Mal tribe in Christ's kingdom that shall at the end time be handed over to the Father (1 Cor. 15:24).

The redeemed from the nations, tribes, peoples, clans, and every other group of this world are God's wealth, his glory in the church and forever more in his everlasting heavenly kingdom.

Application

What is the application of the missionary message of the Old Testament today? Where is the Great Commission leading us? Two tasks lie ahead.

First, pastors, teachers, and theologians must recognize the missionary dimension to the Old Testament and give it priority in preaching, teaching, and interpretation. Theologians must explicate the missionary implications and ramifications of biblical themes and texts in theology and doctrinal studies. Preachers and teachers should emphasize the missionary dimension in the interpretation and application of these themes and texts in personal life and in the life of the church.

In short, the task here is to demonstrate, in the words of David Hesselgrave (1993), how missions is the basis for understanding and applying the Scriptures today.

More important is the second task, evangelism in today's world. The missionary message of the Old Testament for God's people today, now made explicit by the Great Commission, is for us

-to reach the remaining ethnic and people groups with the proclamation of the Gospel and

-to establish his church in every remaining group

-in order to create a ground swell of praise in every language

-so that God will be glorified by every tribe, tongue, language, people, and nation for ever and ever.

Amen.

Questions For Discussion

1. Why is the mission program of a church necessary for that church to fully glorify God?

2. God is glorified in Jesus Christ and in the church. Discuss how both are equally true and necessary.

3. Discuss why the expression "from every nation, tribe, people and language" in Revelation is the ultimate and final expression of giving glory to God both on earth and in heaven forevermore.

References

Agus, Jacob Bernard. 1963. *The Meaning of Jewish History*. London: Abelard-Schuman.

Allen, Diogenes. 1985. *Philosophy for Understanding Theology*. Atlanta: John Knox Press.

Anderson, A. A. 1989. *Word Biblical Commentary, 2 Samuel*. Dallas: Word Books.

Baron, Salo Wittmayer. 1952. *A Social and Religious History of the Jews*, Vol. 1. New York: Columbia University Press.

Barrett, David B. 1992. "Annual Statistical Table On Global Mission: 1993." *International Bulletin of Missionary Research*, Vol. 17, No. 1, pp.22–23.

———— and Todd M. Johnson. 1990. *Our Globe and How to Reach It*. Birmingham, Al.: New Hope.

Bentwich, Norman. 1920. *Hellenism*. Philadelphia: The Jewish Publication Society of America.

Bickerman, Elias. 1962. *From Ezra to the Last of the Maccabees: Foundations of Post-Biblical Judaism*. New York: Schocken Books.

Blauw, Johannes. 1962. *The Missionary Nature of the Church*. New York: McGraw-Hill.

Braaten, Carl E. 1966. *History & Hermeneutics*. New Directions in Theology Today, Vol. II. Philadelphia: Westminster Press.

————. 1977. *The Flaming Center: A Theology of the Christian Mission*. Philadelphia: Fortress Press.

Brantley, Richard E. 1984. *Locke, Wesley and the Method of English Romanticism*. Gainesville: University Presses of Florida.

Bright, John. 1953. *The Kingdom of God: the Biblical Concept and its Meaning for the Church*. New York: Abingdon-Cokesbury Press.

Bruce, F. F. 1988. *The Book of Acts*. Grand Rapids: W. B. Eerdmans Pub. Co.

Burke, D. G. 1982. "Interpret; Interpretation" in *The International Standard Bible Encyclopedia*, Vol. Two, pp. 861–863. Grand Rapids: W. B. Eerdmans Pub. Co.

Burris, Stephen E. 1992. "Building the Mission Bridge: Education for 'People on the Run'." *Mission Frontiers*, Vol. 14, No. 9–2, (Sept.-Dec.), pp. 6–7.

Childs, Brevard S. 1974. *The Book of Exodus*. Philadelphia: Westminster Press.

Croatto, J. Severino. 1987. *Biblical Hermeneutics: Toward a Theory of Reading as the Production of Meaning*. Translated from the Spanish by Robert R. Barr. Maryknoll, N.Y.: Orbis Books.

Danker, Frederick W. 1987. "Biblical Exegesis: Christian Views" in *The Encyclopedia of Religion*, Vol. 2, pp. 142–152. Mircea Eliade, Editor in Chief. New York: Macmillan Publishing Company.

Davis, John J. 1986. *Moses and the Gods of Egypt* (second edition). Grand Rapids: Baker Book House.

Davis, John R. 1993. *Poles Apart? Contextualizing the Gospel*. Bangkok: Kanok Bannasan (OMF Publishers).

De Ridder, Richard R. 1976. *Discipling the Nations*. Grand Rapids: Baker Book House.

De Waard, Jan and Eugene A. Nida. 1986. *From One Language to Another: Functional Equivalence in Bible Translating*. Nashville: Thomas Nelson Publishers.

Derwacter, Frederick. 1930. *Preparing the Way for Paul: The Proselyte Movement in Later Judaism*. New York: The Macmillan Co.

Dimont, Max I. 1962. *Jews, God and History*. New York: Simon And Schuster.

Doble, Peter. 1993. *Luke 23:47—The Problem of DIKAIOS*. The Bible Translator, 44:320–331.

Durham, John I. 1987. *Exodus*. Waco, Tex.: Word Books.

Encyclopaedia Judaica. Vols. 11, 13, 14. Jerusalem: Keter Publishing House, LTD.

Engel, James F. 1993. "Will the Great Commission Become the Great Ad Campaign." *Christianity Today*, Vol. 37, No. 5 (April 26).

Filbeck, David. 1964. "Concepts of Atonement Among the Tin." *Practical Anthropology*, 11:181–184.

———. 1978. "Tin, A Historical Study." *Pacific Linguistics*, Series B - No. 49.

———. 1985. "Social Context And Proclamation: A Socio-Cognitive Study" in *Proclaiming The Gospel Cross-Culturally*. Pasadena: William Carey Library.

Foerster, Werner and Gottfried Queli. 1958. "Lord" in *Bible Key Words*. New York: Harper & Brothers.

Foster, R. C. 1966. *Studies in the Life of Christ*. Grand Rapids: Baker Book House.

Fuller, D. P. 1982. "Interpretation, History of" in *The International Standard Bible Encyclopedia*, Vol. 2, pp. 863–874. Grand Rapids: W. B. Eerdmans Pub. Co.

Gadamer, Hans-Georg. 1975. *Truth and Method*. New York: Seabury Press.

Gesenius' Hebrew Grammar. 1909. Revised by A. E. Cowley. London: Oxford Press.

Giles, Thomas S. 1992. "Did You Know." *Christian History*, 35:2–3 (Vol. XI. No. 3).

Gossey, Arthur John. 1952. "The Gospel According to St. John" in *The Interpreter's Bible*. New York: Abingdon Press.

Grenz, Stanley J. 1993. *Revisioning Evangelical Theology*. Downers Grove, Il.: InterVarsity Press.

Hedlund, Roger E. 1991. *The Mission of the Church in the World*. Grand Rapids: Baker Book House.

Heibert Paul. 1982. "The Flaw of the Excluded Middle." *Missiology*, 10:35–47.

Hekman, Susan J. 1986. *Hermeneutics & the Sociology of Knowledge*. Notre Dame: University of Notre Dame Press.

Hesselgrave, David J. 1993. "A Missionary Hermeneutic: Understanding Scripture in the Light of World Mission." *International Journal of Frontier Missions*, 10:17–20.

Jacobson, Richard. 1958. "The Structuralist and the Bible", in Donald K. McKim 1986.

Jansen, Frank Kaleb. 1989. *Target Earth*. Kailua-Kona, Ha.: University of the Nations.

Jeremias, Joachim. 1958. *Jesus' Promise to the Nations*. Naperville, Il.: Alec R. Allenson, Inc.

Johnson, Sherman E. and George A. Buttrick. 1951. "The Gospel According to St. Matthew" in *The Interpreter's Bible*. New York: Abingdon Press.

Joy, Donald M. 1985. *Bonding: Relationships in the Image of God*. Waco, Tx.: Word Books.

Kaiser, Walter C. Jr. 1977. "The Davidic Promise and Inclusion of Gentiles." *JETS*, 20:97–111.

———. 1978. *Toward An Old Testament Theology*. Grand Rapids: Zondervan.

———. 1983. *Toward Old Testament Ethics*. Grand Rapids: Academie Books, Zondervan.

Keegan, Terence J. 1985. *Interpreting the Bible: A Popular Introduction to Biblical Hermeneutics*. New York: Paulist Press.

Laaser, Mark R. 1992. *The Secret Sin: Healing the Wounds of Sexual Addiction.* Grand Rapids: Zondervan.

Lane, William L. 1974. *The Gospel According to Mark; The English Text with Introduction, Exposition and Notes.* Grand Rapids: W. B. Eerdmans Pub. Co.

Latourette, Kenneth Scott. 1970. *A History of the Expansion of Christianity:* Vol. 2 "The Thousand Years Of Uncertainty", Vol. 3 "Three Centuries Of Advance", Vol. 4 "The Great Century: Europe And The United States." Grand Rapids: Zondervan.

Liddell, Henry George and Robert Scott. 1976. *A Greek-English Lexicon.* London: Oxford at the Clarendon Press.

Linsey, T. M. 1967. "Baptism" in *The International Standard Bible Encyclopedia,* Vol. 1, pp. 418–124. Grand Rapids: W. B. Eerdmans Pub. Co.

Louw, Johannes P. and Eugene A. Nida. 1988. *Greek-English Lexicon of the New Testament Based on Semantic Domains.* New York: United Bible Societies.

Marshall, I. Howard. 1978. *Commentary on Luke.* Grand Rapids: W. B. Eerdmans Pub. Co.

Martens, Elmer A. 1977. "Tackling Old Testament Theology." *JETS,* 20:123–132.

Martin, Grant. 1990. *Regaining Control.* Wheaton, Il.: Victor Books.

Mayers, Ronald B. 1984. *Both/And: A Balanced Apologetic.* Chicago: Moody Press.

McKim, Donald K., Ed. 1986. *A Guide to Contemporary Hermeneutics, Major Trends in Biblical Interpretation.* Grand Rapids: W. B. Eerdmans Pub. Co.

McKinney, Lois. 1993. "Missionaries in the Twenty-First Century." *Missiology,* 21:55–64.

McKnight, Scot. 1990. *A Light Among the Gentiles: Jewish Missionary Activity in the Second Temple Period.* Minneapolis: Fortress Press.

Morris, Leon. 1971. *The Gospel According to John.* Grand Rapids: W. B. Eerdmans Pub. Co.

Neusner, Jacob. 1973. *From Politics to Piety: The Emergence of Pharisaic Judaism.* Englewood Cliffs, N. J.: Prentice-Hall.

Nida, Eugene. 1960. *Mission and Message.* New York: Harper.

Nolland, John. 1989. *Word Biblical Commentary Luke 1–9:20.* Dallas: Word Books.

Oldenburg, Ulf. 1969. *The Conflict Between El and Ba'al in Canaanite Religion.* Leiden: E. J. Brill.

Osborne, Grant R. 1991. *The Hermeneutical Spiral.* Downers Grove, Il.: InterVarsity Press.

Patton, Carl S. 1915. *Sources of the Synoptic Gospels*. New York: Macmillan Co.

Pinnock, Clark H. 1984. *The Scripture Principle*. San Francisco: Harper & Row.

Poythress Vern S. 1978. "Structuralism and Biblical Studies." *JETS*, 21:221–237.

Robertson, A. T. 1934. *A Grammar of the Greek New Testament in the Light of Historical Research*. Nashville, Tn.: Broadman Press.

Sandbach, Francis Henry. 1967. "Hellenistic Thought" in *The Encyclopedia of Philosophy*, Vol. 3, pp. 467–469. New York: Macmillan Publishing Company.

Semmel, Bernard. 1973. *The Methodist Revolution*. New York: Basic Books.

Shenk, Wilbert R. 1993. "Moving Beyond Word And Deed." *Missiology*, 21:65–75.

Shepard, J. W. 1971. *The Christ of the Gospel: An Exegetical Study*. Nashville: The Parthenon Press.

Slager, Donald. 1992. "The Use of Divine Names in Genesis." *The Bible Translator*, 43:423–429.

Smalley, William A. 1991. *Translation As Mission: Bible Translation in the Modern Missionary Movement*. Macon, Ga.: Mercer.

———— and Eugene A. Nida. 1959. *Introducing Animism*. New York: Friendship Press.

Stacy, Walter David. 1977. *Interpreting the Bible*. New York: Hawthorn Books.

Stark, W. 1958. *The Sociology of Knowledge*. London: Routledge and Kegan Paul.

Sterns, Bill & Amy. 1991. *Catch the Vision 2000*. Minneapolis: Bethany House Publishers.

Surburg, Raymond F. 1975. *Introduction to the Intertestamental Period*. St. Louis: Concordia Pub. House.

Taber, Charles R. 1970. "Explicit and Implicit Information in Translation." *The Bible Translator*, Vol. 21, pp. 1–9.

————. 1978. "Is There More Than One Way to Do Theology?" *Gospel In Context*, Vol. 1, No. 1, pp. 4–10.

The New Schaff-Herzog Encyclopedia of Religious Knowledge, Vol. VII. 1977. Grand Rapids: Baker Book House.

Thiselton, Anthony C. 1980. *The Two Horizons*. Grand Rapids: W. B. Eerdmans Pub. Co.

Thomas, Robert L. 1986. "The Hermeneutics of Evangelical Redaction Criticism." *JETS*, 29:447–459.

Titiev, Mischa. 1960. "A Fresh Approach to the Problem of Magic and Religion." *Southwestern Journal of Anthropology*, Vol. 16, pp. 292–298.

Toffler, Alvin. 1980. *The Third Wave*. New York: Morrow.

Verkuyl, Johannes. 1978. *Contemporary Missiology: An Introduction*. Grand Rapids: W. B. Eerdmans Pub. Co.

Von Rad, Gerhard. 1966. *Deuteronomy: A Commentary*. Philadelphia: Westminster Press.

Wagner, C. Peter. 1989. "Territorial Spirits And World Missions." *Evangelical Missions Quarterly*, 25:278–288.

Weingreen, J. 1959. *A Practical Grammar for Classical Hebrew*. London: Oxford Press.

Wenham, Gordon J. 1987. *Genesis 1–15*. Waco, Tex.: Word Books.

Westermann, Claus, Ed. 1963. *Essays on Old Testament Hermeneutics* (Translated by James Luther Mays). Richmond: John Knox Press.

Wieand, Albert Cassel. 1950. *Gospel Records of the Message and Mission of Jesus Christ: A Harmony of the Gospels in the Text of the Revised Standard Version Arranged for Comparative Study*. Elgin, Il.: Brethren Publishing House.

Winter, Ralph D. 1970. *The Twenty-Five Unbelievable Years 1945–1969*. South Pasadena: William Carey Library.

———. 1992. "Facing The Final Frontiers." *Mission Frontiers*, Vol.14, Nos. 9–12, pp. 34–41.

About the Author

Holding an M.A. and a Ph.D. in linguistics from Indiana University, Dr. David Filbeck, along with his wife Deloris, has served in northern Thailand since 1960. He is president and founder of Christian Missions to the Orient and serves on the faculty at Payap University in Chiang Mai, Thailand.

David Filbeck and Deloris were the first missionaries with the Tin tribe, a Mon-Khmer language group located in northern Thailand along the border with Laos. He conducted linguistic research, established alphabets for several dialects, did evangelistic work, taught Bible and theology, and is currently finishing his scripture translation of the New Testament in the Mal dialect.

David Filbeck's dream has been to finish the New Testament translation and to see the church firmly planted among the Tin. After a long interruption of missionary work with the Tin tribe because of the Indochina war in Thailand, God's church has again become established in this group. More than 250 believers now worship in four churches, and three other villages have groups of Christians meeting together.

During his time as Missionary Scholar in Residence at the Billy Graham Center, David pursued another dream—to write a book on the theology of mission based on the Old Testament. He believes that God's purpose for his people in being light for the world is also a command to bring his salvation to the ends of the earth.

David and Deloris have four children, all born in Thailand. Two have returned to Thailand as missionaries while the other two are in mission preparation. In addition, three of their seven grandchildren were born in Thailand, the beginnings of a third generation of missionaries.

266.001
F4794

98847